SCHOOL LEADERSHIP *for* Results

A Focused Model

SCHOOL LEADERSHIP for Results

A Focused Model

2nd Edition

Beverly G. Carbaugh
Robert J. Marzano

With:
Kathleen Marx

Copyright © 2018 by Learning Sciences International

Materials appearing here are copyrighted. No part of this book may be reproduced, transmitted, or displayed in any form or by any means (photocopying, digital or electronic transmittal, electronic or mechanical display, or other means) without the prior written permission of the publisher.

1400 Centrepark Blvd., Ste. 1000
West Palm Beach, FL 33401
717.845.6300
email: pub@learningsciences.com
learningsciences.com

Printed in the United States of America

22 21 20 19 18   1 2 3 4 5

Library of Congress Control Number: 2018944945

Publisher's Cataloging-in-Publication Data
provided by Five Rainbows Cataloging Services

Names: Carbaugh, Beverly G., author. | Marzano, Robert J., author.
Title: School leadership for results, second edition : a focused model / Beverly Carbaugh [and] Robert Marzano.
Description: 2nd edition. | West Palm Beach, FL : Learning Sciences, 2018.
Identifiers: LCCN 2018944945 | ISBN 978-1-943920-53-2 (pbk.) | ISBN 978-1-943920-54-9 (ebook)
Subjects: LCSH: Educational leadership. | Education--Aims and objectives. | School management and organization. | School improvement programs. | Effective teaching. | BISAC: EDUCATION / Leadership. | EDUCATION / Professional Development. | EDUCATION / Educational Policy & Reform / General.
Classification: LCC LB2822.82 .C37 2018 (print) | LCC LB2822.82 (ebook) | DDC 371.2/07--dc23.

To the multitude of leaders, including me, who have learned over time that leadership is an ongoing process and who continue to fine-tune their leadership skills, this book is dedicated to help you continue your pathway to excellence. I hope each person reading this book will find special mentors to serve as confidants and guides in the complex process of developing effective school leadership.

And to the mentors who guided my own path, my father (Franklin Goff), Barbara Franques, and Michael Grego, I thank you.

—Beverly Carbaugh

Table of Contents

About the Authors xiii
Preface xv
    School Leaders Matter xvi
    We Need to Stop the Attrition xvii
    Are Today's School Leaders Getting the Support They Need? xix
    Aligning Expectations for Effective School Leadership xix
    School Leader Evaluation: Getting the Best Results xxi

Introduction
The Marzano Focused School Leader Evaluation Model, 2018 Update 1
    Challenges for Designing School Leader Evaluation 2
    The Instructional/Organizational Leader 3
    New Policies for School Leader Evaluation 5
    Updated Professional Standards for School Leaders 6
    The Basics of Using a Framework Approach for Growth and Evaluation 7
        The Concept of a Framework 7
        A Roadmap for Success 8
        Overview of the Domains 9
        What Do We Mean When We Say *Ensure*? 11
    Updated Sample Protocols 13
    Domain 1: A Data-Driven Focus on School Improvement 14
    The Role of the Evaluator 15
    How to Use This Book 15
    Conclusion 16

CHAPTER 1
Domain 1: A Data-Driven Focus on School Improvement 17
    What Do We Mean by "School Improvement"? 18
    The How and Why of Data 19
    The Elements of Domain 1 20

Domain 1, Element 1: Using Data to Develop Critical Schoolwide Goals 20

Elements 2 and 3: The Big Picture 24

Domain 1, Element 2: Monitoring Progress of Individual Students 25

Domain 1, Element 3: Developing Interventions and Support 32

Conclusion 36

CHAPTER 2
Domain 2: Instruction of a Viable and Guaranteed Curriculum 37

Providing a Clear Vision for Instruction 39

What Do We Mean by a Viable and Guaranteed Curriculum? 40

Unpacking the Concept of Viability 41

Unpacking the Concept of Guaranteed 41

Ensuring Equal Opportunity to Learn the Standards 43

The Elements in Domain 2 43

Domain 2, Element 1: Providing a Clear Vision of Instruction 43

Domain 2, Element 2: Using Predominant Instructional Practices to Improve Teaching 47

Domain 2, Element 3: Aligning Curriculum to Standards 52

Domain 2, Element 4: Ensuring Viability of the Curriculum 56

Conclusion 65

CHAPTER 3
Domain 3: Continuous Development of Teachers and Staff 67

An Effective School Leader Develops Expertise: The Challenges 69

Domain 3, Element 1: Hiring, Supporting, and Retaining Staff 73

Domain 3, Element 2: Conducting Ongoing Evaluations 78

Domain 3, Element 3: Providing Job-Embedded Professional Development 84

Conclusion 87

Chapter 4
Domain 4: Community of Care and Collaboration 89

What Do We Mean by a Community of Care? 90

What Do We Mean by Collaboration? 90

Creating a Social Space for Collaboration to Flourish 94

Learning Organization or Learning Community? 95

Effective Communication Breaks Down Isolation 96

Building Evidence of Cooperation and Collaboration 97

Domain 4, Element 1 97
   Moving from Isolation to Collaboration 97
   Building Evidence of Collaboration 99
   The Role of PLCs 99
   The Role of Collaboration in a PLC 100
   Scales and Evidences for Domain 4, Element 1 101
   A Scenario for Domain 4, Element 1 102
   Feedback 103
Domain 4, Element 2 103
   Shared or Distributed Leadership 104
   Scales and Evidences for Domain 4, Element 2 105
   A Scenario for Domain 4, Element 2 106
   Feedback 107
   Growth and Reflection Questions for Domain 4, Element 2 107
Domain 4, Element 3 108
   Communicating with Parents and Community 109
   The Role of Student Participation 110
   Scales and Evidences for Domain 4, Element 3 111
   A Scenario for Domain 4, Element 3 112
   Feedback 112
   Growth and Reflection Questions 113
Domain 4, Element 4 113
   Scales and Evidences for Domain 4, Element 4 115
   A Scenario for Domain 4, Element 4 116
   Feedback 116
   Growth and Reflection Questions for Domain 4, Element 4 117
Conclusion 117

Chapter 5
Domain 5: Core Values 119
   Building Evidence of a Positive School Climate 121
Domain 5, Element 1 122
   Scales and Evidences for Domain 5, Element 1 124
   A Scenario for Domain 5, Element 1 125
   Feedback 126
   Growth and Reflection Questions for Domain 5, Element 1 126
Domain 5, Element 2 127

The Perception of Integrity 127
　　An Example 128
　　Domain Scales and Evidences for Domain 5, Element 2 130
　　A Scenario for Domain 5, Element 2 130
　　Feedback 131
　　Growth and Reflection Questions 131
　Domain 5, Element 3 132
　　Community Perceptions of Safety and Cultural Responsiveness . 133
　　Scales and Evidences for Domain 5, Element 3 135
　　A Scenario for Domain 5, Element 3 136
　　Feedback 137
　　Growth and Reflection Questions for Domain 5, Element 3 137
　Conclusion 138

Chapter 6
Domain 6: Resource Management 139
　Domain 6, Element 1 141
　　The Scales and Evidences for Domain 6, Element 1 141
　　A Scenario for Domain 6, Element 1 142
　　Feedback 143
　　Reflection and Growth Questions for Domain 6, Element 1 143
　Domain 6, Element 2 144
　　Scales and Evidences for Domain 6, Element 2 144
　　A Scenario for Domain 6, Element 2 145
　　Feedback 146
　　Growth and Reflection Questions 146
　Domain 6, Element 3 147
　　The Scales and Evidences for Domain 6, Element 3 147
　　A Scenario for Domain 6, Element 3 148
　　Feedback 149
　　Growth and Reflection Questions for Domain 6, Element 3 149
　Conclusion 149

CHAPTER 7
Implementation and Scoring 151
　Planning the Process of Implementation 151
　Planning Support for Implementation 153
　The Five Steps of the Evaluation Cycle 153

Deliberate Practice as an Added Measure.. 155
Scoring 155
Using Parallel Models of Evaluation... 158
Establishing Inter-rater Reliability.. 158
Data Management and Feedback Systems with the Marzano
  Models 159
About Hierarchical Evaluation.. 159
Conclusion... 161

Appendix A
The Map for the Marzano Focused School Leader Evaluation Model... 165

Appendix B
The Protocols for the Marzano Focused School Leader
Evaluation Model 171
  Marzano Focused School Leader Evaluation Model....................... 171
    Domain 1: A Data-Driven Focus on School Improvement 171
    Domain 2: Instruction of a Viable and Guaranteed Curriculum ... 174
    Domain 3: Continuous Development of Teachers and Staff 180
    Domain 4: Community of Care and Collaboration....................... 183
    Domain 5: Core Values 187
    Domain 6: Resource Management 190

Appendix C
Review of Leadership Studies 195
  The Research Base of the Marzano School Leader Evaluation
    Model 196

Appendix D
Further Resources for the Marzano Focused School Leader
Evaluation Model 199
    Aligned Evaluation Models... 199
    Videos and Webinars 199
    White Papers... 199
    Blogs, Books, and Articles 200

Appendix E
Crosswalk for PSEL Standards and the Marzano Focused School
Leader Evaluation Model 203
  Alignment: Marzano Focused School Leader Evaluation Model
    and the 2015 Professional Educator Leadership Standards 203

Works Cited... 205

About the Authors

Dr. Beverly G. Carbaugh, Senior Advisor and Vice President, Learning Sciences Marzano Center

Beverly G. Carbaugh, EdD, specializes in school- and district-level leadership. She is coauthor of white papers, books, and the Focused Evaluation models with Dr. Robert Marzano. Before joining Learning Sciences International, she was deputy superintendent of Florida's Osceola County School District. She began her career in 1979 as a teacher and served as a principal of Mintz Elementary in Tampa, Florida; charter principal of the National Blue Ribbon School Colleen Bevis Elementary; and Tomlin Middle School.

Dr. Carbaugh's expertise includes executive leadership in school administration, human resources, and business/finance. She also has extensive experience in professional development and presenting at state and national forums. She earned her doctorate of education in education leadership at the University of South Florida and her BS in elementary education from the University of Arizona.

Dr. Robert J. Marzano, Executive Director, Learning Sciences Marzano Center

Robert J. Marzano, PhD, is a nationally recognized education researcher, speaker, trainer, and author of more than thirty books and 150 articles on topics such as instruction, assessment, writing and implementing standards, cognition, effective leadership, and school intervention. His practical translations of the most current research and theory into classroom strategies are widely practiced internationally by both teachers and administrators. Dr. Marzano serves as an adviser for Learning Sciences Marzano Center research and pilot projects.

Dr. Marzano has partnered with Learning Sciences International to offer the Marzano Focused Teacher Evaluation Model, the Marzano Focused School Leadership Evaluation Model, and the Marzano Center Focused Instructional Support Personnel and District Leader Evaluation Models. Dr. Marzano received his doctorate from the University of Washington.

Kathleen Marx, Senior Staff Developer

Kathleen Marx, MSEd (educational leadership), MSEd (school counseling), is a leading expert in personal development across industries. Her background of classroom teaching, gifted education consulting, school counseling, life-success facilitation, and building administration gives her unique insight into leading-edge strategies in implementing research-based instructional and evaluation models. She is a graduate of Miami University (Ohio) and the University of Dayton.

Preface

The word *leadership* evokes images of strength, courage, and fortitude. These are especially apt words to describe qualities that school leaders need to cultivate in today's culture of high-stakes accountability. Sadly, though, there is abundant literature showing that school leaders—no matter how strong or courageous they may be—are leaving the profession almost as quickly as they are appointed. Overwhelmed, overworked, and discouraged, a staggering 50 percent of school leaders choose to leave the profession after only three years at the helm of a school (Tyre, 2015). School systems, foundations, and researchers are all working hard to study and address the problem of school leadership attrition and leadership pipelines in the United States. This complex issue seems forbidding and sometimes impossible to solve. But perhaps there is a silver bullet, or a way past and through the many challenges facing school leaders, challenges that dampen their enthusiasm and often force them from the profession.

In this book, we propose that the silver bullet resides not necessarily in a program or policy or pilot project but within every aspiring leader, every struggling leader, and every school leader who desires to push through the many challenges of school leadership to a successful and rewarding career. With the right focus and support, leadership skills can be *acquired*, so long as we are committed to helping leaders build the skills they need to succeed. The capacity for growth that leads to satisfaction in the profession is available to every leader—regardless of district size and support, pipeline preparation, or university degrees. Previous leaders have paved the path and are staying the course.

In *Developing the Leader Within You*, John Maxwell (2012) distinguishes born leaders from those who develop their leadership capacity over time. Maxwell notes that we are all familiar with the kinds of leadership families—the Roosevelts, Kennedys, and Bushes—who see leadership qualities modeled throughout their lives, have learned leadership skills through specific training, or have the kind of innate self-discipline that contributes to leadership skills. Maxwell calls these the "Leading Leaders." But he also identifies the "Latent Leaders" and the "Limited Leaders," those individuals who have had limited or no access to model leaders or leadership training but who nevertheless possess the desire to lead. In *The 21 Irrefutable Laws of Leadership*, Maxwell (2007) notes that while 10 percent of leaders surveyed believed that they had natural abilities, 85 percent of leaders became leaders due to the inspiration and mentoring of at least one other leader. In other words, the vast majority of leaders are not naturals! They develop the skills they need to succeed.

This should be good news for public education. It means that we ought to have, potentially, a very large leadership pool to draw from.

To help leaders develop growth and evaluation frameworks such as the one we discuss in this book, the Marzano Focused School Leader Evaluation Model, updated in 2018, draw on the most current and thorough research in school leadership. The Focused Model emphasizes school leader behaviors most likely to have the greatest impact on student learning. At the same time, the new Professional Standards for Educational Leaders (PSEL) and research tell us that leader growth and evaluation systems need to restore the right balance between critical leadership behaviors (National Policy Board for Education Administrators, 2015). While instructional leadership is still crucial, the most effective systems will take care to address the many, many roles the school leader must play beyond leader of instruction.

We propose that the right school leader growth and evaluation model has the capacity to address many of these challenges. If potential and practicing school leaders adopt a framework grounded in evidence and contemporary research, then the model should have the capacity to be used as a growth tool for self-reflection as well as a measurement tool for formal evaluation. It should also align language and expectations throughout the educational system. When these pieces are in place, the potential for school improvement is greatly enhanced.

> "As a district administrator, my personal philosophy has been to never see evaluation systems in terms of just compliance. Evaluation feedback should always be about growth. We chose the Marzano model because it is a growth-based model. And while there may be some tension with state policy that emphasizes compliance, the role of Central Office is to help administrators understand that the true purpose of the model is to support professional growth."
>
> —R. J. Webber (2018), Assistant Superintendent for Academic Services, Novi Community School District

School Leaders Matter

When we published the first edition of *School Leadership for Results* in 2015, we began with a straightforward premise: school leaders are crucial to the success of schools. That premise has not changed in the past three years; if anything, it has been strengthened, thanks to abundant new literature on school leadership. We know without a doubt that although a school leader's impact on student learning is indirect, mediated through teachers, staff, and other factors, the impact is nevertheless profound. Numerous studies have found that after effective teachers, the principal has the second-largest impact on student achievement (Hallinger & Heck, 1998; Leithwood, Louis, Anderson, & Wahlstrom, 2004; Waters, Marzano, & McNulty, 2003).

The challenges for school leaders are now more urgent than ever. International Programme for International Student Assessment (PISA) scores have remained mostly stagnant for students in the United States, with math scores declining below the international average. A 2017 PISA report found, additionally, that US students were only moderately successful collaborative problem solvers, coming in thirteenth, well below Singapore, Japan, and Hong Kong (Programme for International Student Assessment, 2017). We now know that in order to be effective as twenty-first century citizens, students must not only have solid math and language skills, but they also must be skillful at solving problems in collaborative teams—yet another challenge school leaders will be called on to address directly, and be held accountable for, in the coming years.

Liz Wiseman (Weisman, Allen, & Foster, 2013) has identified how good leaders can have a "multiplier effect" that exponentially increases the success of the organization, as capacity fans out from the leader to teacher teams, parents, and students. A 2012 report from the American Institute for Research called this expanding circle of impact "the ripple effect," where school leader behaviors *directly* influence school conditions, teacher quality, district and community contexts, and classroom instruction, and *indirectly* affect student achievement (Clifford, Behrstock-Sherratt, & Fetters, 2012). Recognizing the potential a school leader has to exert influence, the Gates Foundation, the Wallace Foundation, and a host of others have continued to pump millions of dollars into studies and pilot projects to examine and test how best to maximize the school leader's impact, examining ways to train, support, and retain current and future school leaders so they are fully equipped to lead K–12 schools to improved student learning. We would propose that a growth and evaluation model, when used as a guide for reflection and improvement, will ultimately have a positive effect on the school leader's personal growth and potential impact.

We Need to Stop the Attrition

Developing school leadership is more critical than ever. As we noted above, research has shown that there is tremendous turnover and attrition of principals and assistant principals in K–12 schools. A 2014 report, *Churn: The*

High Cost of Principal Turnover, released by the School Leaders Network, finds that 25,000 principals leave the profession each year, fully a quarter of the country's school leaders. Half of principals quit their jobs by their third year. And those who do stay eventually tend to leave high-poverty schools for more affluent schools, a further contribution to our stubborn achievement gap (School Leaders Network, 2014). The authors note that "the job is simply too complex, too poorly constructed, too isolating. School leaders lack the ongoing support and development required to maintain and foster sustained commitment" (School Leaders Network, 2014, p. 1). They go on to say, "Leaders are effectively being thrown into the deep end of the pool without adequate continued support, impacting schools, teachers, students, and our country."

Furthermore, principal attrition is expensive. Mariah Cone, vice president of knowledge with the School Leaders Network, estimated in a 2014 Marketplace interview that it costs approximately $75,000 to recruit and train each replacement for a departing principal (Scott, 2014). Marketplace summarized Cone's contention that "studies have shown precipitous drops in student scores on math and English achievement tests when a principal departs." We would only modify Cone's assertion with the caveat that test scores do drop when an average or effective principal departs but likely do not when an ineffective principal moves on. Cone further estimated that once a school leader is replaced, it takes three to five years for a school to begin to show achievement gains. The $75,000 figure that Cone cites does not include the significant investment that school leaders themselves have made in their own education and training, or the economic impact of careers derailed or stalled, or the much greater long-term economic impact of half a decade of declining test scores. A 2017 National Assessment of Educational Progress report found that the achievement gap continues to widen (Balinget, 2018). We propose that it is both necessary and possible to stop the churn with the right support for principals, and one element of that support is the right growth and evaluation system.

The Wallace Foundation (2011) has emphasized that investments in good principals yield a high return on investment when it comes to improving teacher practice and student achievement. Or, as a 2014 National Conference of State Legislatures (NCSL) (2015) Policy Brief summarized, "Targeted investments in good principals can be a particularly cost-effective way to improve teaching and learning because principals ensure that excellent teaching and learning spread beyond single classrooms. They also play a critical role in implementing schoolwide reform efforts." The same brief noted that effective leaders attract and retain effective teachers and that twenty-four out of twenty-five teachers say that the number-one factor in whether they stay at a school is their principal.

A 2016 nationwide study that surveyed principals in large urban districts to analyze reasons for high attrition rates found that, along with having a competent teaching staff and good work/life balance, "having an effective supervisor and collegial support from other principals were helpful supports; and having adequate resources, time for long-term planning, and teacher support and resources were critical working conditions" (Anthony, 2016).

Are Today's School Leaders Getting the Support They Need?

A 2016 National Association of Elementary School Principals (NAESP) (2016) presentation claimed that evidence from the field indicates that too few principals are, in fact, getting the training and mentoring support that they need to be effective. Only 4 percent of Local Education Agencies (LEAs) use Title II funds to support professional capacity in principals. Sixty percent of principals report spending less than 1 percent of their workdays per year in state- or district-sponsored professional development. And 43 percent of principals report that their district does not tailor professional development opportunities to meet their specific needs. A preliminary answer to the question of whether or not school leaders are receiving adequate support to be successful would be: *Not yet*.

Aligning Expectations for Effective School Leadership

Clearly, one of the challenges we face in public education is stanching the flow of school leaders leaving the profession and ensuring a steady pipeline of competent and well-trained individuals to lead our schools into the future. The solution to this challenge is to provide adequate support in the form of professional development and mentoring opportunities and to emphasize continuous improvement. But at the same time, we face another, related challenge: we must continue to clearly define and align expectations for the role of an effective school leader throughout our educational systems. Too often, there is a disconnect between professional expectations and actual practice—when expectations between districts and schools are misaligned, for instance. Just as often, school leaders enter the profession with one idea about the job, only to find a daily reality that seems to bear no resemblance to the work they'd hoped to do.

In part, the cause for this disconnect may be due to the ways our conception of principal leadership roles and responsibilities has shifted and evolved over time. Clifford (2012) and Walker (2002) have summarized these many shifts, from early conceptions of the school leader as "traditional manager," to the "supervisor of standards," to the "adaptive leader," the "instructional leader," and finally "leader among leaders"—the place that principal leadership has now settled in the twenty-first century. In *The Ripple Effect* (Clifford, Behrstock-Sherratt, & Fetters, 2012), the authors note that leaders among leaders "recognize their limitations and the limitations of their position and the capacity of others to lead. Leaders work to establish organizational systems that distribute leadership and support organizational learning." The measure of effectiveness for such leaders is how well they facilitate "democratic decision making and processes to take place among communities of professionals" (p. 2).

Nationally, structures are now fully in place to help align a unified vision of effective school leadership, most notably with the Interstate School Leaders Licensure Consortium Standards (ISLLC) of 2008 and the updated PSEL standards of 2015. Evidence continues to accrue that school leaders must be instructional leaders—they must set and maintain an instructional vision that is coherent and consistent from classroom to classroom. But new leader standards do reflect that strong instructional leadership is not the end of the story. School leaders must also devote a significant percentage of their energies to *organizational* leadership, maintaining the necessary and delicate balance between instruction, organizational processes, and vision. In their rationale for the 2015 standards, the PSEL authors note:

> The profession of educational leadership has developed significantly. Educators have a better understanding of how and in what ways effective leadership contributes to student achievement. An expanding base of knowledge from research and practice shows that educational leaders exert influence on student achievement by creating challenging but also caring and supportive conditions conducive to each student's learning. They relentlessly develop and support teachers, create positive working conditions, effectively allocate resources, construct appropriate organizational policies and systems, and engage in other deep and meaningful work outside of the classroom that has a powerful impact on what happens inside it. Given this growing knowledge—and the changing demands of the job—educational leaders need new standards to guide their practice in directions that will be the most productive and beneficial to students (National Policy Board for Educational Administration, 2015, p. 1).

Although PSEL standards were published in 2015, an informal survey we conducted of school leaders in a large urban district of more than 150 school leaders revealed that less than 50 percent of school leaders were aware of the standards, and of those 50 percent, only 10 percent were actively using the standards to guide their practice.

School Leader Evaluation: Getting the Best Results

Has the excellent research and literature we now have available trickled down to influence the *actual practice* of school leaders in real classrooms across the nation? How do we translate research into action? And how do we help leaders internalize, practice, and adopt national leadership standards so that our school leaders become truly reflective, continuously improving professionals? One key to helping school leaders internalize and practice professional standards is in the focus and support provided by districts and the implementation of a framework that helps transfer national standards into actionable evidence-based practices. Superintendent Ember Conley of Park City, Utah, School District says that such alignment is key to school improvement. "Alignment sets the game rules before the game begins, meaning that when school and district leaders have clear objectives, it yields accountability and improved results" (Conley, 2017).

Continuous, systematic improvement of leadership capacity requires ongoing organizational change. The perennial problem, one that never seems to go away, is the great difficulty of implementing deep structural change throughout an organization. Fullan (2000) acknowledged this challenge when he noted that organizational change requires a three-year timeline for elementary schools and a six-year timeline for secondary schools. And even so, he writes, we recognize that "there has been strong adoption and implementation, but not strong institutionalization" (Fullan, 2000, p. 581) of the leadership and instructional changes necessary to foster strong and permanent results. More recently, McKinsey & Company has made the controversial claim that 70 percent of all organizational changes fail and that the root cause of the failure is communication (Bucy, Finlayson, Kelly, & Moye, 2016).

To have real value, professional development and other supports for school leaders require an aligned system, a unified vision that runs through national professional standards, to state or district growth and evaluation systems and other initiatives, to school vision, mission, and policies. The question we raised in the 2015 edition of this book remains vital and, as yet, not entirely resolved: how do we ensure that school leaders have the support, training, vision, and tools to facilitate performing at the highest levels of effectiveness?

From national PSEL standards and federal initiatives such as the Every Student Succeeds Act (ESSA) to state guidelines, district policies, school programs, and the vision of individual school leaders—total alignment may feel like it is beyond our capacity. But such alignment is, indeed, a major goal of effective school leader growth and evaluation systems. Frameworks such as the Marzano Focused School Leader Evaluation Model draw on the most current and thorough research in school leadership; they focus school leader behaviors on those behaviors most likely to have the greatest impact on student learning. As we have noted, PSEL standards and research tell us that leader evaluation systems need to restore the right balance among critical leadership behaviors. While instructional leadership is still crucial, the most effective growth and evaluation systems will take care to address the many, many roles the school leader must play beyond leader of instruction. The Marzano Focused School Leader Evaluation Model balances instructional and organizational duties and recognizes their interrelated influence on improving student achievement.

At the same time, we acknowledge that while the silver bullet to resolve the challenges every school leader faces is elusive, it is still attainable. Leaders still have to juggle the many responsibilities inherent in the job—evaluating data, ensuring standards-driven curriculum and instruction, developing teachers, instilling values and fostering community, and managing resources. Nevertheless, we do believe that nearly every school leader has the potential for growth—excellent leaders can be *made* as well as born. Given the right tools and support, school leaders will find a path to success, cultivating mentorships with districts, universities, or outside partners. Leaders will find their way to the resources they need to grow and evolve their practice and to continuously improve their performance. As we will discuss in detail in the following chapter, the key is finding the right balance between organizational and instructional leadership. In this book, we lay out one such path.

SCHOOL LEADERSHIP for Results

A Focused Model

INTRODUCTION

The Marzano Focused School Leader Evaluation Model, 2018 Update

A 2017 Rand report, *School Leadership Interventions Under the Every Student Succeeds Act: Evidence Review* (Herman et al., 2017), identified the Marzano School Leader Evaluation Model as one of only two leader evaluation models that meet ESSA criteria for evidence-based leader evaluation systems.

A 2016 Mid-Atlantic REL study, *Measuring Principals' Effectiveness: Results from New Jersey's First Year of Statewide Principal Evaluation* from the Mathematics Policy Research Institute (Herman & Ross, 2016), also reported on the effectiveness of the model based on first-year implementation data of 212 principals in 209 schools. One of the study's conclusions was that principal ratings with the model and median student growth percentiles had moderate to high year-to-year stability.

Introduced in 2018, the Marzano Focused School Leader Evaluation Model is an update to the original Marzano School Leader Evaluation Model, drawing on lessons learned, current research, and new standards. Refined over five years, the Focused Model is designed to support school leaders to continuously improve their practice, concentrating on focused, research-based elements correlated to school improvement and restoring the right balance between instructional and organizational leadership. The model was designed as a framework to break down large domains of responsibility into individual elements in order to guide professional practice and help leaders self-assess and improve. As part of the process, the school leader is evaluated on how effectively he or she is getting the desired results of implementing these elements. The 2018 Marzano Focused School Leader Evaluation Model is complex enough to provide specificity and objectivity, yet streamlined enough to support ease of adoption and use.

This conceptual framework undergirds both the Focused Model and the premise of this book. The Focused Model supports improved performance and professional growth; thus, evaluation becomes the measurement of the school leader's progress toward specific growth goals and the desired effects of each element. If a school leader wants to find the silver bullet to grow his or her practice and achieve sustained results in student achievement, the Focused Model serves as a roadmap.

> "I have used the model as a roadmap to reflect on my practice, going through each domain and then figuring out how to use my reflection to identify areas where I want to get better. For me, it is a mindset type of thing—this is my blueprint and my path and it helps me identify an area where I can grow. The model also gives me concrete examples. You can look at the evidences and see yourself in those, and you take that and look at the scale to ask yourself: Am I just really implementing, or am I implementing and also monitoring for the desired effect?"
>
> —Lori Connery, PhD, Principal, Norman, OK

Dr. Robert Marzano and Dr. Beverly Carbaugh developed and field-tested the original Marzano School Leader Evaluation Model over a period of several years and have updated the objectives in the new Focused Model.

Key Objectives of the 2018 Updated Focused Marzano School Leader Evaluation Model

- To recognize the responsibility of the school leader to find balance and synergy between instructional and organizational leadership
- To recognize the importance of supporting diversity, inclusiveness, and equal opportunity for each student
- To clearly define the role of the school leader in keeping the school focused on its core values
- To support a caring and collaborative culture where all stakeholders embrace a growth mindset
- To keep a constant focus on results

Challenges for Designing School Leader Evaluation

As we noted in 2015, although a great deal of research has been compiled on school leader effectiveness over the past several decades, the research on school leader *evaluation* has been "surprisingly thin" as indicated by a review of the literature conducted in 2011. Davis, Kearney, Sanders, Thomas, and Leon published a comprehensive review of the existing literature on school leader evaluation that identified the challenges most districts were facing as they began to implement new evaluation systems as required by Race to the Top. The report summarized the research from 1980 to 2010. From a total of sixty-eight publications, the authors drew a number of important conclusions about school leader evaluation and the requirements around implementing new evaluation systems.

Davis et al. (2011) went on to identify the most common recommendations and suggestions for reforming principal evaluation. Among their findings were the following:

- Evaluation should guide professional development.
- Evaluation criteria and standards should be clear and should align with school and district goals and student outcomes.
- Principals should collaborate in their evaluation goals, planning, and assessment.
- The tools should be reliable and valid.
- The evaluation system should be built on a foundation of research on effective school leadership and organizations.
- A balance of formative and summative functions would best ensure school leader buy-in and collaboration.
- Evaluations conducted by multiple stakeholders, and drawing on multiple measures, appear to be most effective (pp. 33–35).

The 2018 Marzano Focused School Leader Evaluation Model is correlated with all these criteria, as we will discuss in some detail as we delve into the six domains and twenty-one elements in the ensuing chapters of this book.

The Instructional/Organizational Leader

We have updated the objectives of the 2018 Focused Model *to balance a dual focus on instructional and organizational leadership*. Instructional leadership requires a large skill set, but as any school leader will tell you, mastery of those skills alone will not guarantee a school's success. There must be a critical balance between instructional leadership and organizational leadership. Multiple factors create this balance and interplay, and the updated Focused Model recognizes those factors and their importance.

We will discuss the specifics of the domains, elements, desired effects, and the sample evidences in some detail below. But before our discussion of the specific domains, it's important to understand what we mean by *instructional leadership* and *organizational leadership* and how these two leadership capacities are interdependent and critical to the successful functioning of the school.

Various definitions of *instructional leadership* have been proposed over the years, but there is general agreement that the term implies a deep involvement with teaching and learning. Because the literature on instructional leadership does not always define instructional leadership consistently, our own definition of *instructional leadership* has continued to evolve under the impetus of new research. The updated elements in the Focused Model reflect this evolution. True instructional leadership requires a deep understanding of, and commitment to, the interconnected areas of instruction, curriculum, and assessment in the service of optimizing student learning (DuFour & Marzano, 2011).

The school leader's involvement may take many forms, including leading and supporting teacher learning teams and motivating teachers to continue to grow and provide the most effective classroom environments for each student. The instructional leader identifies effective instructional practices and provides rich classroom observation feedback. He or she organizes professional development opportunities, supports the concept of standards-based instruction, and ensures equal learning opportunities for each student. In these capacities, the instructional leader is highly visible and accessible, distributing necessary resources and clearing distractions so that everyone in the school can focus on what matters most: student learning.

Organizational leadership is how the leader organizes and operates all aspects of the functioning of the school: culture, climate, safety, and budget.

It's not much of a stretch to see how instructional leadership is intimately connected to organizational leadership. For example, Standard 9 (Operations and Management) of the PSEL makes explicit that the goal of streamlined operations is to ensure students' academic success and well-being. The elements of this standard include optimizing teachers' professional capacity to address each student's learning needs; acquiring resources to support curriculum, instruction, and assessment; protecting teacher time from disruption; maintaining data systems to provide actionable information for classroom and school improvement; and developing systems for managing conflict resolution. It's quite clear how these aspects of organizational leadership would directly impact instruction and the conditions for student learning.

Research on how a school leader's organizational capabilities and resource management practices impact student achievement or school growth is still somewhat scarce. But a 2009 Stanford University study conducted on Miami-Dade Public Schools concluded:

> Time spent on Organization Management activities is associated with positive school outcomes, such as student test score gains and positive teacher and parent assessments of the instructional climate; whereas Day-to-Day

Instruction activities are marginally or not at all related to improvements in student performance and often have a negative relationship with teacher and parent assessments. This paper suggests that a single-minded focus on principals as instructional leaders operationalized through direct contact with teachers may be detrimental *if it forsakes the important role of principals as organizational leaders* [our italics]. (Horng, 2009, p. iv)

Additionally, some researchers have made a distinction between management and leadership that may be useful here. School leaders must be *leaders*, not managers, even when designing and executing organizational systems. Citing 2011 research by Shamas-ur-Reman Toor in the engineering field, Stein (2013) in the *Journal of Leadership Education* notes three significant themes that emerge in thinking about the difference between leadership and management:

In his extensive research on the differences between managers and leaders, Toor (2011) concluded that there are three significant themes: "First, leadership pursues change that is coupled with sustainability, while management endeavors to maintain order that is tied with the bottom line. Second, leadership exercises personal power and relational influence to gain authority, whereas management banks on position power and structural hierarchy to execute orders. Third, leadership empowers people, whereas management imposes authority" (p. 318). It is no coincidence, therefore, that America's highest performing schools are the products of good leadership as opposed to effective management. (Stein, 2016, p. 23)

In this vein, the authors of the 2018 Marzano Focused School Leader Evaluation Model have conceptualized school management of resources and operations as part of the evidence of effective organizational leadership, the emphasis of the new Domain 6.

The Focused School Leader Evaluation Model has also been updated to make these connections between instructional and organizational leadership explicit and to balance these interconnected responsibilities. As with the original model, the 2018 model has an accompanying protocol that explains the element and provides sample evidences. The updated model's protocols have been revised to include a specific desired effect for each element and an increased number of sample evidences. The Focused Model is aligned to the 2015 PSEL, discussed below (for a crosswalk between the model and PSEL, see appendix E).

New Policies for School Leader Evaluation

We published the first edition of *School Leadership for Results* in 2015, just a few months before President Obama signed the Every Student Succeeds

Act (ESSA) on December 10, 2015. ESSA represented a further step in the long evolution of our understanding of effective school leadership. Along with the new PSEL released that same year, ESSA set a high bar for evidence-based initiatives for school improvement. New ESSA guidelines have shifted the burden and the freedom to develop and sustain evaluation systems back to the states. At the same time, they emphasize research- and evidence-based systems for improving school leader performance, through training, evaluation systems, and preparation. A 2017 Rand report, *School Leadership Interventions Under the Every Student Succeeds Act: Evidence Review*, identified the Marzano School Leader Evaluation Model as one of only two leader evaluation models that meet ESSA criteria for evidence-based leader evaluation systems.

A Wallace report notes that ESSA evidence on the positive effects of school leadership activities include principal evaluation, principal preparation, academies, professional learning, working conditions, and school improvement models (The Wallace Foundation, 2016). School leader evaluation has a large role to play in developing effective school leadership, for evaluation models are, at best, tools to frame leadership responsibilities, to measure leader performance, and to guide and support focused professional development.

Updated Professional Standards for School Leaders

Researchers have taken a growing interest in not only what fosters and constitutes principal effectiveness but also what constitutes best design and implementation of effective principal evaluation systems. The most prudent school leader growth and evaluation models should align with the ten PSEL standards released by the National Board for Education Administration in 2015:

Standard 1. Mission, Vision, and Core Values

Standard 2. Ethics and Professional Norms

Standard 3. Equity and Cultural Responsiveness

Standard 4. Curriculum, Instruction, and Assessment

Standard 5. Community of Care and Support for Students

Standard 6. Professional Capacity of School Personnel

Standard 7. Professional Community for Teachers and Staff

Standard 8. Meaningful Engagement of Families and Community

Standard 9. Operations and Management

Standard 10. School Improvement

These widely agreed-on national standards have helped shape the "what" of school leader effectiveness. They clearly define a school leader's goals and areas of focus. Getting to the "how" is another matter. Aspiring leaders, assistant principals, and principals also require systems to support them to reach these levels of effective leadership, as well as systems to accurately measure progress toward their goals. Thus, accurate measurement of leader practice and support for professional growth must be the twin pillars of today's school leader evaluation systems, and these pillars are emphasized in the updated Marzano Focused School Leader Evaluation Model. These pillars, measurement and growth, also serve as a guide for aspiring leaders as they strike their path toward effective leadership.

The Basics of Using a Framework Approach for Growth and Evaluation

We will begin our discussion of school leader evaluation with perhaps a deceptively simple definition of school leader effectiveness: *an effective school leader achieves desired results*. To identify and measure desired results, a robust, well-defined school leader evaluation model based on research is essential. (Note: in this book, we will use the terms *desired results*, *desired effects*, and *desired outcomes* synonymously.)

The Concept of a Framework

As we noted in our preface, a comprehensive growth and evaluation system should be a *framework* that addresses all the actions, decisions, and work that school leaders do in their multifaceted roles. School leaders can use such a framework to measure all their actions and to self-assess their behaviors and understand their responsibilities. We see using a systematic framework as the potential silver bullet for self-assessment and growth.

> As a quick illustration of how a framework can be used to organize all the actions and responsibilities of a school leader, complete the following exercise. Write down all leadership responsibilities performed by a school leader, and sort them into large categories of behavior. You should then be able to match the responsibilities to the domains and elements on the following Focused Model map. As a quick reflection, ask yourself: Where do I see the majority of my work? Where am I placing most of my emphasis, and perhaps what is being left out? Principal Olivia Dean says, "I fit all of my work into the framework. I constantly think about what I am doing and what I need to do to move to the next level."

The second valuable aspect of a framework is that it encourages every educator in the system to use a common professional language and to use common names for specific behaviors. A framework allows everyone in a system to recognize and talk about behavior using common descriptors related to instruction or key performance indicators. Just as in the professions of law or medicine, for example, educators need to have a common language to speak with accuracy about what they are doing and observing.

High school principal Peter Liesenfeld (2018) shared with us that the Marzano School Leader Model "is compiled in such a way that I can identify specific elements, and when engaging in conversation with my supervisor, we are using the language from the elements. The language in the scale has become an essential part of our regular common language."

A Roadmap for Success

Figure I.1: **The 2018 Marzano Focused School Leader Evaluation Model.**

Marzano Focused School Leader Evaluation Model

 **A Data-Driven Focus on School Improvement**

Element 1:
The school leader ensures the appropriate use of data to develop critical goals focused on improving student achievement at the school.

Element 2:
The school leader ensures appropriate analysis and interpretation of data are used to monitor the progress of each student toward meeting achievement goals.

Element 3:
The school leader ensures the appropriate implementation of interventions and supportive practices to help each student meet achievement goals.

 Instruction of a Viable and Guaranteed Curriculum

Element 1:
The school leader provides a clear vision for how instruction should be addressed in the school.

Element 2:
The school leader uses knowledge of the predominant instructional practices in the school to improve teaching.

Element 3:
The school leader ensures that school curriculum and accompanying assessments align with state and district standards.

Element 4:
The school leader ensures that school curriculum is focused on essential standards so it can be taught in the time available to teachers.

Element 5:
The school leader ensures that each student has equal opportunity to learn the critical content of the curriculum.

 **Continuous Development of Teachers and Staff**

Element 1:
The school leader effectively hires, supports, and retains personnel who continually demonstrate growth through reflection and growth plans.

Element 2:
The school leader uses multiple sources of data to provide teachers with ongoing evaluations of their pedagogical strengths and weaknesses that are consistent with student achievement data.

Element 3:
The school leader ensures that teachers and staff are provided with job-embedded professional development to optimize professional capacity and support their growth goals.

Marzano Focused School Leader Evaluation Model

 **Community of Care and Collaboration**

Element 1:
The school leader ensures that teachers work in collaborative groups to plan and discuss effective instruction, curriculum, assessments, and the achievement of each student.

Element 2:
The school leader ensures a workplace where teachers have roles in the decision-making process regarding school planning, initiatives, and procedures to maximize the effectiveness of the school.

Element 3:
The school leader ensures equity in a child-centered school with input from staff, students, parents, and the community.

Element 4:
The school leader acknowledges the successes of the school and celebrates the diversity and culture of each student.

 Core Values

Element 1:
The school leader is transparent, communicates effectively, and continues to demonstrate professional growth.

Element 2:
The school leader has the trust of the staff and school community that all decisions are guided by what is best for each student.

Element 3:
The school leader ensures that the school is perceived as safe and culturally responsive.

 **Resource Management**

Element 1:
The school leader ensures that management of the fiscal, technological, and physical resources of the school supports effective instruction and achievement of each student.

Element 2:
The school leader utilizes systematic processes to engage district and external entities in support of school improvement.

Element 3:
The school leader ensures compliance to district, state, and federal rules and regulations to support effective instruction and achievement of each student.

The Focused Model integrates the criteria and behaviors leaders need to demonstrate into more focused elements and emphasizes the organizational responsibilities necessary to support optimal conditions for student learning. As with the original Marzano School Leader Evaluation Model, the updated model is an objective, evidence-based model that evaluates school leader performance against specific criteria aligned to professional standards and specific evidences.

Overview of the Domains

The 2018 Focused Model now contains six, rather than five, domains that define the major job responsibilities of the school leader, and the language of the domains has been adapted to reflect current literature and research regarding school leaders (see the review of research in appendix C).

As illustrated in figure I.1, Domain 1 is now A Data-Driven Focus on School Improvement (previously A Data-Driven Focus on Student Achievement), a shift that reflects a broader perspective regarding student achievement while continuing to emphasize the use of data to drive student achievement, which drives school improvement. The five elements in the original model are now compacted into three elements; however, the sample evidences have been expanded.

The Focused Model Domain 2 (Instruction of a Viable and Guaranteed Curriculum) collapses Domains 2 and 3 of the original model (incorporating two elements from Continuous Improvement of Instruction and three from A Guaranteed and Viable Curriculum). This change reflects the interconnectedness of curriculum and instruction as well as the necessity that both align with new state and national standards. A major part of an instructional leader's job begins with a clear vision of what teaching should look like in the school. This domain focuses on implementation of the school leader's vision of teaching and learning.

Domain 3, Continuous Development of Teachers and Staff, is a new domain focused on human capital management. Although the school leader's primary focus is on improving teacher practice, all staff must grow in their areas of responsibility. The new Domain 3 makes that balance clear: it is critical for the school leader to manage and grow all people in the building. In the original model, this focus was addressed by Elements 2, 4, and 5 of Domain 2.

Domain 4, Community of Care and Collaboration, retains its emphasis from the previous Domain 4 (Cooperation and Collaboration) with a slight shift in focus. The aim is to promote a more inclusive way to think about the school leader's role in establishing a community of care, including the responsibility to ensure equity in instruction, the celebration of diversity, and an emphasis on collaborative teamwork for teachers to plan effective instruction. Domain 4 addresses the way a school does its work, looking at how staff forms a unified, transparent, and collaborative environment so that the school functions at optimal levels. Domain 4 now contains four, rather than five, elements. This domain represents part of the shift in this model to a focus on organizational management, or how the school leader operates the school. The elements in this domain specifically focus on the way the leader establishes a community of care and collaboration. All of the attributes in the elements in Domain 4 work together to define the culture of the school.

Domain 5, Core Values, represents a shift from the previous domain name of School Climate to more expansive ways of thinking about the values that the school leader is committed to: transparency, trust, cultural responsiveness, and safety. These are the values that the school leader instills within the school so that all stakeholders perceive them. Domain 5 is based on the understanding that what the school leader values and models influences the school community's perception of the school and how it feels to be a part of the school. The three elements that comprise Domain 5 are compacted from the prior version of the model. Core values set the tone for school climate. For example, if the leader is transparent, is an effective communicator, and establishes trust in the building, the school climate should reflect those values. Conversely, if those positive core values are not in evidence, the school climate will suffer.

Domain 6, Resource Management, is a new domain that recognizes the important role organizational and resource management plays in instructional leadership and school improvement. In the original model, the three elements now in Domain 6 were captured in the single Element 5 of Domain 5 ("The school leader manages the fiscal, organizational, and technological resources of the school in a way that focuses on effective instruction and the achievement of all students"). As part of our emphasis on striking the right balance between organizational and instructional duties, we have added this domain and broken the elements out for further clarity. Domain 6 focuses on how school leaders manage all of the fiscal and physical resources necessary at the school to support optimal student learning, including attention to and compliance with district and federal mandates. John Kotter (2001) has written that "management is about coping with complexity. Leadership, by contrast, is about coping with change." It is in this sense that the school leader's resource management duties outlined in Domain 6 contribute to the larger vision of the school in their specific and targeted support of school improvement, instruction and curriculum, continuous improvement, collaboration and care, and core values. The three elements of Domain 6 specifically emphasize the desired outcome of improving student achievement and school growth.

What Do We Mean When We Say *Ensure*?

As evaluators and school leaders begin to familiarize themselves with the elements of the Focused School Leader Evaluation Model, it will be helpful to note important recurring words and phrases and to formulate definitions for clear understanding. For example, all elements indicate the school leader needs to "ensure" that certain practices, methods, strategies, and actions are in place—he or she does not need, necessarily, to personally perform the actions.

Understanding what we mean by *ensure* allows the school leader to distribute leadership and to develop leadership talent in others. The word *ensure* implies that the school leader has ultimate responsibility for outcomes. Yet, when appropriate, the school leader directs other school personnel to perform the tasks necessary to create the desired results. For instance, one look at the body of possible evidences quickly reveals the need for shared leadership responsibilities, so that others are enlisted to perform many of the expected tasks.

Rarely does the school leader work in isolation, but the buck stops at his or her desk. The school leader is ultimately responsible for the outcome of all measures taken, making it critical to constantly monitor progress and measure results. The school leader should develop a data system to monitor that the desired results are achieved, as the leader has the final responsibility to ensure that the actions of each domain are completed.

Key Terms in the Common Language of the Marzano Focused School Leader Evaluation Model.

Domain: A large category of responsibility or an area of expertise.

Element: A specific set of behaviors within a domain. An element can be thought of as a standard that breaks down leader actions into specific constructs.

Protocol: Guidelines to provide deeper exploration of the elements. Each element has a specific protocol to further explain the requirements and expectations of the element.

Focus or Element Statement: A statement (included in the protocol) that defines and specifies the constructs of a particular element. It also identifies the behaviors the school leader should demonstrate at the Developing level on the rating/feedback scale. The element and the focus statement are synonymous in this model.

Desired Effect / Desired Result: The expected or desired outcome as a result of the school leader's implementation of the element. The desired effect is the measurement component when demonstrating growth or mastery of the element.

Scale: Describes novice to expert performance (level of skills) for each of the elements included in the six domains of the Marzano Focused School Leader Evaluation Model. Scales provide a means for school leaders to gauge their use of particular strategies and for evaluators to provide feedback to school leaders regarding their use of the strategies. The developmental scale is embedded within the observation protocol using the labels: Not Using (Level 0), Beginning (Level 1), Developing (Level 2), Applying (Level 3), and Innovating (Level 4).

Sample Evidences: Specific observable artifacts or behaviors listed in each protocol that provide samples for leaders to help guide the implementation of each element. The evidences are designed for use by both the school leader and the evaluator. They may also be used as look-fors to guide school leaders and evaluators in assessing the leader's progress toward desired behaviors. The evidences are *not* designed for use as a checklist requiring school leaders to demonstrate each evidence. Rather, they serve as a menu to guide growth. Aspiring leaders will find sample evidences helpful as they build their knowledge base and their repertoire of leadership skills.

Updated Sample Protocols

As part of the roadmap system, every key indicator or element in the model has a corresponding protocol. It may be helpful to think of an *element* as a standard that is unpacked to identify the critical behaviors that the school leader should demonstrate. The protocols are procedural guidelines that provide a deeper explanation of the element. The protocol for each element includes the element or focus statement, which identifies the specific behaviors the leader must demonstrate to satisfy the requirements for that element. The element statement can also be used as a reflective tool when the leader transforms the statement into a question by asking, "What am I doing to ensure . . . ?" This stem can be used with every element in the model. For example, "What am I doing as a school leader to ensure the appropriate use of data is being used to develop critical goals focused on improving student achievement?" As a result of implementing the behaviors in the focused statement, every element has a desired effect/outcome. One can think of the desired effect, or desired result, this way: *if* the leader performs the actions in the element statement, *then* the desired effect of that behavior is what should be evidenced.

The 2018 update of the Marzano School Leader Evaluation Model employs the same five-point scales (0–4) as the original model, and the model may be implemented as part of an aligned Marzano evaluation system. However, the model is agnostic in that it is designed and may be used in conjunction with any teacher or district leader evaluation system. The updated protocols provide broader evidences with more behaviors identified, so that as the leader uses the model for self-assessment and reflection, the evidences serve as a guide to the process.

As with the original model, a school leader who meets the criteria for the element statement would be said to be functioning at Developing, or Level 2, of the scale. Providing evidence of the desired effects indicates a score at Applying, or Level 3. Updated evidences and desired effects are included in the protocols. The following example is the protocol for Domain 1, Element 1. Note that the desired effect is specifically stated for each element beneath the focus statement.

Domain 1: A Data-Driven Focus on School Improvement

Figure I.2: **Sample focus statement, desired effect, scales, and evidences for the Marzano Focused School Leader Evaluation Model.**

The school leader ensures the appropriate use of data to develop critical goals focused on improving student achievement at the school.

Desired Effect: Everyone understands the school's most critical goals for improving student achievement.

Scale Value	Description
Innovating (4)	The school leader ensures adjustments are made or new methods are utilized so that all stakeholders sufficiently understand the critical goals.
Applying (3)	The school leader ensures the appropriate use of data to develop critical goals focused on improving student achievement at the school AND regularly monitors that everyone understands the critical goals for improving student achievement.
Developing (2)	The school leader ensures the appropriate use of data to develop critical goals focused on improving student achievement at the school.
Beginning (1)	The school leader attempts to use appropriate data to develop critical goals focused on improving student achievement at the school but does not complete the task or is not successful.
Not Using (0)	The school leader does not attempt to use appropriate data to develop critical goals focused on improving student achievement at the school.

Sample Evidences for Element 1 of Domain 1
- Published goals focus on a plan for eliminating the achievement gap for each student. - Goals support the vision and mission of the school. - School improvement goals are established as a percentage of students who will score at a proficient or higher level on state assessments or benchmark assessments. - Multiple sources of data are used to develop critical goals. - Schoolwide achievement goals are posted and discussed regularly at faculty and staff gatherings. - Written goals address the most critical and severe achievement deficiencies. - Written timelines contain specific benchmarks for each goal including who provides support for achieving the goal. - A school improvement or strategic plan delineates the critical goals.

- Faculty and staff can explain how goals support and eliminate differences in achievement for students at different socioeconomic levels, English language learners, and students with disabilities.
- Faculty and staff can describe why the identified schoolwide achievement goals are the most critical.
- Data are available to identify how the most critical achievement goals of the school are supported.

The Role of the Evaluator

A district leader evaluating a school leader will use the protocol to guide conferences and goal setting with the school leader; the protocol provides sample evidences that can also serve as questions. You might think of the evidences as sources of questions to ask school leaders for documentation to support their actions for each element. The role of the evaluator should not just be to evaluate but also to support, to give honest and accurate feedback, and to serve as a coach for growth.

How to Use This Book

This book is intended for school leaders and their evaluators, district leaders, and policy makers interested in improving school leader performance and retention in the context of school leader evaluation and growth. It also can be used by aspiring leaders who are still forming and refining their craft. It is written as a self-help guide for leaders in search of the silver bullet.

Chapters 1 through 6 look at the literature and research for each domain. Each chapter then explains the Focused Model's elements and evidences in some detail, with sample scenarios for each element, sample scoring, and feedback with reflection and growth questions for each element.

Scenarios are based on examples gathered from the field and can be used as practice on how to self-score or to help readers learn how to use the scale accurately. We encourage reading them as practice even if the specifics of the scenarios do not directly apply.

The model's emphasis on continuous individual development is supported by samples of evidences to guide performance and growth, which makes it unique among leader evaluation models and positions it as an optimal tool for improving school leadership skills and capacities. The scenarios, sample scores, and reflection questions will help school leaders create their own silver bullet for reflection and growth.

The growth and reflection questions for each element of the model are questions for aspiring leaders to ask themselves as they develop leadership skills. Current leaders can use them as personal reflection questions as they continue to grow in their practice. Supervisors may also refer to these questions in conversations with a school leader to guide them in probing and reflecting on whether the leader is demonstrating evidence of the desired effect of the element.

Finally, chapter 7 discusses guidelines for implementation and scoring. It also provides information about the virtual platform and tools to support the model. We also discuss the model as part of an aligned evaluation system for teachers, district leaders, and non-classroom-certificated personnel.

Conclusion

New research and practice necessitates that evaluation models undergo regular examination and revision to maintain alignment to best practices in the education field. Updating an evaluation model requires a delicate balance: the model must identify the essential behaviors required, define clear measurement standards, and perhaps most critically, be built to support feedback and growth objectives. Our goal in this model update has been to provide a set of criteria to help current or potential school leaders reflect on and improve their practice while remaining true to our vision of leadership qualities most likely to impact whole-school improvement and student achievement.

CHAPTER 1

Domain 1: A Data-Driven Focus on School Improvement

Figure 1.1. **The three elements of Domain 1 guide the school leader to ensure appropriate use of data to monitor and improve student achievement.**

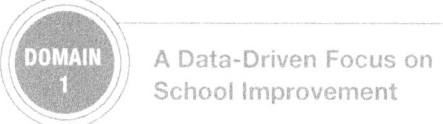

A Data-Driven Focus on School Improvement

Element 1:
The school leader ensures the appropriate use of data to develop critical goals focused on improving student achievement at the school.

Element 2:
The school leader ensures appropriate analysis and interpretation of data are used to monitor the progress of each student toward meeting achievement goals.

Element 3:
The school leader ensures the appropriate implementation of interventions and supportive practices to help each student meet achievement goals.

Domain 1 of the Focused Model represents a highly aligned process that drives overall school improvement, as the behaviors represented in the three elements work together to create a focus on student achievement. In this domain, the actions of the school leader in setting schoolwide goals and using data to monitor progress are *leading indicators* for ensuring the desired result/outcome of the *lagging indicator* of overall school improvement. Because the Focused Model as a whole is designed to move the leader and school away from a compliance mentality toward an approach that values and monitors measurable results, the elements in Domain 1, as well as those in the other domains in the model, are specifically focused on leader actions and oriented toward results.

What Do We Mean by "School Improvement"?

School improvement is a topic of much current discussion and interest. But how do we know what we mean when we talk about improving schools? A review of the literature finds multiple definitions of the phrase, many focused on the process of improvement but lacking an exact definition.

The Glossary of Education Reform (2013) offers a definition of *continuous improvement* that closely aligns with the goal of school improvement articulated in Domain 1 of the Focused Model:

> The term *continuous improvement* refers to any school- or instructional-improvement process that unfolds progressively, that does not have a fixed or predetermined end point, and that is sustained over extended periods of time. The concept also encompasses the general belief that improvement is not something that starts and stops, but it's something that requires an organizational or professional commitment to an ongoing process of learning, self-reflection, adaptation, and growth.

Although this definition does not address the use of data, it does describe the process. We propose that data is the driver of the continuous school improvement process.

It should be noted that *continuous improvement* has become something of a buzzword in education, but schools and school systems are challenged in actually executing, in any practical or authentic sense, a continuous improvement process.

A report from Hanover Research (2014), Best Practices for School Improvement Planning, indicates a key finding regarding school improvement. The authors stress that "effective school improvement planning models emphasize comprehensive needs assessments, strategic prioritization of needs, and data-driven decision-making" (Hanover Research, 2014, p. 4). They emphasize that "throughout the school improvement process, leaders should communicate objectives, progress, and results with all relevant stakeholders" (p. 4).

The school improvement process outlined previously can be applied within the structure of Domain 1 if we think of analysis of data as the "comprehensive needs assessment" and identifying critical goals as "strategic prioritization of needs," both the focus of Element 1. The data are then used to drive decision making for interventions, the focus of Element 3. Throughout the process, the school leader should monitor progress (Element 2) and continually communicate results with relevant stakeholders.

It's important to emphasize that the collection and monitoring of data are not exercises designed to exert control over students, teachers, or school leaders. Rather, effective leaders view data as a means not only to pinpoint problems but also to understand their nature and causes. Data collection serves one primary purpose: to allow school leaders and teachers to track progress toward goals and design interventions when necessary to get struggling students back on track. The path to school improvement begins in Domain 1 of the Marzano Focused School Leader framework.

The How and Why of Data

In the context of school leader growth and evaluation, both school leaders and their supervisors need to understand how and why they use data. As we noted previously, data collection allows school leaders and teachers to track progress toward goals and design interventions when necessary to get struggling students back on track. School leaders often get caught in the trap of using large-scale summative testing data as the primary vehicle to drive goals and interventions. However, we propose that in order to isolate and identify the most critical goals, the leader must mine through data at the individual student level to look for data trends and patterns for individual and groups of students. Finally, the school leader uses that disaggregated data to form a micropicture of achievement gaps and critical needs within the school's student population.

Use of appropriate, relevant data could lead the school to redefine its most important student achievement goals. This redefinition might move the school away from its current overarching goals to more specific, granular goals. Those granular goals, when aggregated, might very well lead to the reformulation of *different* overarching goals.

For example, we have seen schools identify a large overarching goal to improve reading comprehension. But that goal is so bulky that it may not actually help a teacher zero in on the most critical aspects of comprehension. It is the leader's responsibility to ensure that goals are not just specific but also focused on the most critical achievement needs.

Use of appropriate data is vital to the school improvement process. Leaders need to use appropriate data to identify struggling learners in order to design early interventions. Leaders also need to use appropriate data to monitor *response to interventions* (RTI) and to provide *multitiered systems of support* (MTSS). Designing specific interventions based on data and continually monitoring the results of the interventions are the practices most likely to produce results. Appropriate use of data helps a school leader meet a school's academic growth goals and narrow achievement gaps. Building a culture that continually seeks and utilizes multiple sources of data is pivotal to driving school improvement.

Let's look at an example of how to use data to plan specific interventions. In a school where ninth-grade English language arts (ELA) midyear test scores have declined and many students do not meet the standards, a principal might work with a committee to mine the data to determine if scores declined in all classes or specific classes, to analyze any gender differences, and to see if the daily or other formative grades of individual students were predictive of how they scored on the midyear test. The committee could then conduct an item analysis process to determine if particular concepts were problematic for any or all of the failing students. Using the data from the item analysis, very specific interventions with systematic progress monitoring could be designed and implemented. This type of process moves interventions from one-size-fits-all to specific, results-oriented interventions.

In summary, Domain 1 has three major criteria: establishing the most critical goals, using the right data to monitor progress toward those goals, and designing intervention programs to meet the needs of individual students. In this growth and evaluation model, school leaders must keep their eyes on the nonnegotiable goal: steady growth in student achievement that leads to attaining school improvement goals.

The Elements of Domain 1

Domain 1, Element 1: Using Data to Develop Critical Schoolwide Goals

The school leader ensures the appropriate use of data to develop critical goals focused on improving student achievement at the school.

Desired Effect: Everyone understands the school's most critical goals for improving student achievement.

Most school leaders have an understanding that the collective goal of all educators—from teachers to superintendents—is, as Stiggins (2016) noted, "to help the largest possible percentage of our students get 'there.' . . . Any energy a school leader . . . invests in becoming clear about targets will pay big dividends" (p. 304). Element 1 is about defining, first of all, where "there" is, and second, how to use data appropriately to support those goals.

This cornerstone element asks the school leader to establish critical goals that are specific and clear enough to be understood by all staff and stakeholders, which is the desired effect. The goals must be developed based on data and thus be measurable, not just broad-based statements of improvement. And the focus of the goals must be on the critical achievement needs of the school as a whole.

Determining the Most Critical Goals

Successful leaders begin by determining the most critical achievement needs at the individual student level and then aggregating that data to compile a schoolwide data set. This data might include summative student achievement scores, benchmark scores, formative assessments, or student/parent surveys. To establish the most critical goals, the process typically involves data disaggregation—or analysis of data by content disciplines and then by broad descriptors such as student subpopulations, gender, socioeconomic status, and proficiency levels—so that school leaders may determine areas of critical need for the school as a whole. In this process, school leaders are drilling down from overarching goals to more specific critical goals for improving student achievement.

The process described in Element 1 aligns the development of schoolwide goals to goals that are SMART: specific, measurable, attainable, results oriented (requiring evidence of higher levels of student learning in order to be achieved), and time bound (Dufour & Marzano, 2011).

Once the school leader has identified critical goals, the next step is to identify the who, what, when, where, and how—the factors necessary to determine how the goals will be accomplished. Domain 1 leads the school leader through this process element by element.

The Scales and Sample Evidences for Domain 1, Element 1

Figure 1.2 details the performance scale and sample evidences for Element 1 of Domain 1.

Figure 1.2: **The scales and sample evidences for Domain 1, Element 1.**

Scale Value	Description
Innovating (4)	The school leader ensures adjustments are made or new methods are utilized so that all stakeholders sufficiently understand the critical goals.
Applying (3)	The school leader ensures the appropriate use of data to develop critical goals focused on improving student achievement at the school AND regularly monitors that everyone understands the critical goals for improving student achievement.
Developing (2)	The school leader ensures the appropriate use of data to develop critical goals focused on improving student achievement at the school.
Beginning (1)	The school leader attempts to use appropriate data to develop critical goals focused on improving student achievement at the school but does not complete the task or is not successful.
Not Using (0)	The school leader does not attempt to use appropriate data to develop critical goals focused on improving student achievement at the school.

Sample Evidences for Element 1 of Domain 1
• Published goals focus on a plan for eliminating the achievement gap for each student.
• Goals support the vision and mission of the school.
• School improvement goals are established as a percentage of students who will score at a proficient or higher level on state assessments or benchmark assessments.
• Multiple sources of data are used to develop critical goals.
• Schoolwide achievement goals are posted and discussed regularly at faculty and staff gatherings.
• Written goals address the most critical and severe achievement deficiencies.
• Written timelines contain specific benchmarks for each goal including who provides support for achieving the goal.
• A school improvement or strategic plan delineates the critical goals.
• Faculty and staff can explain how goals support and eliminate differences in achievement for students at different socioeconomic levels, English learners, and students with disabilities.
• Faculty and staff can describe why the identified schoolwide achievement goals are the most critical.
• Data are available to identify how the most critical achievement goals of the school are supported.

Collecting Evidence and Providing Artifacts

In order to move from leadership focused on compliance to leadership focused on desired results within an evidence-based growth and evaluation model, both the school leader and his or her supervisor must be clear about the kinds of evidence and artifacts that demonstrate the school leader is meeting the desired results for each element. For the learning or aspiring leader, this set of evidences can be used as a self-learning guide to generate questions for mentors and as a menu of sample evidences that, when fully understood and anticipated, can help ease the transition into the role of school leader.

As part of the school leader's preparation for evaluation, he or she will want to start planning what kinds of evidences or artifacts to present for each of the three elements in Domain 1. The school leader and supervisor may collaborate or conference to obtain general agreement on what kinds of evidence determine each level of performance, from Not Using to Innovating. The Focused Model does offer sample evidences for each element. But these sample evidences may not be all-inclusive; individual schools and districts may use them whole-scale or adapt them. Most important, evidences should be designed to help a leader focus on achieving desired results. They should not be designed for use as a checklist system but rather as samples of the types of artifacts or evidences that would help the leader ensure the desired results.

Planning Exercise for Evaluators of School Leaders

As a preconference exercise, for this domain or any domain in the model, a supervisor might ask the following questions:

- Has the leader met all the constructs (or parts) described in the element statement?
- What is the desired effect/outcome for this element?
- What does it mean for the school leader to *ensure*?
- What evidence/documentation supports a score on the scale?

The scenario below offers a sample for school leaders and their evaluators to use in pre- and postconferences as a guide to acquire familiarity with scoring. School leaders can also use scenarios to learn how to meet the constructs of an element and to score themselves on obtaining desired results. A practice scenario will be provided for each element in the model.

A Scenario for Domain 1, Element 1

Principal Wentz has provided his supervisor, Ms. James, with the school improvement plan from River Elementary as documentation of his actions in using data to develop the most critical goals for the school. When reviewing the plan, Ms. James notes that clear goals were established based on achievement data from the statewide assessment, as well as from their district and building assessments. She also notes that the building's plan sets specific percentage goals to close achievement gaps, with timelines for achievement of the goals. In the plan, it was noted that the leadership team took part in development of the goals and was given responsibility for providing support. Mr. Wentz has also provided pictures of a data wall established in a secure room in the media center so that all teachers would have easy access to it. Pictures and posters in the building's hallways state the school's academic achievement goals for the year.

Score: *Developing*

Feedback

Ms. James congratulates Mr. Wentz for working with his leadership team to develop specific goals based on data from multiple sources. They discuss why this triangulation of data is so important, and Mr. Wentz shares that he was surprised at some of the insights the team had about gaps in student achievement when they dug deeper and used other sources of data in addition to statewide assessments. Ms. James also notes the steps taken to display the goals and to assign leadership team members to provide support. Ms. James then has Mr. Wentz consider the desired effect of this element, "Everyone understands the school's most critical goals for improving student achievement," and asks what information he has to confirm that everyone understands the goals. Mr. Wentz agrees that he does not really know how many teachers, other than those on the leadership team, actually view the data wall, nor how many would be able to tell what the goals are. Ms. James and Mr. Wentz agree that he has made a very good start in this element. To move the score on the developmental scale to the next level, the principal would need to provide evidence that he is achieving the desired effect of the element.

Growth and Reflection Questions for Domain 1, Element 1

- How are school improvement goals effectively communicated to the school community?
- What evidence would demonstrate that everyone understands the most critical goals for improving student achievement?
- If the leader discovers that some staff are unaware of the critical school goals, what adjustments or interventions should be taken?
- What sample evidences support that teachers understand which goals are most critical?
- How do the goals support increasing achievement for students at different socioeconomic levels, English language learners, and students with disabilities?
- Are there ways to involve more people, other than the leadership team, in developing the goals?
- What action does the school leader need to take to move to the next level?
- What evidence would demonstrate the leader is achieving the desired effect of the element?

Elements 2 and 3: The Big Picture

Elements 2 and 3 of Domain 1 focus on setting individual student goals, monitoring and analyzing data, and using that data to determine appropriate interventions. These elements have been strategically designed to keep the school leader shifting his or her focus between individual student goals and whole-school goals. In order to monitor goals and individual student performance, school leaders need ongoing formative, diagnostic, and benchmark data with a process for multiple levels of data analysis. We will discuss multiple levels of data analysis later in this chapter.

> *"One of the things that I started focusing on was, I had to be more data driven in my decision making. So I created some tools to help me look specifically at each student's data. That has allowed me to facilitate conversations with teachers and*

monitor the data with students. Our school has jumped two letter grades [in Florida's school accountability system]. I think a lot of that success goes back to the data conversations and monitoring of our work—we have been very purposeful in our conversations. I would tell teachers, 'You need to be honest with yourself; we need to step back from our pride and look at ourselves honestly.' You have to make yourself vulnerable to allow growth to happen."

—Michael Feeney, Principal, High Point Elementary, Pinellas County, FL

Domain 1, Element 2: Monitoring Progress of Individual Students

The school leader ensures appropriate analysis and interpretation of data are used to monitor the progress of each student toward meeting achievement goals.

Desired Effect: Data confirm students are making progress toward meeting their achievement goals.

Our discussion of Element 1 of Domain 1 focused on using data to create schoolwide goals. Element 2 focuses on using data to monitor whether each student is making progress toward meeting achievement goals.

With Element 2, teachers and students all need to be aware of individual student achievement goals. The school leader must also ensure that teachers have a deliberate plan to monitor progress toward these goals. To this end, teachers disaggregate individual student data for the students in their classes to determine which students may be highly proficient or proficient and, conversely, where there may be achievement gaps. Having access to disaggregated data allows the teacher to adjust instruction to the appropriate level of rigor for individual students and to set appropriate goals for each student in the class.

About Data Analysis

Element 2 sets the expectation for the leader to ensure that data are collected, organized, analyzed, and interpreted to monitor individual students' progress toward achievement goals. Leaders and teachers are often overwhelmed with sources of data, including state assessments in multiple disciplines, district-generated end-of-course exams, benchmark tests, and formative assessments created and used by teachers. To analyze data, school leaders will find it helpful to have a systematic process for data analysis and ongoing progress monitoring.

We suggest thinking in terms of levels of data analysis, or steps in a protocol to analyze data (Preuss, 2003). These steps for analyzing data are meant for practitioners in the field to go into *deeper levels of analysis* on their data sets. If we want to get to the *root causes* of an issue, these levels constitute a process to identify those root causes. Equipped with this understanding, the leader and school teams may then take steps toward a solution.

Level One Data Analysis

School leaders will often begin the process with *level one data analysis*—in other words, quantifying by category to describe the data set. Paul Preuss (2003) has defined level one data as the initial aggregated data set: most often "prior to disaggregation or further analysis." Level one data is used to identify "red flag issues" (Preuss, 2003, p. 201).

The data examined in level one analysis answer basic questions, such as: How many students are proficient or meet benchmarks? Is attendance improving, or are there changes in behavioral data? This data is typically *descriptive* in terms of the quantities in any given category.

Level one data analysis can be important for specific purposes. For example, in analyzing a summative assessment or even a student survey, the school leader will look at percentages of students who answered in the same way. The school leader would consider the percentage of the total survey population and compare those numbers with the percentages in subgroups.

Examples include, but are not limited to, disaggregating the number of graduates by demographic subgroups, the percentage of proficient students by grade level on an assessment, and the number of students attending an intervention and their rate of attendance. This is probably the level of data analysis with which we are most familiar and, oftentimes, the level of analysis at which we make important decisions—perhaps shortsightedly. Although level one data analysis provides much demographic and broad achievement information and is useful in setting schoolwide goals, it may not help a leader interpret data at a level that will inform instruction or assist in making intervention decisions.

Level Two Data Analysis

Level two data analysis is a process that questions and examines the strengths and weaknesses in the data in terms of their intended use. Preuss (2003) defines level two data as data that has been disaggregated from an initial set of aggregated data for a deeper understanding of the issue. Analysis of level two data may also include looking at "the who" and "on what" in terms of a data set. For example, we may want to examine the names of students who have failed one or more classes during the first quarter and whether or not they are enrolled in an intervention program. Or, we might examine the students participating in a specific intervention in relationship to their performance on a current assessment. This level of analysis could include identifying students who have not been proficient on the state assessment and have low value-added scores. We would emphasize that state assessment results alone would not be the most relevant data to determine specific interventions for specific students. More timely data, such as benchmark or formative assessment, would be a far better source of data for placing a student in a specific intervention.

The questions at level two data analysis focus on whether the data we are analyzing provide us with enough specific information to plan for appropriate interventions or to make changes in core programs or instructional strategies. It is the responsibility of the school leader to identify the appropriate level of data analysis and to ensure that staff examine the data as thoroughly as necessary for the task at hand.

To illustrate: If staff are attempting to monitor whether the school is closing the achievement gap, it will be appropriate to use *level one analysis* to look at the percentage of proficient students on an assessment over time. However, if staff are trying to determine who may need additional opportunities to learn a particular area of content, they would be remiss if they did not engage in *level two analysis* to identify to *which* students *what* specific content and *how much* additional instructional time should be provided.

Level Three (Root Cause) Data Analysis

A process of level three data analysis, which often draws on multiple sources of data, is recommended for a school leader to discover *root causes*. The root cause, according to Preuss (2003), is "the deepest underlying cause or causes of positive or negative symptoms within any process, which, if dissolved, would result in elimination, or substantial reduction, of the symptom" (p. 204). It is important to distinguish between symptoms (the *results* of a problem) and the root cause of the problem. For example, poor attendance is a *symptom* of a root cause; the root cause itself could turn out to be a high incidence of bullying, widespread drug use, lack of engagement, and so on.

This synthesis process, using multiple sources of data to determine root cause, is probably the least-used level of data analysis. But in reality, level three analysis will allow school leaders to address, and even remedy, specific root causes of negative symptoms. As noted, this level of analysis usually involves using information from multiple data sources to answer specific questions.

For example, a data team reviews the names of students, by teacher, who have not shown any percentile increases on the benchmark assessment from the first to second quarters. They analyze proficiency levels for specific items related to a skill or standard. Finally, they identify the items, by level of complexity, on which students show proficiency or are below proficiency. They consider this information in relation to prior assessments, to the curriculum, and perhaps even to other sources of data.

Using this type of analysis, the data team can zero in on instructional or curriculum changes that should be implemented. The root cause in the earlier case would be identified as a problem with the curriculum or with the implementation of the curriculum. Perhaps the implemented curriculum did not reach the same level of complexity as items on the benchmark test. Once the root cause has been identified, specific feedback can be used by the team or even a specific teacher. It advances the process from merely *having* the data to *using* the data to determine how to adapt presentation of classroom content to the required level of complexity.

To further illustrate: A secondary school principal shared an example of level three data analysis. At the end of the first quarter, more than 50 percent of the students taking algebra were failing the course. A data team meeting was convened to analyze why the school was experiencing such a high failure rate. The team began by reviewing the absence rates, number of tardies, and behavior incidences for each failing student. The team also analyzed and compared the periods and teachers with the most failing students and the formative assessment data for each student (i.e., multiple data sources). With an eye on discovering the root cause, the team began asking questions to determine why students were failing.

The team discovered a group of first-period students who rode a bus that routinely arrived late. When reviewing the students' formative assessments, it was apparent that interventions should have been implemented but had not been put in place. In the process, the data team also discovered most algebra classes were scheduled during the first period of the school day; the failing students had high tardy rates. When they interviewed the students, most students said they did not find algebra relevant or engaging, so they avoided coming to first period. Once the data team discovered the root causes, changes were made to the master schedule so that algebra classes met later in the day, and teachers in the department worked on engagement strategies to make algebra relevant to their students.

With level three or root cause data analysis, a leader can make intervention decisions that focus on root causes (late buses, lack of engagement) rather than symptoms (low algebra scores). Deeper levels of data analysis are what help school leaders make better decisions. These systematic processes will ensure the school leader has the appropriate data to monitor disaggregated student data and also to aggregate data to monitor schoolwide progress.

Goal Setting and Tracking

In Element 2, we see the focus of drilling down to include setting, maintaining, and monitoring goals for individual students. Effective leaders know that it takes more than just setting individual student goals to drive improvement. For a school to reach its overall goal, the school leader must pay careful, ongoing attention to individual student data.

The school leader's job is to ensure that teachers not only know the critical achievement goals of their students and monitor data to determine progress but also that students, in turn, know their own critical achievement goals. And to go one step further, the test of Element 2 will be whether the *desired effect* has been achieved: that data confirm students are making progress toward meeting their achievement goals.

To formulate goals for individual students, teachers must have a solid knowledge of grade-level expectations or standards. Here, the school leader can help teachers understand and focus on ways to plan for discrepancies in student performance in relation to grade-level expectations, a likely subset of overall goals for student achievement. The Common Core State Standards and other college and career readiness standards were designed as grade-level expectations. To monitor critical achievement goals, a teacher must first consider the expectations for the grade level and set the right goals for individual students.

Students, of course, should participate in the process and know their own goals for individual achievement; they should also track their own progress toward the goals.

Student participation not only helps students buy in to the goals, but ideally it also helps them stay focused on the end goal—to improve achievement and to meet their grade-level expectations.

A principal we know shared a schoolwide process that she implemented during the first two weeks of school as a first step to students knowing their individual proficiency targets. Every student was presented with his or her achievement data from the prior year. Teachers then made students aware of the school/state proficiency targets in each tested subject. Each student set goals to meet his or her proficiency targets. Students recorded the process in their daily homework or agenda notebooks, then teachers and school leaders used this information to informally monitor and track progress toward students' individual goals.

This process could be the beginning phase of working with students to not only know their long-term achievement targets but also to know their goals for units or even courses.

The Scale and Sample Evidences for Domain 1, Element 2

Figure 1.3: **Scales and sample evidences for Domain 1, Element 2.**

Scale Value	Description
Innovating (4)	The school leader ensures that multiple sources of data are analyzed to provide the most relevant information and readdresses achievement goals using accrued achievement data.
Applying (3)	The school leader ensures appropriate analysis and interpretation of data are used to monitor the progress of each student toward meeting achievement goals AND monitors the extent to which student data are used to track progress toward goals.
Developing (2)	The school leader ensures appropriate analysis and interpretation of data are used to monitor the progress of each student toward meeting achievement goals.
Beginning (1)	The school leader attempts to ensure appropriate analysis and interpretation of data are used to monitor the progress of each student toward meeting achievement goals but does not complete the task or is not successful.
Not Using (0)	The school leader does not attempt to ensure appropriate analysis and interpretation of data are used to monitor the progress of each student toward meeting achievement goals.

Sample Evidences for Element 2 of Domain 1
• Reports, charts, graphs, and other relevant data for each student are available for tracking status and growth.
• Data are routinely analyzed for learning gaps.
• Individual student results from multiple types of assessments are regularly reported and used (e.g., classroom formative, benchmark, summative / end of year).
• Individual student reports, graphs, and charts are regularly updated to track the progress of each student.
• Teachers regularly meet to analyze school growth data for individual students.
• School leadership teams regularly meet to analyze individual student performance.
• Teachers utilize multiple sources of individual student data in planning to close achievement gaps.
• Teachers regularly analyze data of their individual students, including all subgroups.
• Students keep data logs regarding their individual goals and for tracking progress.
• Student-led conferences focus on the student's achievement goals.
• Parents have access to student achievement data systems to track student progress.
• Parent-teacher conferences focus on individual student goals and progress.
• Teacher plans address the learning goals of their students.
• Each student has recorded achievement goals for classroom formative, benchmark, and summative assessments.

Domain 1: A Data-Driven Focus on School Improvement

A Scenario for Domain 1, Element 2

When the principal of Crest High School, Ms. Gain, meets with her supervisor in February, she shows evidence of how the school is using data to improve student achievement. She provides copies of professional learning community agendas and notes that show analysis of student data is happening on a regular basis in these teams. The notes also provide evidence that teachers are developing unit and lesson plans based on information they obtain from reviewing multiple assessments to include classroom assessments and benchmark and summative tests. There is evidence in the notes that teachers discuss and make plans for individual students who are struggling and for students who are achieving at higher levels.

To track progress, Ms. Gain provides samples of individual charts that students and their teachers update at regular intervals. Finally, Ms. Gain shows her supervisor notes from staff meetings in which content teams/PLCs report and notate the overall progress of each student toward meeting his or her goals. The latest data demonstrate that the school's goal of 5 percent growth in math has been met based on a standardized benchmark assessment used in the district and that the ELA scores increased by 2 percent (the goal is 5 percent). In addition, PLC teams have data showing individual growth.

Score: Applying

Feedback

As the supervisor examines the evidence Ms. Gain presents, it clearly meets the criteria for the Developing level. The staff at Crest High analyzes and uses data to monitor student progress, at both the schoolwide and the individual student levels. Ms. Gain and her supervisor then look at the desired effect of the element to determine that the staff continually analyzes data throughout the year and can document that students are making progress toward their goals. Sharing documents from data reviews and taking a look at the updated data wall, Ms. Gain and her supervisor determine that the criteria for the Applying level is the correct feedback score.

Growth and Reflection Questions for Domain 1, Element 2

- What assessments other than district benchmark tests can a principal use to analyze student growth?
- How does one determine what sources of data are most appropriate for monitoring student growth in math and ELA? Can it be different at different grade levels?
- How does a school leader help teachers use the data from ongoing progress monitoring or data reviews?

- In cases below the level of Innovating, what would the school leader need to do to move his or her score to the next level?
- What evidence would demonstrate the leader is achieving the desired effect of the element?

Domain 1, Element 3: Developing Interventions and Support

The school leader ensures the appropriate implementation of interventions and supportive practices to help each student meet achievement goals.

Desired Effect: Data confirm interventions help each student meet achievement goals.

As we touched on earlier in this chapter, data collection allows school leaders and teachers to track progress toward goals and design interventions such as RTI, MTSS, and other specific interventions when necessary to get struggling students back on track. These strategies allow us to design programs focused on academic goals and to narrow achievement gaps.

Once the school leader has a process for monitoring individual data and recognizes its impact on overall school data, he or she must ensure that appropriate school-level intervention programs are in place.

Interventions are typically just a first step, but the most critical component of any intervention is how the leader knows whether the intervention is yielding results. For every intervention established—whether schoolwide or for individual students—both the desired results and the criteria for success should be determined early in the process. Establishing the criteria for success allows the school leader a definitive way to measure results.

The school leader might, for example, implement a program to improve students' organization skills to facilitate a readiness to learn. If the leader puts in place such a schoolwide intervention, requiring that all students use organizational notebooks, the leader ought to know both the desired result (e.g., all students use notebooks) and how to measure the desired result (e.g., a teacher survey indicates that students are better prepared for class). In other words, for every element, the leader should begin with the end in mind and a plan for monitoring progress toward that end.

Determining Individual Student Interventions

How does a leader determine appropriate and necessary individual student interventions? Such interventions are dependent on the data analyzed and interpreted as part of Element 2. Interventions for individual students may include small-group or one-on-one interventions, but the key is that they must be based on data and aligned to narrow students' individual achievement gaps.

The real problem is that schools sometimes plan a menu of intervention options and then try to plug students into the available options. We suggest, instead, an approach that uses multiple sources of data analyzed for root causes, followed by interventions planned to address individual root causes. Data analysis should be at a level that helps a school leader and teachers drill down to root causes.

Let's look at a hypothetical example. The school leader has examined data for an individual student and recognized that Student A has not made progress toward a specific reading goal. In a worst-case scenario, the teacher might assign the student to participate in a tiered reading group that does not focus on the student's specific reading proficiency. But perhaps when doing root cause analysis, the school leader and teacher discover that Student A needs targeted help in analyzing story elements and text features. If the student has been homogeneously grouped with Students B, C, and D, who have different proficiency needs, the group has not been differentiated for Student A's critical needs. Student A needs targeted instruction that will address specific deficits. Remember, the purpose of the intervention is to increase proficiency in the targeted skill. The teacher will use formative assessments to track Student A's progress toward achieving specific goals.

Again, when planning individual student interventions, the school leader must begin with the end in mind and have specific measures identified to clearly determine if the desired outcomes have been met.

The Scale and Sample Evidences for Domain 1, Element 3

Figure 1.4: **The scale and sample evidences for Domain 1, Element 3.**

Scale Value	Description
Innovating (4)	The school leader continually examines and expands the options for individual students to make adequate progress toward meeting their achievement goals.
Applying (3)	The school leader ensures that appropriate interventions and supportive practices are implemented to help each student meet achievement goals AND monitors whether interventions help each student meet achievement goals.
Developing (2)	The school leader ensures the appropriate implementation of interventions and supportive practices to help each student meet achievement goals.
Beginning (1)	The school leader attempts to ensure the appropriate implementation of interventions and supportive practices to help each student meet achievement goals but does not complete the task or is not successful.
Not Using (0)	The school leader does not attempt to ensure the appropriate implementation of interventions and supportive practices to help each student meet achievement goals.

Sample Evidences for Element 3 of Domain 1
• Processes are in place to identify students who need interventions.
• Interventions take place during the school day or in extended-day programs (e.g., Saturday school, summer school).
• Response to intervention measures and/or multitiered systems of support are in place and routinely measured for producing results.
• Enrichment programs are in place.
• Intervention, including enrichment, programs are constantly monitored to measure their effect on student achievement.
• Completion rates of programs designed to enhance academic achievement are monitored (e.g., gifted and talented, advanced placement, STEM).
• Processes for ongoing progress monitoring are used to appropriately place students and, when appropriate, redirect students into intervention support groups.
• Push-in or other in-class interventions are utilized when appropriate.
• Interventionist and classroom teachers regularly work together to track student progress.
• Teachers can explain how implemented interventions help individual students meet their goals.
• Students and/or parents can identify how interventions helped close their achievement gap.

A Scenario for Domain 1, Element 3

At the midyear evaluation conference, Principal Manley meets with his supervisor, Ms. Sharps, and shares evidence that teachers have identified students who require interventions in specific content areas. He gives examples of how the teachers used statewide and classroom data to identify the students. Then Principal Manley gives Ms. Sharps a copy of a memo in which he communicated to teachers the need to provide appropriate interventions for these students. He also shows her a list of online and text-based intervention programs that he has purchased for teachers to use with these students. As teachers are working to implement the interventions, personnel challenges, such as leaves of absences and unfilled teacher positions, make it difficult to follow up on progress of the students. Mr. Manley doesn't know if all the interventions are being implemented as he had planned. Ms. Sharps and Mr. Manley examine the focus statement for this element: "The school leader ensures the appropriate implementation of interventions and supportive practices to help each student meet achievement goals." They agree that the criteria/constructs in the focus statement have not been met.

Score: Beginning

Feedback

Using the evidence presented by Mr. Manley, Ms. Sharps points out several examples of evidence that he is attempting to implement interventions but does not ensure the appropriate implementation and provide support for the interventions. Mr. Manley did make an attempt by citing different sources of data that were used to identify the students in need of interventions, and he also noted that several intervention programs were identified and purchased. However, there is no evidence that the school leader has actually *ensured* the interventions are in place, and he does not present evidence of the desired result: that interventions help each student meet achievement goals. Thus, he scores at the level of Beginning.

To move his score to the Developing level, Mr. Manley needs to create a process for actually implementing the interventions that were purchased and then provide support by monitoring the progress of each student receiving the interventions. He should also be prepared to put in place structures to monitor the progress of the students and determine if the interventions are actually affecting student achievement. Mr. Manley makes a commitment to create schedules and a plan for grade-level teams to meet and plan for student interventions and how they will monitor intervention programs for their effect on each student meeting his or her learning goals.

Growth and Reflection Questions for Domain 1, Element 3

- How can a leader manage resources, including human and traditional, to help with the implementation of intervention programs?
- How does a leader communicate to teachers the structure and procedures required for the implementation of interventions?
- What is the system or process for maintaining and reporting ongoing student progress data? Is it the responsibility of the teacher delivering the intervention?
- How can a school calendar and/or master schedule be adjusted to provide support for intervention initiatives during the day, after school, or on Saturday?
- What action does the school leader need to take to move to the next level?
- What evidence would demonstrate the leader is achieving the desired effect of the element?

Conclusion

Domain 1 of the Marzano Focused School Leader Model emphasizes goal setting and appropriate levels of data analysis, both on the big-picture, or macro schoolwide level and on the micro level of individual students. School leaders then use the analyzed data to target specific students with tailor-made interventions. In the original school leader model, Domain 1 was titled "A Data-Driven Focus on Student Achievement" and included five supporting elements. The Focused Model reflects an update to the title, A Data-Driven Focus on School Improvement, and has compacted the five original elements into three more focused elements. Elements 1 and 2 of the original model now are compiled to form Element 1. Original Elements 3 and 4 are now represented in Element 2. Finally, Element 5 of the original model is Element 3 of the updated model.

Thus far, we have been focusing on principal behaviors that impact the achievement of whole-school and individual student goals. In the next chapter, we will turn to Domain 2, "Instruction of a Viable and Guaranteed Curriculum," to examine the practices and actions a principal takes to support improved teacher practice and to ensure alignment of pedagogy, assessments, and curriculum to state and district standards. These actions, in turn, impact Domain 1 for whole-school improvement.

CHAPTER 2

Domain 2: Instruction of a Viable and Guaranteed Curriculum

Figure 2.1: The five elements of Domain 2 support a clear vision of instruction and a viable and guaranteed curriculum.

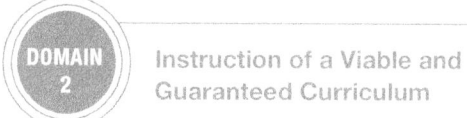

Instruction of a Viable and Guaranteed Curriculum

Element 1:
The school leader provides a clear vision for how instruction should be addressed in the school.

Element 2:
The school leader uses knowledge of the predominant instructional practices in the school to improve teaching.

Element 3:
The school leader ensures that school curriculum and accompanying assessments align with state and district standards.

Element 4:
The school leader ensures that school curriculum is focused on essential standards so it can be taught in the time available to teachers.

Element 5:
The school leader ensures that each student has equal opportunity to learn the critical content of the curriculum.

The Focused Model positions the school leader as an instructional leader whose primary purpose is, above all others, to help teachers improve their classroom practice by implementing a coherent, standards-aligned curriculum and instructional strategies and thus drive growth in student achievement. As Hallinger and Heck (1998) have noted, the behaviors of the school leader "have a measurable, though *indirect* effect on school effectiveness and student achievement" (p. 186). School leader behaviors support and facilitate teacher effectiveness.

More recently, in a paper published by the Wallace Foundation, Goldring et al. (2007) have articulated the core challenge facing America's schools as decreasing the achievement gap. The authors note that such improvement

> ultimately depends on improving teaching practice. The available evidence suggests that schools that cultivate particular in-school processes and conditions such as rigorous academic standards, high quality instruction, and a culture of collective responsibility for students' academic success are best able to meet the needs of all students (Bryk & Driscoll, 1985; Newmann & Wehlage, 1995, Purkey & Smith, 1983). School leadership, especially principal instructional and transformational leadership, is widely recognized as important in promoting these school processes and conditions (Lieberman, Falk, & Alexander, 1994; Louis, Marks, & Kruse, 1996; Rosenholtz, 1989; Sheppard, 1996). Hence, meeting the excellence and equity challenge in urban schools depends on school leaders who effectively guide instructional improvement (Barth, 1986; Leithwood, 1994). (Goldring et al., 2007, p. 1)

Domain 2 emphasizes that the school leader must, first of all, have a vision for what effective classroom instruction looks like when aligned to a standards-based curriculum and what the desired outcomes of effective instruction should be. The elements in Domain 2 are the leading indicators, or the actions a school leader must take to ensure the instruction of a viable and guaranteed curriculum and then to obtain the desired results. This domain helps create a comprehensive approach to planning, implementing, reflecting, sharing, and mentoring around a common vision of instruction. Additionally, the leader must guarantee a viable curriculum and equal opportunity for each student to have access to critical content. As with the original model, the Focused Model supports and prioritizes the development of both teacher and leader capacity as instructional leaders within the classroom and the school.

Domain 2, Instruction of a Viable and Guaranteed Curriculum, restructures Domains 2 and 3 of the original model, incorporating two elements from Continuous Improvement of Instruction (formerly Domain 2) and three elements from A Guaranteed and Viable Curriculum (formerly Domain 3). This revision reflects the interconnectedness of curriculum and instruction, as well as the necessity that both align with new state standards. Note another shift: a Viable and Guaranteed Curriculum reverses the order in Marzano's original (Guaranteed and Viable) so that the viability of the curriculum is the first order of business. The school will first analyze the curriculum, identifying essential standards, and the critical components of the curriculum to ensure that the curriculum can be taught in the time allotted—in this sense, the curriculum is *viable*. Once a viable curriculum is adopted, the school leader ensures that the critical content is taught and available to all students. Guaranteeing all students have an equal opportunity to learn critical content is an essential role of the school leader.

Providing a Clear Vision for Instruction

As we have stated, the school leader must be an *instructional leader*. In Domain 2, the first element, which is an overarching element for the entire domain, begins with the leader providing a clear vision for how instruction should be addressed in the school.

The idea of instructional leadership has a long legacy, and our definition of an instructional leader continues to evolve. As early as 1930, for example, the superintendent of St. Louis public schools was emphasizing both managerial and instructional leadership for principals, noting that the school principal was responsible for "all phases of management and instruction. It is the business of the principal to secure the best possible educational results and to do this with the utmost efficiency" (Pierce, 1935, p. 56). By the early 1980s, as the school accountability movement was beginning to take shape, the tide had turned toward a focus on principals who were taking responsibility for the instructional climate of their schools. The decade of the 1980s was characterized by a renewed interest on the part of researchers and policy makers, as many educators struggled with the thorny issues of what made principals effective.

In 1983, Cheryl Chase and Michael Kane found, for instance, that a review of the literature devoted to principal practices demonstrated a good deal of confusion about what, exactly, the job description entailed. Chase and Kane determined that the literature focused on three dilemmas related to the school leader's role: (1) how the principal determined his or her relationship to teachers and students, (2) how principals managed their time compared to managers in industry, and (3) what characteristics were shared by effective principals. Instructional leadership, they found, was largely left to the principal's discretion—as Elmore (2000) put it later, to the principal's individual interest (or lack of) in pedagogy. Chase and Kane concluded that instructional leadership could be improved by a more structured definition of the role, a defined evaluation system, and a district plan for professional development. In our work in the field with teacher groups, we continue to hear a cry for more principals who are experts in pedagogy, who can lead discussions about instruction, and who can provide accurate, constructive feedback.

Other researchers of the period wrestled with similar questions about the role of instructional leadership. Is it possible, for instance, for a school leader to make the difference between a successful and an unsuccessful school (as measured in increased student achievement scores), and to what extent did the administrator influence instruction? In a report published in July 1978, Jean Wellisch and colleagues identified five differences in successful schools based on their assessment of twenty-two elementary schools. In successful schools, the administrator was highly concerned with instruction, communicated instructional views openly, took responsibility for instructional decisions, coordinated instructional programs, and emphasized academic standards (Wellisch, MacQueen, Carriere, & Duck, 1978). These emphases are addressed in Elements 1 and 2 of Domain 2.

Subsequent studies supported these general precepts. Caroll Persell, in her analysis of school effectiveness literature, found common threads in underlying assumptions about school leader effectiveness: effective principals generated consensus and commitment to academic goals, set high academic expectations, displayed strong instructional leadership capabilities, and facilitated learning objectives by maintaining order (Persell, 1982).

For our purposes in this chapter, an instructional leader must guarantee the implementation of rigorous instructional practices and actively articulate a vision for what instruction should look like in the school. We suggest that leaders use an instructional framework such as the Art and Science of Teaching or Essentials for Achieving Rigor to provide a common language regarding instruction. In the absence of a common instructional language communicated by the school leader, teachers typically continue using the same strategies and practices they have learned over time.

The subsequent elements of Domain 2 address recent, rapid changes as schools and districts strive to meet multiple demands, including adopting new rigorous college and career readiness standards and other state and federal curriculum reform efforts.

What Do We Mean by a Viable and Guaranteed Curriculum?

In order to fully understand this domain, we should establish and clarify our definitions. Marzano (2003) coined the phrase *a guaranteed and viable curriculum* in *What Works in Schools*, based on his analysis of the literature on effective schools. The term has strong implications for what should be expected of effective leaders. Marzano defined *curriculum* as the "essential content to be addressed in specific courses at specific grade levels." Further, a *guaranteed curriculum* is designed to "optimize learning for all students" (the focus of Element 5) by ensuring that classroom teachers follow the curriculum and address specific content in specific courses at specific grade levels that align with state and district standards (the focus of Element 3). In other words, a guaranteed curriculum imposes the expectation that this content is available to *all* students, not just specific populations, and guarantees that teachers teach the essential curriculum. And finally, we want to further define the concept of *viability*, which says that teachers have time to address the essential content of the standards in the time allocated for teaching (the focus of Element 4).

We might summarize our definition with the following formula: Curriculum + Time + Opportunity to Learn (OTL) = A Viable and Guaranteed Curriculum.

Unpacking the Concept of Viability

A viable curriculum is one that can be taught in the instructional time available to teachers.

New standards can appear daunting at the outset. Many principals may wonder how teachers will still manage to cover so much material at the appropriate level of rigor within given time constraints. For most instructional leaders, it is not simply a question of exposing students to content—it's also about maximizing the instructional time available to teachers.

Indeed, one of the most common long-term complaints we hear from teachers is that they don't have time to teach all the required content for their standards. Even with the adoption of college and career readiness standards, we are still in a situation where the standards are not as manageable as they should be (Schmoker & Marzano, 1999).

As a result, teachers often feel that, by necessity, their approach is to apply a broad brush when it comes to content. Teachers may cover many topics, but with less depth than is really optimal to ensure that students are able to learn and apply their learning to authentic learning experiences. In many cases, teachers continue to have more standards in a given year than it is ultimately possible to teach (Senechal, 2011). The challenge will be to shift the focus from an emphasis on simply covering content to an emphasis on depth of content, which requires more time for students to process and utilize knowledge. The true issue is for the school leader to protect instructional time so that teachers have time to teach the essential content.

Unpacking the Concept of Guaranteed

A guaranteed curriculum ensures that all students have an opportunity to learn the essential curriculum. For example, in the absence of a guaranteed curriculum, it is possible for triplets attending the same school but with different teachers to be taught a widely divergent curriculum. Until the advent of standards, teachers tended to teach lessons that were more or less idiosyncratic—lessons derived from individual textbooks and from favorite sources or units that reflected their own choices. While these lessons may well have been approved by individual schools and may have inspired and motivated students, there was not a focus on ensuring that a standards-based curriculum was being taught across all classes, frequently even at the same grade level. In this scenario, we could not guarantee that the triplets would learn the same curriculum.

A guaranteed curriculum may mean that occasionally teachers must give up cherished lessons they've relied on for many years, of course, if those lessons cannot be uniformly applied across a grade or subject or if they do not teach the concepts needed to meet required standards. Lessons that do not incorporate the complexity of today's standards will no longer do. Teachers must develop new, standards-aligned instructional units and lessons and identify new resources that they may not have used in the past. The school leader's pivotal role is to ensure alignment of planning and teaching to adopted standards.

In "Ambitious Leadership: How Principals Lead Schools to College and Career Readiness" (2016), the authors note that new college and career readiness (CCR) standards have upped both the stakes and the challenges for principals attempting to ensure instructional and curricular alignment to standards. The authors write that "what principals must know and be able to do in regards to the instructional core has increased dramatically. . . . for the new generation of assessments, the only effective preparation is a challenging, well-designed curriculum and strong teaching" (p. 10). Their study further found that principals who were successfully advancing mastery of standards had the three following qualities. To summarize the findings, these principals:

1. Had a deep grasp of the demands of CCR standards and aligned assessments
2. Understood—in a detailed and concrete way—the components of ambitious instruction that could support students in developing the necessary capabilities
3. Had command of instructional leadership "best practices" such as building buy-in and teacher capacity to enact more rigorous pedagogical practices

In order to apply a guaranteed curriculum, school leaders must ensure that *all* students in the same grade are exposed to the same *essential content* and that the agreed-on essential content is aligned to required standards.

Ensuring Equal Opportunity to Learn the Standards

Another relevant question for Domain 2 is this: How can the school leader guarantee that every student has an equal opportunity to learn to the required standards (Element 5)?

A principal relates a painful story about an honors advanced algebra class in her school that brought this question home for her. Visiting district personnel sat in on the advanced class. At the end of it, they asked the principal if only the white kids at her school were smart.

The principal was taken aback. She asked what they meant.

"The kids in this math class are all white," the visitors pointed out. "No African Americans. No Latinos."

The principal realized to her chagrin that the criteria for entrance into the advanced math class set the bar so high that it was effectively preventing some student subpopulations from learning the higher math skills they would need to succeed in college and career readiness courses. Rather than *all* the students in the school learning the critical content, only *some* were provided the opportunity. The realization shook her, and she was able to make appropriate corrections to ensure that the students in her school would have the opportunity to learn critical content.

This principal is hardly alone. It seems it was not uncommon for students to be required to score above the eightieth percentile on a norm-referenced test in order to take Algebra 1. In states that maintain these stringent requirements, Algebra 1 is still a gateway to advanced mathematics classes. In such cases, it may be necessary for the school leader to reevaluate the structure of that gateway and to adjust the necessary requirements to allow all students an equal opportunity to pass through it.

The Elements in Domain 2

Domain 2, Element 1: Providing a Clear Vision of Instruction

The school leader provides a clear vision for how instruction should be addressed in the school.

Desired Effect: Teachers use the instructional model.

Element 1 of Domain 2 asks that the school leader establish a *clear vision of instruction*—what good teaching looks like and how to get there. To this purpose, the school leader will likely implement a model of instruction or at the very least a framework that establishes a common language of instruction. The logic of this model would say that if the leader articulates a vision for instruction, then the desired outcome is that teachers know and implement the instructional model.

Thus, it is extremely important to implement and support a schoolwide common language of instruction and to encourage an understanding of and agreement about best classroom practices—specifically those practices most closely correlated to gains in student achievement.

A compact model of instruction like the Marzano Essentials for Rigor Model, for example, can go a long way to iron out the misunderstandings and pedagogical misalignments between teachers and teachers, teachers and supervisors, and teachers and the community. Our position is that a robust model of instruction provides a frame, a vocabulary, and a research base, and can form the basis for a measurement system to ensure that every member involved in the school knows what is expected of teachers' behaviors and practices—and what the intended results, or desired effects, are of those behaviors. In such a system, each teacher is provided feedback using the common language of instruction.

New Heights Elementary Assistant Principal Chris Boulanger (2018) made the following connections: "The Marzano Leader Model aligns so well to our district initiatives, and to the teacher evaluation model, and it has helped us create a common vocabulary and a common vision for instruction so that we are all working together."

Characteristics of a Model of Instruction

In our research and field experience, we have identified five major characteristics of the most effective models of instruction. The model should set clear definitions and measurements, help inform decisions, facilitate collaboration, and allow for efficient use of data, as outlined here:

- The model of instruction defines and describes effective teaching based on the most current research on classroom strategies to improve student learning. This foundation allows for successful unit and lesson planning along with the strategies to meet instructional objectives.
- The model provides a means for assessment, reflection, and deliberate practice. (We will discuss this in more detail below.)
- The model functions as a transparent framework for making decisions about how to adjust instruction based on student data, formative and summative assessments, and other feedback.
- The model provides a framework and common language for professional conversations, collaboration between teachers, and coaching.
- And finally, the most useful models will incorporate a system to collect, analyze, and distribute data.

One major advantage of a schoolwide (or districtwide) instructional model is that formative and summative feedback may be more focused, specific, and actionable. Because teachers in classrooms across the school intentionally implement agreed-on classroom strategies to improve student learning, feedback from formal or informal observations, walk-throughs, and teacher visits has common ground. This shared understanding and focus makes it possible for observers or supervisors to provide the type of feedback most likely to help teachers show growth on a performance scale, and as the leading indicator of teacher effectiveness improves, so will the lagging indicators of student achievement.

The Scale and Sample Evidences for Domain 2, Element 1

Figure 2.2: **Scale and sample evidences for Domain 2, Element 1.**

Scale Value	Description
Innovating (4)	The school leader continually examines and provides updates so that all teachers use the instructional model.
Applying (3)	The school leader provides a clear vision for how instruction should be addressed in the school AND monitors the extent to which the teachers use the instructional model.
Developing (2)	The school leader provides a clear vision for how instruction should be addressed in the school.
Beginning (1)	The school leader attempts to provide a clear vision for how instruction should be addressed in the school but does not complete the task or is not successful.
Not Using (0)	The school leader does not attempt to provide a clear vision for how instruction should be addressed in the school.

Sample Evidences for Element 1 of Domain 2
- A written document articulating the schoolwide model of instruction is in place.
- The schoolwide language of instruction is used regularly by faculty in their professional learning communities and in faculty and/or department meetings.
- The schoolwide language of instruction is used regularly by faculty in their informal conversations.
- Professional development opportunities are provided for new and experienced teachers regarding the schoolwide model of instruction.
- Implementation of the instructional model is evident in daily classroom instruction.
- Intentional planning to use the instructional model is evident in teacher lesson plans.
- New initiatives are prioritized and limited in number to support the instructional model.
- Teachers can describe the major components of the schoolwide model of instruction.
- Teachers can explain how strategies in the instructional framework promote learning for the school's diverse population.
- Data are available to support teacher implementation of the instructional model (e.g., lesson plans, observations, PLC notes).
- The vision for instruction is shared throughout the school and community.

A Scenario for Domain 2, Element 1

Dr. Alonzo is a member of a district committee tasked to select a new instructional model for districtwide implementation. The committee selects a research-based instructional model that will guide teachers in moving from the use of foundational instructional strategies to strategies that result in students thinking and producing work at higher taxonomy levels. With great excitement, Dr. Alonzo spends the summer preparing to introduce this model to the staff. She believes the model exemplifies the way teachers should teach in the school.

Dr. Alonzo starts the school improvement plan by identifying the instructional model as the primary vehicle to help the school accomplish its goals. She also has a series of meetings with the leadership team to introduce the model and sends them to training in the summer. At the beginning of the new year, teachers are introduced to the model during multiple staff meetings. Teachers from the leadership team assist in rolling out the training to their colleagues. Dr. Alonzo wants everyone in the school community to learn about the new model, so she displays posters featuring the structure and common language of the model throughout the school. She visits planning meetings to determine if teachers are using the new model as part of their planning process.

Then, at a faculty meeting, she asks teachers to explain the model in an exit ticket. All teachers can explain the model. In addition, when conducting classroom observations and walk-throughs, she listens for use of the common language. She notes a few teachers still struggling with using the common language and provides feedback to them. During the course of the year, she constantly looks at walk-through and other data to confirm that all teachers are using the instructional model and gaining a deeper understanding of how it can impact student achievement.

Score: Innovating

Feedback

When meeting with her supervisor, Dr. Alonzo has multiple pieces of evidence to support that teachers are using the model. She has documents to confirm all the training and meetings she and the teachers attended, pictures on her phone, samples of the exit tickets, and a summary of observational data. She shares how she hears teachers routinely using the common language and digging deeper in how to implement the instructional strategies. The supervisor notes how clearly the vision for the use of a common instructional model has been shared and communicated in multiple ways throughout the school community. Dr. Alonzo has clearly met the desired effect of the element and is at the innovating level, because when she notices teachers who can explain the model but are not using its common language or instructional strategies in their classrooms, she intervenes by giving them feedback. During subsequent walk-throughs, she notes how teachers are implementing more strategies from the common model of instruction.

Growth and Reflection Questions for Domain 2, Element 1

- Is there a written document articulating the common language regarding instructional strategies?
- How does the school leader make sure that all teachers understand the model of instruction?
- What evidence would be used to monitor teachers' understanding and effective use of the model of instruction?
- When teachers discuss and plan instruction, do they use the common language of instruction?
- Is it critical to include the use of an instructional model in a school improvement plan?
- What is the plan for teachers who may resist moving to a common instructional model?
- How does a leader intervene with teachers who are not implementing or who do not demonstrate that they understand the model?
- What fiscal and human resources can be utilized to assist all teachers to implement a leader's vision for instruction?
- Is there evidence that teachers see a relationship between their use of instructional strategies and student achievement?
- What action does the school leader need to take to move to the next level?
- What evidence would demonstrate the leader is achieving the desired effect of the element?

Domain 2, Element 2: Using Predominant Instructional Practices to Improve Teaching

The school leader uses knowledge of the predominant instructional practices in the school to improve teaching.

Desired Effect: Teachers improve instructional practices when the leader provides feedback regarding predominant instructional practices.

The authors of this book maintain an expectation that all teachers can increase their expertise from year to year, which can produce gains in student achievement from year to year, with a powerful cumulative effect. The majority of classroom teachers enter their classrooms at the beginning of each day and start the daily process of teaching and learning. Some call it an isolated process, but we suggest that if we want teachers to embrace a vision for a schoolwide model of instruction, and perhaps embrace the practice of adding new instructional strategies to their pedagogical tool kit, the first step is for school leaders to identify the predominant instructional practices in the school and make teachers aware of these practices. In Element 2, we explore why teachers should be aware of and understand the school's predominant instructional practices, what can happen with that information, and how it can be one of the first steps to improve teaching. To foster this awareness, the school leader will have to help break down a long-standing tendency toward teacher isolation and potentially resistance to more frequent in-class observations.

As Jacob Mishook noted in a 2011 commentary for the Annenberg Institute:

> The traditional "egg-crate" model of teaching and learning has been dominant in the United States for decades, where individual teachers are isolated behind the closed doors of their classrooms (Johnson 2010). This traditional model has been discarded by most of the world's successful school systems, which recognize that having highly qualified but isolated teachers is not enough (Fullan 2010). Developing schools with a high level of human capital (i.e., a staff of individual teachers who have advanced skills and knowledge) *and* a high level of social capital (i.e., where teachers interact regularly with each other) is necessary for all teachers and students to succeed. But new human capital reforms, which evaluate teachers individually, and district decentralization, which isolates schools from one another and pits them against one another as competitors, actively work against the notion of teachers utilizing each other to become better practitioners. (p. 1)

Although Element 2 says that the school leader must know the predominant practices, before this can happen, we assert that a set of identified instructional practices should be in place, as we have advocated in Element 1. The key to Element 2 is that the leader must be able to accurately identify instructional strategies during walk-throughs and informal and formal observations. For example, after completing several weeks of walk-throughs, a principal notes that during the majority of time teachers are in front of their classes, they are reviewing past content and then introducing new content. Teachers are not spending sufficient time *processing* or *practicing* before rushing on to yet more new content. The leader would then share this trend data with teachers to make them aware of the need for students to have opportunities to process and elaborate on content before introducing additional content. One of the first steps to making improvement or changes is to make people aware of current behavior.

If the leader is accumulating data about predominant instructional practices within the school, the desired outcome is that teachers will change and improve instructional practices when the leader provides feedback. Unfortunately, even in this modern period of social media and virtual tools for collaboration, teachers often continue to work in relative isolation and can be unaware of how others in their building and grade level use instructional strategies, so this process of data collection and sharing is the first step in making changes to teachers' use of instructional strategies.

To demonstrate the interconnections of the elements within the model, note that part of the process in helping teachers change instructional practice is to provide meaningful professional development, which we will discuss in more detail in Domain 3. But the process begins with teachers and leaders knowing the school's instructional patterns and trends. Then, the school leader and teachers use these data to design and implement individual or schoolwide professional development plans.

The Scale and Sample Evidences for Domain 2, Element 2

Figure 2.3: **The scale and evidences for Domain 2, Element 2.**

Scale Value	Description
Innovating (4)	The school leader regularly intervenes to ensure that ineffective instructional practices are corrected and effective instructional practices are implemented.
Applying (3)	The school leader uses knowledge of the predominant instructional practices in the school to improve teaching AND monitors the extent to which teachers improve their instructional practices.
Developing (2)	The school leader uses knowledge of the predominant instructional practices in the school to improve teaching.
Beginning (1)	The school leader attempts to use knowledge of the predominant instructional practices in the school to improve teaching but does not complete the task or is not successful.
Not Using (0)	The school leader does not attempt to use knowledge of the predominant instructional practices in the school to improve teaching.

Sample Evidences for Element 2 of Domain 2
• Walk-through or other observation data are aggregated to disclose predominant instructional practices in the school.
• Accurate feedback is provided to each teacher regarding instructional practices.
• Systems are in place to monitor the effect of predominant instructional practices for each subgroup.
• Feedback is provided to each teacher regarding instructional practices needed to address learning gaps and diverse student populations.
• Predominant instructional practices and trends are documented and regularly shared with teachers.
• Effective instructional practices and problems of practice are accurately described by the school leader.
• Data show teachers implement new instructional strategies when provided feedback.
• Data regarding predominant instructional practices are used to inform professional development opportunities.
• Observation data confirm that teachers improve instructional practices.
• Student achievement data improve as teachers improve in the use of instructional strategies.
• Teachers can describe the predominant instructional practices used in the school and how they affect student achievement.

A Scenario for Domain 2, Element 2

Dr. Goff has been the principal of the same middle school for almost ten years. A colleague has asked her what the most common instructional strategy used in her school is. The question takes her by surprise, as she has never really thought about specific instructional strategies. When conducting walk-throughs, she usually only notes if the teacher is teaching and if the students are engaged in the lesson.

The question has prompted a lot of thinking. Dr. Goff begins to work with teacher leaders to conduct frequent informal observations in the building. Together, they note what instructional strategies they observe and discuss building trends. Dr. Goff shares the information with the whole staff and has them identify areas of strength and areas for growth.

They note that all teachers in the building are consistently posting learning targets and bringing student attention to them. They also see that there are only a few teachers using grouping structures to encourage students to interact about content. Rather, whole-group direct instruction is the dominant strategy. In other words, teachers continue to teach additional critical content without allowing students time to actively process the content. Dr. Goff provides training and resources to help teachers build their skills in using different instructional strategies. Any issues with resistance to changing the predominant instructional practices are addressed with individual teachers. She provides additional trainings for small groups of teachers who have not been implementing the new strategies effectively.

Dr. Goff tracks the results of walk-throughs and other observations and gives teachers feedback throughout the year. The school's instructional specialist is tasked with providing resources and modeling for two teachers who have struggled to implement new strategies. After several weeks of working on moving from teacher-centered instruction to more student-centered activities, the number of classrooms using grouping structures has increased by 20 percent.

Score: Innovating

Feedback

The superintendent who evaluates Dr. Goff commends her for the structured approach to identifying and providing feedback on the use of predominant instructional strategies in the school. The evidence is clear that she has worked to help her teachers identify effective instructional strategies and is continuing to provide training. In addition, Dr. Goff has continued to check for the use of effective strategies, including watching for evidence that some ineffective practices have decreased. The fact that effective uses of grouping strategies have increased significantly is evidence that Dr. Goff's feedback to teachers has resulted in the implementation of new instructional strategies.

Growth and Reflection Questions for Domain 2, Element 2

- How does a leader plan to change instructional practices at a school?
- How does a leader provide the training and support for the implementation of new instructional strategies?
- What data sources are used to track instructional strategies in the building?
- How are teachers made aware of the predominant instructional strategies used throughout the building?
- How does the school leader address problems with instructional strategies that are not being used appropriately?
- What types of resources should be provided to support teacher growth in implementing new instructional strategies?
- What evidence would demonstrate the leader is achieving the desired effect of the element?

Domain 2, Element 3: Aligning Curriculum to Standards

The school leader ensures that the school curriculum and accompanying assessments align with state and district standards.

Desired Effect: Assessments accurately measure student progress toward achieving the adopted standards.

One of the primary jobs of the school leader is to ensure that the curriculum is aligned to essential state and district standards. It is imperative for all teachers to have a solid understanding, first, of what content is essential to teach for each grade level or course and, second, the level of rigor required to meet state standards. If the district has not already done so, the school leader can put processes in place to examine state standards with groups of teachers and curriculum directors to determine which standards are essential. Resources such as test specifications, released test items, or previously released tests can be invaluable to leaders in determining essential standards.

A principal recently shared a personal story with the authors. He said that although his district provided standardized scales and pacing charts to help make sure teachers could teach the required standards, he felt like he had to go out on a limb and adapt what the district provided for his school. He described a process whereby teachers took the published standards and created action boards with different performance levels and then created short formative assessments. He said the process of owning and aligning the learning targets to their teaching has been a powerful process and a lot of hard work, but "we see the results when we look at achievement data."

There are currently commercial resources such as the LSI Standards Tracker (see appendix D) that eliminate much of the burden on schools to unpack standards and drill down to the essential standards, so that assessments can be written to align with the most essential parts of the standards.

Using Formative Assessments to Keep Curriculum on Track

In this era of high-stakes accountability, where teachers and school leaders are typically held responsible for student achievement outcomes on state assessment tests, school leaders must guarantee testing measures that can be administered periodically and are so closely aligned with the tested standards that these tests show student progress toward achieving the standards. One way a school leader can ensure that the school curriculum and accompanying assessments are aligned to state and district standards is by using a *formative approach* to testing.

In *District Leadership That Works*, Marzano and Waters (2009) cite Black and Wiliam's (1998) definition of *formative assessment*: "All those activities undertaken by teachers and/or by students which provide information to be used as feedback to modify the teaching and learning activities in which they are engaged" (pp. 7–8). Wiliam and Leahy (2007) emphasize that the purpose of formative assessment is determined by "the extent that information from the assessment is fed back within the system and actually used to improve the performance of the system in some way (i.e., that the assessment *forms* the direction of improvement)" (p. 31).

Therefore, the formative assessments teachers develop and use must be tightly aligned to college and career readiness standards. It is critical for teachers to ensure that their assessments incorporate items at all levels of the taxonomy. In other words, teacher assessments should measure more cognitively complex thinking skills and knowledge utilization. In the past, too many assessments have fallen short of rigor and therefore failed in the formative sense defined earlier—as a tool to provide feedback and guide modifications in pedagogy. As Black and Wiliam (1998b) note, "The tests used by teachers encourage rote and superficial learning even when teachers say they want to develop understanding; many teachers seem unaware of the inconsistency" (p. 5).

Brookhart (2010) suggests that:

> Observing and discussing student reasoning directly can be a powerful way to assess higher-order thinking. Give students an assessment, and use it formatively. Have conversations with students about their reasoning, or give substantive written feedback. The conversations and feedback should be based on your learning target and criteria. Exactly what sort of thinking were you trying to assess? How should students interpret the quality of their thinking? What are some ways they might extend or deepen that thinking? (p. 31)

Formative assessments can be an extremely valuable tool to give teachers early feedback on whether the time allotted to a lesson or unit has been sufficient. School leaders will have to be sure that teachers are utilizing formative assessments that are rigorous and specific enough to give teachers the targeted feedback they need to hone their lessons and identify struggling students.

We might say that the desired result of Element 3 is that there is universal alignment between taught curriculum in the school, state standards, and the accompanying assessments that measure the progress toward the standards.

The Scales and Sample Evidences for Domain 2, Element 3

Figure 2.4: **Scales and evidences for Element 3, Domain 2.**

Scale Value	Description
Innovating (4)	The school leader ensures that the assessment and reporting system focuses on state and district standards and intervenes with teachers who do not utilize the adopted standards.
Applying (3)	The school leader ensures that the school curriculum and accompanying assessments align with state and district standards AND monitors the extent to which the assessments accurately measure student progress toward achieving the adopted standards.
Developing (2)	The school leader ensures that the school curriculum and accompanying assessments align with state and district standards.
Beginning (1)	The school leader attempts to ensure that the school curriculum and accompanying assessments align with state and district standards but does not complete the task or is not successful.
Not Using (0)	The school leader does not attempt to ensure that the school curriculum and accompanying assessments align with state and district standards.

Sample Evidences for Element 3 of Domain 2
• An understanding of the alignment of curriculum and assessments is demonstrated by the school leader.
• Curriculum documents are in place that correlate the written curriculum to state and district standards.
• Resources to support curriculum align to standards.
• Rubrics or scales are in place that clearly delineate student levels of performance on essential standards.
• Classroom/formative, benchmark, and summative/end-of-year assessment data are consistently analyzed for alignment to standards.
• School teams regularly analyze the relationship between the written curriculum/standards, taught curriculum, and assessments and make adaptations when needed.
• Assessments accurately measure adopted standards.
• Interventions are in place when standards are required and not incorporated.
• Implemented assessments reflect knowledge of child development and learning theories.
• Teachers can describe the essential standards for their subject area and/or grade level.

A Scenario for Domain 2, Element 3

Principal Durant knows that the district has implemented new standards, and he has bought assessments to accompany the standards. He is relieved that he doesn't have to get involved in testing, as his schedule is already overloaded. As he prepares for his evaluation conference, he makes a copy of the state standards and an assessment schedule that shows statewide and district testing dates. PLC teams have developed a testing schedule that is available for review. In addition, other staff members volunteer to help administer tests. Teachers also use the adopted textbook series to prepare their students for the upcoming tests. A few teachers are developing a set of short-cycle assessments using objectives from the textbooks.

Score: Beginning

Feedback

Principal Durant does not question or evaluate whether the school curriculum and assessments are aligned with the required standards because resources are provided by the district. Taking a hands-off approach will not ensure alignment. Although the district is providing support and resources, the school leader is responsible for ensuring that the curriculum and assessments are aligned with the standards. Assessments typically include more than district benchmark tests or large summative tests, and can include formative, short-term assessments created by teachers to assess standards-based units. Content teachers and PLCs must continually review all assessments for alignment to standards. Teachers and leaders could also use scales and rubrics to clearly delineate student levels of performance to determine if assessments accurately measure student progress toward achieving the standards.

Growth and Reflection Questions for Domain 2, Element 3

- How can a leader help teachers analyze their curriculum and lesson plans to ensure alignment to state and district standards?
- Since this type of work may be new to teachers, what resources and/or trainings do teachers need to successfully align assessments and the curriculum?
- What is the process to verify that assessments are aligned to state and district standards?
- How does the leader ensure that all staff members have copies of the most current curriculum standards?
- Who is responsible for providing formative assessments correlated to the rigorous, standards-based curriculum?
- What evidence would reveal that current formative assessments adequately prepare students to meet state standards?
- What action does the school leader need to take to move to the next level?
- What evidence would demonstrate the leader is achieving the desired effect of the element?

Domain 2, Element 4: Ensuring Viability of the Curriculum

The school leader ensures that the school curriculum is focused on essential standards so it can be taught in the time available to teachers.

Desired Effect: Teachers have time to teach the core or essential standards.

Element 4 addresses the viability of the curriculum, which we discussed in some detail early in this chapter. The relevant question for school leaders is whether they have created a focused curriculum with the essential standards that can be accomplished in the scope of a school year. We would say the essential standards and content must be determined collaboratively, not by individual teachers.

Savvy school leaders examine data and talk to teachers about how to design a plan so that they have enough instructional time in class to meet the standards. Research compiled by Learning Sciences Marzano Center, based on classroom observation data logged in its virtual platform, the iObservation database, suggests that teachers are currently spending the majority of their instructional time introducing new content or reviewing and far too little time on deepening knowledge and cognitively complex thinking skills. As little as 4 to 6 percent of class time is devoted to the kinds of complex thinking skills—analysis, compare and contrast, generating hypotheses, and problem solving—that are the foundation of what we mean when we use the term *rigor*. Some like to call this misallocation of classroom time the "mile-wide, inch-deep" syndrome.

The intention of college and career readiness standards is to narrow the standards so that mile-wide and inch-deep lessons become less prevalent. Standards alone, however, are not enough to overcome a long history of pedagogical focus on new content.

Again, this element aligns to the work we do in Element 2 around ensuring effective instruction in our classrooms. Recently, a survey of teachers in one district indicated that the teachers felt they did not have enough time to teach the standards identified in district curriculum guides. A visit to the classrooms by school leaders revealed opportunities where instructional time could have been used more efficiently. Teachers were spending inordinate amounts of time on activities that were developed with loose connections to the standards. For example, one grade-level team was implementing lessons that required students to *identify* whether a statement was a fact or an opinion. But the standard required students to *analyze* the impact of the statement as to whether it was a fact or an opinion with the goal of comprehending the text. Teachers were spending time on lower-level activities that did not impact the students' mastery of the standards. The principal had the opportunity to help teachers better understand standards-aligned instruction through feedback connected to lesson planning.

The School Leader Determines What Is Nonnegotiable

The taught curriculum must be aligned with district and state standards, as we have discussed, but the school leader must also determine which elements of district and state standards are nonnegotiable.

In order to determine what curriculum content is nonnegotiable, a school leader might consider the following questions:

1. Who currently does the work of developing standards-based content in your district or school? Who determines which content is essential and is responsible for alignment? Who ensures the opportunity to learn the content in the classroom? Who instructs in the essential content? What type of professional development is offered, and is it aligned to the school's nonnegotiable goals?
2. How do teachers, building leaders, and district leaders share in these aspects of education? *What evidence might be considered to measure the effectiveness of that involvement?*
3. How is your school leadership regarding curriculum positively affecting student outcomes?
4. What sources of evidence could demonstrate that these practices are effective in creating a viable and guaranteed curriculum?

It's important to emphasize that one role of the school leader in Elements 3, 4, and 5 of Domain 2 is as a curriculum communication channel and sometimes as a buffer between the district and teachers. Teachers are not, for the most part, equipped to create curriculum guides or common summative assessment items on their own or to deal with thorny issues of developing and aligning curriculum to standards. This is not to say that teachers should not participate in decision-making processes about curriculum. But a school leader who has his or her ear to the ground, in terms of the kind of help teachers want and need, can be a voice in the district to ensure that the necessary curriculum mapping and accompanying assessments are developed. The school leader then becomes a guide or coach who can support teachers to determine how to group standards into effective units and so on.

The Written versus the Taught Curriculum

Although not a new concept, it's important to stress that there is often a conflict in school buildings between the *written* curriculum and the *taught* curriculum (Gehrke, Knapp, & Sirotnik, 1992), or more recently in the Second International Mathematics Study (SIMS) model, between the *intended* curriculum, the *implemented* curriculum, and the *attained* curriculum. As Marzano (2003) noted in *What Works in Schools*:

> The intended curriculum is content specified by the state, district, or school to be addressed in a particular course or at a particular grade level. The implemented curriculum is content actually delivered by the teacher, and the attained curriculum is content actually learned by students. The discrepancy between the intended curriculum and the implemented curriculum makes OTL [opportunity to learn] a prominent factor in student achievement—a factor that since SIMS has continued to show a very strong relationship with student achievement (Brewer & Stacz, 1996; Herman, Klein, & Abedi, 2000; Robitaille, 1993). (p. 22)

There may still be a gap between what teachers are actually teaching in the classroom (for example, a favorite third-grade dinosaur unit) and the agreed-on curriculum for that grade or unit (for example, the organization and development of living organisms, including growth and reproduction). In this case, the school leader will help the teacher adjust instruction to ensure that dinosaur lessons will happen in the context of, perhaps, comparing the reproductive behaviors of mammals and reptiles. Students taught in this unit will have the same essential knowledge about living organisms as students in other third-grade classes when it comes time to take a formative assessment or end-of-year achievement test.

These conflicts and confusions often arise when teachers or administrators conflate textbooks with curriculum, rather than perceive textbooks as one *resource* toward implementing the intended curriculum. There may be many resources dedicated to implementing an agreed-on curriculum—but resources do not a curriculum make.

To unpack this a bit further, the point is to ensure that there is consistency in the material teachers cover in the same subjects between classrooms and that it is covered at the level of rigor required by the state standards. Common formative assessments will supply the proof in the measured outcomes.

Figure 2.5 illustrates the scales and possible evidences for ensuring that critical content and cognitively complex thinking skills can be addressed in the time allotted. Possible evidences might include that the school leader has conducted a curriculum audit; that teams meet regularly to assess pacing guides, curricular maps, and the like; and that student surveys indicate that students feel they have enough time to learn the expected material.

Domain 2: Instruction of a Viable and Guaranteed Curriculum

The Scale and Sample Evidences for Element 4, Domain 2

Figure 2.5: **Scale and evidences for Domain 2, Element 4.**

Scale Value	Description
Innovating (4)	The school leader ensures that essential standards are regularly examined and revised to ensure teachers have time to teach the essential standards.
Applying (3)	The school leader ensures that school curriculum is focused on essential standards so it can be taught in the time available to teachers AND monitors the extent to which the essential standards are few enough to allow adequate time for students to learn them.
Developing (2)	The school leader ensures that school curriculum is focused on essential standards so it can be taught in the time available to teachers.
Beginning (1)	The school leader attempts to ensure that the school curriculum is focused on essential standards so it can be taught in the time available to teachers but does not complete the task or is not successful.
Not Using (0)	The school leader does not attempt to ensure that the school curriculum is focused on essential standards so it can be taught in the time available to teachers.

Sample Evidences for Element 4 of Domain 2
• A written list of essential standards is in place and available to each teacher.
• The written curriculum has been unpacked in such a manner that essential elements/standards have been identified.
• A curriculum audit has been conducted that delineates how much time it would take to adequately address the essential standards.
• Teams regularly meet to discuss the progression and viability of documents that articulate essential content and timing of delivery (e.g., pacing guides, curriculum maps).
• Time available for specific classes and courses meets the state or district specifications for those classes and courses.
• Schedules are protected to allow teachers time to teach the essential curriculum/standards.
• A plan is in place to monitor that the essential curriculum is taught in the time available to teachers.
• Teachers can describe which elements are essential and can be taught in the scheduled time.
• Students report they have time to learn the essential curriculum/standards.
• Processes are implemented at the school to ensure teachers teach the essential curriculum/standards.
• Data are available to show that teachers teach the essential curriculum/standards.
• Technology systems support essential standards.

A Scenario for Domain 2, Element 4

Principal Fields and a team of teachers have worked with the district curriculum department to complete a vertical alignment of state standards for all grade levels at Starr Elementary. Teachers learn to identify the standards evident at all grade levels and those standards common to several grade levels but not all. In addition, they have found documents shared by other districts that developed lists of essential standards in all content areas. The teachers have studied these lists and made adjustments based on district input, so that they end with a final list of critical, essential standards to use as the basis for unit and lesson planning. In addition, they have grouped standards to ensure they can plan their instructional time to sufficiently address all. During his monthly visits to each PLC team, Principal Fields discusses with teachers their current status and pacing with the plan to address the most essential standards. He also assigns the assistant principal to review unit plans and lesson plans developed in the PLC teams and to apprise him of any issues with addressing the identified standards in the designated time. The school's instructional coach reports to Mr. Fields that teachers are feeling positive about being able to teach the required essential standards.

Score: Developing

Feedback

When Mr. Fields is self-assessing his progress on this element, he notes the progress of the development of the curriculum documents. He is proud of the important work teachers have accomplished in unpacking their standards, determining which are essential and grouping those standards into units. Teachers also added an informal chart to help them pace the implementation of their units so at the end of the year they will not find standards left untaught. This evidence would place Mr. Fields at the Developing level for this element. To move to the next level on the scale, Mr. Fields needs to review the actual implementation of the units and determine if teachers actually have time to adequately address the essential standards and stay on pace. These actions, of monitoring for the desired result of teachers having time to teach the core or essential standards, would move Mr. Fields to the Applying level.

Growth and Reflection Questions for Domain 2, Element 4

- What is the plan to review and revise unit and lesson plans if they cannot be implemented in the time allotted? What resources and/or personnel are needed to assist with that process?
- How does a leader assess whether teachers are implementing the essential standards and communicate the expectation for teachers to address all the essential standards?

- How can input from students help address whether teachers have time to teach the core standards?
- What is the school leader's role in assessing whether the essential standards are in place?
- How does the school leader monitor whether teachers are using standards as the basis for unit and lesson planning?
- What indicators are monitored to determine whether teachers have enough time to teach the required standards?
- What action does the school leader need to take to move to the next level?
- What evidence would demonstrate the leader is achieving the desired effect of the element?

Element 5: Ensuring Opportunity to Learn Critical Content
The school leader ensures that each student has equal opportunity to learn the critical content of the curriculum.

Desired Effect: Each teacher teaches the essential standards so every student has the opportunity to learn the essential standards.

We touched on the focus of Element 5 earlier in this chapter with the story of the principal who realized her school had set the bar too high for entrance into an essential math class. If the focus of the new state standards is college and career readiness, it can't be emphasized often enough that this means readiness for *all* students.

In his survey of college and career readiness, K. J. Pittman (2010) outlined the sobering results of the "readiness gap" between student subpopulations and what the inevitable consequences of that gap might be:

> **Up to a fourth of all first-year students at four-year colleges do not return for their second year.** The dropout rates are particularly high for African-American, Hispanic and first-generation college students, according to a report by the Urban Institute and the Harvard Civil Rights Project. As many as 30 percent of students will take at least one remedial class during their college years, according to national studies.
>
> **Employers, while acknowledging the need for 21st-century skills, are not equipped to train in these deficiency areas.** According to a 2009 Corporate Voices for Working Families study, 40 percent of the business respondents that offer some workforce-readiness training have no on-the-job trainings to offer in these high-need areas.
>
> **Youth, especially low-income minorities, are having a hard time finding quality jobs during and after high school.** Teen employment is now the

lowest it has been in more than half a century. Low-income, minority youth are least likely to find work, even with high school diplomas. And those jobs that are available are typically in lower-level service industries, often lacking benefits, training and opportunities for advancement, according to a study of teen joblessness by Northeastern University's Center for Labor Market Studies.

Another aspect of a school leader's responsibility is to foster a school culture where teachers have high expectations for each student. Students should be placed in appropriately rigorous classes, and the school leader should ensure that honors and AP classes are not available to one subset of students at the expense of others.

Such a mission sounds very clear in theory, but it can become murky in practice. The building leader's role is that of an arbiter, the person who makes sure, in the final count, that no student is denied the opportunity to succeed in college and career. For example, if Jake needs a reading intervention, and the reading specialist is only available during Jake's math class, then either Jake is going to miss math or the reading intervention. Such conflicts are not insoluble if everyone, from teachers to parents to instructional support staff, is aware that missing either vital math or equally vital reading instruction is simply not an option.

The other aspect of guaranteed curriculum is ensuring that each teacher is teaching the essential critical content of the curriculum or the standards. This may be tougher than it seems if multiple teachers are teaching the same subject and each teacher does not adhere to the essential standards. When teachers plan units and lessons collaboratively, it's a step toward the process of guaranteeing that teachers teach the essential curriculum.

So how does the school leader ensure that each teacher stays true to teaching the critical content? The leader must begin with clearly setting the expectation. Then, constant monitoring of what teachers are teaching and analysis of student work are the real keys to ensuring a guaranteed curriculum.

The Scale and Sample Evidences for Domain 2, Element 5

Figure 2.6: **Scale and evidences for Domain 2, Element 5.**

Scale Value	Description
Innovating (4)	The school leader intervenes with teachers who do not teach essential standards that guarantee students have equal access to learning the critical content of the curriculum.
Applying (3)	The school leader ensures that each student has equal opportunity to learn the critical content of the curriculum AND monitors the extent to which each teacher teaches the essential standards to each student.

Domain 2: Instruction of a Viable and Guaranteed Curriculum

Developing (2)	The school leader ensures that each student has equal opportunity to learn the critical content of the curriculum.
Beginning (1)	The school leader attempts to ensure that each student has equal opportunity to learn the critical content of the curriculum but does not complete the task or is not successful.
Not Using (0)	The school leader does not attempt to ensure that each student has equal opportunity to learn the critical content of the curriculum.

Sample Evidences for Element 5 of Domain 2
• Tracking systems are in place that examine each student's access to the essential elements/standards of the curriculum.
• Parents are aware of their child's current access to the essential standards/elements of the curriculum.
• Each student has equal access to advanced placement or other rigorous courses.
• Each student has a prescribed program of study that documents access to appropriate courses.
• Data are available to show teachers have completed appropriate content area training in their subject area courses.
• Each student has equal access to courses that directly address the essential elements/standards of the required curriculum.
• Data are available to verify student achievement in critical content and standards.
• Teachers can describe the content strategies that result in the highest student learning for specific courses and topics.
• Student data/feedback reveal that they are given the opportunity to learn the critical content of the curriculum.
• Data are available to show that students are ready to be contributing members of society and participate in a global community (e.g., graduation rates, CTE certifications, post-graduation enrollment).
• Data are available to show that students are college and career ready.
• Appropriate technology is in place to support and enhance instruction and curriculum.
• The process in place to ensure that each student has an equal opportunity to learn the critical content/standards can be explained by the school leader.

A Scenario for Domain 2, Element 5

The principal of Tuttle Middle School is proud of her school's passing rate in physical science and other advanced courses that the district requires in eighth grade. As the new school year begins, her supervisor questions her about the number of students enrolled in advanced courses as compared to the overall enrollment of the school. The principal begins to see a major discrepancy between enrollment in advanced classes and standard and even remedial classes. The subject area team leaders in the school had always set the criteria for placement in any advanced classes. On review of the criteria, only students who were performing at top levels on state assessments were enrolled in advanced classes. The only criteria for placement was one state summative test score from the prior year. The supervisor asks the principal if it is possible to accelerate the achievement of students by teaching them an advanced curriculum. The principal agrees that the school has not been focused on making sure all students have equal opportunity to learn the critical content of the curriculum. But she is concerned that teachers will not agree with a change to the criteria.

The principal assigns the assistant principal and school counselor to research other schools and districts for the criteria used for placement in advanced classes. The team then revises their placement criteria for advanced classes and adjusts student placement accordingly.

Score: Developing

Feedback

During a midsemester conference, the supervisor checks the data and notes students are enrolled in the courses and classes that will give them equal opportunity to learn the critical content of the curriculum. He commends the principal for studying the data and utilizing his assistant principal and counselor to gather information about more appropriate entrance criteria and for using that information to make adjustments to the entrance criteria of multiple courses. He also notes the steps the principal took to place students in appropriate classes, even though classes were ready to begin. Together, they examine the desired effect of this element to determine if the principal met the criteria of Developing. The supervisor asks one question: "What evidence shows that all teachers are maintaining focus on the essential standards in their unit and lesson plans?"

Growth and Reflection Questions for Domain 2, Element 5

- How does a leader ensure teachers are addressing essential standards in unit and lesson plans and in classroom instruction?
- Is there a system to track if any students are being pulled out of core instruction for assistance in other subjects?
- If it is determined that teachers are not teaching the core standards, what interventions will be put in place to ensure that teachers plan, instruct, and assess the essential standards for all students?
- What structures are in place to track whether all students have the opportunity to learn the critical content of the curriculum?
- What criteria or structures are in place to determine which students will have access to advanced-level courses?

- What structures are in place to ensure that parents are aware of their child's current access to the essential elements of the curriculum?
- What action does the school leader need to take to move to the next level?
- What evidence would demonstrate the leader is achieving the desired effect of the element?

Conclusion

Domain 2 in the Focused Model combines elements from Domains 2 and 3 of the original model. Domain 2 also sets the expectation for instruction of a viable and guaranteed curriculum. In this updated domain, the school leader needs to remain cognizant of the big picture of teaching and learning.

Element 1 begins with the leader having a clear vision of instruction; this cornerstone element remains the same. The updated Element 2 was previously Element 3 of Domain 2. It says that a leader needs to know the predominant instructional practices in the school and use this baseline data to help teachers improve instructional practices. Elements 3, 4, and 5 were previously found in Domain 3, A Guaranteed and Viable Curriculum, and the constructs remain unchanged. However, please note that the authors have realigned the order of the elements; Element 4 in the new Domain 2 now focuses first on the viability of the curriculum, followed by Element 5, which guarantees that each student has equal opportunity to learn the critical content of the curriculum. The constructs of Elements 3, 4, and 5 remain unchanged. Only the order has been updated.

This domain reflects that a school leader's role, now more than ever, is to create a culture where teachers and leaders can support each other in teaching and ensuring a viable and guaranteed curriculum.

In our next chapter, on Domain 3, we turn to a discussion of how the role of the leader is to provide opportunities for staff members—including teachers and all other personnel at the school—to continue to grow in their unique roles. Chapter 3 will also highlight a shift in the focus of the school leader as primarily an instructional leader to a leader who finds the right balance with aspects of organizational leadership.

CHAPTER 3

Domain 3: Continuous Development of Teachers and Staff

Figure 3.1: Domain 3 supports continuous development of all staff.

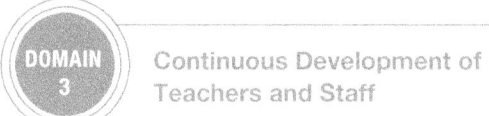

Continuous Development of Teachers and Staff

Element 1:
The school leader effectively hires, supports and retains personnel who continually demonstrate growth through reflection and growth plans.

Element 2:
The school leader uses multiple sources of data to provide teachers with ongoing evaluations of their pedagogical strengths and weaknesses that are consistent with student achievement data.

Element 3:
The school leader ensures that teachers and staff are provided with job-embedded professional development to optimize professional capacity and support their growth goals.

"We have to put the best teacher in front of students for students to learn. And likewise, we have to put the best principal in front of teachers in order for teachers to improve. I take the Marzano model elements and look at how they fit my school, what I need to do to grow my school, and how to align it all. Coming to a turnaround school, for example, in addition to knowing schoolwide instructional practice and digging into data, I really had to improve on giving feedback to teachers to help them grow."

—Lisa Freeman, Pinellas Park Elementary School, Florida

In Domain 3, the principal ensures that teachers and school personnel are working on continuously improving their practice. In this sense, the principal is a "human capital developer" (Donaldson, 2013), where "human capital refers to the skills and competencies that individuals acquire and are valued in the marketplace" (p. 841). Donaldson notes that, in the corporate world, studies have shown that human capital management has been tied to organizational outcomes and is a predictor of a company's performance. Donaldson concedes that because schools are "loosely coupled systems" rather than "tightly coupled," the effects of successful human capital management are not easily teased out from other factors that influence student achievement. Even so, teacher and other staff hiring and appropriate assignment is undoubtedly an area of principal influence on student learning that cannot be underestimated.

A 1987 study by Richard Andrews and Roger Soder made a clear connection between principal leadership and student achievement. The authors found that principals who set expectations for continual improvement of instruction within their schools and actively engaged in staff development had an impact on classroom practice that demonstrably improved student learning. Their findings suggested that "teacher perceptions of the principal as an instructional leader are critical to the reading and mathematics achievement of students, particularly low achieving students" (p. 11).

The actions and behaviors in Domain 3 work to ensure that the staff as a whole, as well as individual teachers, perceive their skills and expertise as powerful instruments in enhancing student learning and that they are continuously working to improve those skills. Element 1 of Domain 3 emphasizes that a growth mindset for teachers is nonnegotiable, that professional growth plans are in place, and that teachers and staff who continuously grow and reflect are retained in the school. In the Focused Model, this element has been broadened to include all school personnel. To make a school better, the principal cannot simply focus on producing better teachers but must also ensure that *all* staff are improving in their jobs.

Since schools work as a unit, a weak link can have a ripple effect on other systems and personnel. An effective leader keeps an eye on all aspects of hiring, supporting, and continually improving the entire staff.

Element 2 requires that principals conduct ongoing teacher evaluations and provide feedback consistent with student growth data. Additionally Element 3 ensures that job-embedded PD supports growth goals for all personnel at the school. Teachers need professional development, but so do support staff and other personnel who work as part of the school unit.

The three interrelated elements that comprise Domain 3 of the Focused

School Leader Evaluation Model have been identified by research as crucial practices and behaviors for successful school leadership and improving student achievement. The Wallace Foundation report *Learning from Leadership*, for example, detailed the school leader practices that best supported improved classroom instruction (Seashore-Louis, Leithwood, Wahlstrom, & Anderson, 2010). Those practices included focusing the school on goals and expectations for student achievement (behaviors that correspond to Element 1 of Domain 1 but are also relevant to all three elements of Domain 3). Blase and Blase (2004) identified three primary elements of successful instructional leadership, all of which are addressed in Domain 3: conducting instructional conferences (Element 2), providing staff development (Element 3), and developing teacher reflection (Element 1).

New Standard 6 of PSEL states that "effective educational leaders develop the professional capacity and practice of school personnel to promote *each* student's academic success and well-being." One of the indicators of this standard includes the responsibility to "develop teachers' and staff members' professional knowledge, skills, and practice through differentiated opportunities for learning and growth."

The three interrelated elements together form a cohesive plan to support, monitor, measure, and ensure that all teachers and staff share a commitment to ongoing growth, that the leader is able and willing to provide consistent and actionable feedback to help them grow, and that teachers have access to professional development that supports them to meet their growth goals.

An Effective School Leader Develops Expertise: The Challenges

In our work with school leaders, we have identified a number of the most common and significant challenges a school leader faces in helping teachers develop their expertise so as to impact student achievement. Leaders should be aware of these four points of tension in advance, so as to devise creative strategies to mitigate their effect:

1. **Creative tension between roles**

   As we have indicated, the school leader wears multiple hats. In one role, the school leader is an *instructional leader*, a lead learner and teacher, a person with a clear implementation plan for the common language or model of instruction. Simultaneously, the school leader is also called on to *evaluate* teachers, to make decisions about hiring, promotion, and tenure. And finally, the school leader plays an important *managerial* role to ensure the smooth operations of the school.

There are naturally some challenges for a school leader who expects to fully support continuous improvement of instruction and the other duties of personnel within the school. First and foremost, the leader must walk the delicate line between the role of instructional leader, on the one hand, and that of evaluator/supervisor on the other.

We attest that tension may arise as school leaders desire to maintain strong interpersonal relationships and also continually improve the craft knowledge of teachers. Craft knowledge is the "wisdom of teaching"; as in any profession, craft knowledge is developed over time with practice, reflection, and feedback (Van Driel & De Jong, 2001). Leaders must support teachers in their professional growth, but they must also evaluate teachers. The divide between these roles may create tension.

Tension, however, is not always necessarily a bad thing. It's possible to resolve tension so that *meaning* is created within the space of conflict—so that the tension results in growth. In *The Fifth Discipline*, Peter Senge (1990) identified this tension between reality and what could be—calling it "creative tension."

Creative tension is the difference between shared vision and current reality. When dissatisfaction occurs with the current state, such that one is driven to change it, creativity will result. The gap between where we are and where we want to be results in a desire for change. Creative tension will drive committed group members toward organizational goals, closing the gap.

In other words, the tension between the school leader's roles as lead learner/teacher and evaluator can open the door for positive, systemwide growth. Steps toward resolving this tension might include formal and informal conversations, dialogue, active listening, questioning, and other collaborative strategies common to mentoring relationships.

Developing positive mentoring relationships with teachers requires the leader to have productive, collegial conversations. Effective leaders become coaches to their teachers and know how to effectively communicate goals and objectives that support professional growth and student achievement. One administrator who uses the Marzano Teacher Evaluation Model calls these conversations "courageous conversations." It is a delicate balance to faithfully implement an evaluation system that produces professional growth while maintaining effective relationships.

2. **Hiring, retention, and termination**

The instructional leader must hire teachers and staff most likely to demonstrate an eagerness to develop professionally and retain teachers who are committed to growth. A 2011 study from MetLife found that only 44 percent of teachers are "very satisfied" with their jobs (an 18 percent decline since 2008) and that, depending on demographics, as many as 66 percent planned to leave the profession in the next five years (MetLife, 2012). A report on America's top K–12 teachers from The New Teacher Project (TNTP) noted that, in a survey of the most distinguished teachers in the United States, a full 60 percent said they were planning to leave the profession within five years (TNTP, 2013). In almost any other industry or profession, such a planned exodus would constitute a crisis (imagine 60 percent of surgeons leaving the profession or 60 percent of engineers!).

Hiring and retaining teachers who are willing to self-assess, reflect, and implement personal growth plans may be a significant challenge. Conversely, an emphasis on professional growth often leads to increased autonomy, personal pride, and job satisfaction—which may result in more teachers remaining in the profession for longer periods. In addition to hiring the right teachers, school leaders also empower and motivate teachers and staff to the highest levels of professional practice and to continuous learning and improvement.

3. Becoming a reliable observer

Most school leaders need training, practice, and feedback to become reliable observers. In this way, the learning curve for a school leader implementing a model of instruction is as steep as it is for teachers. A school leader conducting an observation has to be able to identify evidence that the teacher is using strategies effectively; but more than that, the observer must also note when strategies were called for but not used in that particular lesson or unit.

Further, to be truly helpful, an observer has to diagnose which teacher behaviors contribute to weaknesses (and strengths) of instruction and formulate a plan for improvement. Which practices should the teacher continue to use? Which should be retired? Which need more reflection to produce desired results? And which new strategies or behaviors should the teacher start to incorporate?

4. Providing formative feedback

School leaders who hope to foster an environment in which instruction is continually improving also make sure that assessments or evaluations are formative as well as summative. When teachers can assess their skills early in the year, they have the opportunity to practice and refine. Good teachers are aware of the value of practice: In response to the TNTP (2013) survey, 100 percent of America's best teachers strongly agreed that "practice in the form of trying different lessons and teaching methods over time" had the highest impact on helping them improve (p. 12). Ninety-three percent found observation of other teachers very helpful. Advice and feedback from colleagues and students were close behind.

Although 83 percent of teachers surveyed agreed that their evaluator's honest feedback had helped them improve, "a significant subset of respondents indicated that they are not receiving useful feedback on a regular basis. Almost one in four teachers (27 percent) at least somewhat disagreed that they 'get regular, constructive feedback on their teaching'" (TNTP, 2013, p. 12).

In regard to feedback, Blase and Blase (2004) have noted that "a central and powerful element of principals' interactions with teachers" constitute "imperative" verbal forms—both suggestions and requests. Suggestions, they note, at least to some extent, break down the power dynamic—one person in authority and another under authority—and allow a chink through which creative insights may emerge. Such suggestions and requests are quite different from the usual orders and demands, but even suggestions require some finessing. Blase and Blase found that teachers respond most positively when the suggested action is *purposeful*, when the teacher has the *ability to perform* it, and when the suggestion does not offend the teacher (pp. 30–31).

One school leader we know takes this idea a step further. She tells us that she stopped offering teachers suggestions entirely—she only asked them questions. She resolved that she would *never* offer solutions. Instead, she framed the issue she had seen during classroom observations (for example, students who never spoke in class), then asked the teacher to think through possible solutions to that specific challenge. This school leader found that teachers were far quicker and more willing to change their practice and implement new strategies when they had brainstormed their *own* solutions! Which perhaps, knowing human nature, should not come as such a surprise.

In an informal survey we conducted with leaders from more than thirty districts, leaders reported that the number-one reason they failed to give teachers accurate feedback regarding their teaching practices was "relationships"—in other words, school leaders worried that honest feedback might damage or strain an otherwise good working relationship. Finding the right balance between targeted, honest feedback and collegial support will continue to be an ongoing challenge for school leaders, but it is also an opportunity to create a culture of openness, transparency, and trust.

To summarize, Domain 3 fosters the kind of internal accountability that Michael Fullan, quoting Richard Elmore, has identified as necessary for sustained professional growth:

> Richard Elmore said 15 years ago, "No amount of external accountability will be effective in the absence of internal accountability." So what's internal

accountability? It's when the group individually and collectively has a sense of responsibility about their work. When we look at collaborative cultures, the districts, the schools, even some of the systems that have strong degrees of collaboration, they have built in a growing and increasing sense of responsibility about what they're doing and how they need to explain themselves—not just to themselves, but to the wider system.

To have accountability that works means to have a framework of goals, to monitor the results that come from those goals, but to be transparent and specific about the evidence that people themselves are using to improve. And once you have trust, transparency, specificity, evidence, and nonjudgmentalism, you get a constellation of conditions that make progress possible. In effect, this turns accountability on its head. Such accountability is built at the level of action, which in turn interfaces with the external accountability system—inside-out more than the reverse. (Thiers, 2017)

Domain 3, Element 1: Hiring, Supporting, and Retaining Staff

The school leader effectively hires, supports, and retains personnel who continually demonstrate growth through reflection and growth plans.

Desired Effect: Teachers and staff continue to grow as they meet their growth goals.

Element 1 begins with the basic practice of hiring the right people. Human capital is undoubtedly the most critical factor in setting the stage for improving student achievement. Hiring can be a monumental task in high-needs schools, in schools with low student achievement, and for novice leaders. Although hiring is embedded among other constructs in Element 1, it should not be overlooked. Having processes and procedures in place to hire the right personnel is the motor to drive a school forward.

This element also explores how a school leader supports personnel, then drills down to which personnel the leader retains. In this case, the leader retains personnel who continue to grow, using a reflection process, but even more specifically, retains personnel who have growth plans. Using growth plans can be either a formalized or informal process. But the underlying premise emphasizes that all personnel in a school, including noncertificated support staff, need to continuously improve. Ineffective personnel in other departments can consume a school leader's time and rob attention that could be directed at building better teachers.

Deliberate Practice for Deliberate Growth

[School leaders] *realize that most teachers expand their teaching range only with carefully designed support and assistance. This is a startling revelation for principals who had always assumed intuitively that when given minimal information and assistance most teachers would analyze their own teaching and formulate and act on growth plans in a self-directed and constructive manner.* —Blase and Blase (2004, p. 22)

One of the most effective ways for teachers to enhance their pedagogical skills is through a method of deliberate practice, first identified by Anders Ericsson as a proven route to expertise for athletes, musicians, and other high performers. More recently, deliberate practice—a system where the practitioner identifies specific skills for improvement and hones those skills based on feedback from a coach—has been applied as a way to improve teacher pedagogy. In the past, it seems feedback to improve teacher performance has been intermittent or, at worst, nonexistent in many schools and districts. Many states require teachers to develop individualized professional development plans. These are often viewed as compliance documents but in fact should be deliberate practice.

As Marzano (2011) notes,

> Research suggests that the supervisory and feedback systems in place in many districts do little to systematically enhance teacher expertise (Toch & Rothman, 2008; Weisberg, Sexton, Mulhern, & Keeling, 2009). Fortunately we can develop expertise through deliberate practice (Ericsson, Krampe, & Tesch-Romer, 1993). Deliberate practice involves more than just repetition; it requires activities that are designed to improve performance, challenge the learner, and provide feedback. (p. 82)

Deliberate practice, when applied to teaching, is a mindful, systematic, highly structured effort to relentlessly seek solutions to clearly defined problems. Rather than getting stuck in a loop of trial and error, teachers and school leaders use deliberate practice to grow expertise through a series of planned activities, reflection, and collaboration.

In other words, it is a focused plan to improve, no matter how high the level of current expertise. We begin with the assumption that we can all get better at our craft with a growth mindset. Then, a process for reflection and deliberate practice empowers teachers to grow. To work effectively, deliberate practice requires

- *Effort.* Individuals are motivated to practice because practice improves performance.
- *Perseverance.* Expert performance doesn't happen overnight.
- *Brainpower.* Experts' practice causes brains to develop better systems for storing, organizing, and accessing information.

- *Metacognition.* The learner must possess a keen awareness of his or her own thinking processes.
- *Feedback.* A coach provides suggestions, questions, and prompts to improve thinking about performance.

In summary, Marzano (2011) identifies four major components of deliberate practice in schools: a common language of instruction, a focus on specific strategies, tracking teacher progress, and opportunities to observe and discuss teaching expertise.

Tracking Teacher Progress to Improve Pedagogical Skills

Once a teacher has chosen which strategies to practice deliberately, then coaches, observers, and supervisors can track improvement using a generic scale. We suggest using a developmental scale or rubric like the Marzano scale that starts with the basic concept of Not Using with a scale value of 0 and moves up the scale to Innovating, which is a level 4. The goal of the coach will be to help the teacher by giving accurate feedback and other support that results in the teacher moving forward on the developmental scale or rubric. For example, once an element for deliberate practice is identified, it is likely that the teacher would begin at the level of Not Using, which means the teacher has never tried or is not using the strategy. Once the teacher tries a strategy, the feedback on the scale may likely be at a Beginning level. Here, the teacher is trying to use the strategy but is using the strategy incorrectly or with parts missing. With practice and coaching, the teacher can move to Developing, or Level 2, indicating that the teacher is using the strategy with no major errors or omissions but in a mechanical way.

Level 3 of the Marzano scale—Applying—is the minimum target for developing expertise. At this level, the teacher not only uses the strategy without error but also monitors to see whether the strategy has the desired effect on students. At the highest level of the scale—Innovating—the teacher knows the strategy so well that he or she has developed adaptations specific to the needs of every student in the class.

A teacher's scores may initially be quite low—either Not Using (unsatisfactory, needs improvement, and so on) or Beginning—because the teacher is focusing on areas where he or she would like to improve. Throughout the year, teachers can monitor their progress through self-ratings, walk-throughs conducted by administrators and instructional coaches, and comprehensive observations conducted by supervisors.

Although our focus here refers only to teachers, as we have noted previously, the effective school leader will have a similar process for all personnel so the school as a whole is focused on getting better—person by person.

Scales and Evidences for Domain 3, Element 1

The descriptions above provide guidance for evaluators to gather evidence for Element 1. Evaluators can expect to see evidence of a comprehensive system for hiring, supporting, and growing all personnel in the schools of effective leaders.

Figure 3.2: **The scale and evidences for Domain 3, Element 1.**

Scale Value	Description
Innovating (4)	The school leader provides interventions and support for teachers and staff who are not meeting their growth goals.
Applying (3)	The school leader effectively hires, supports, and retains personnel who continually demonstrate growth through reflection and growth plans AND monitors the extent to which teachers and staff achieve their growth goals and continue to grow.
Developing (2)	The school leader effectively hires, supports, and retains personnel who continually demonstrate growth through reflection and growth plans.
Beginning (1)	The school leader attempts to effectively hire, support, and retain personnel who continually demonstrate growth through reflection and growth plans but does not complete the task or is not successful.
Not Using (0)	The school leader does not attempt to effectively hire, support, and retain personnel who continually demonstrate growth through reflection and growth plans.

Sample Evidences for Element 1 of Domain 3
• Each teacher provides written pedagogical growth goals.
• Teachers regularly track their progress toward meeting pedagogical growth goals.
• Evaluation results, growth plans, and interventions for struggling personnel are available.
• Meetings are regularly scheduled with personnel regarding their growth goals and tracking progress.
• A teacher induction program is in place to support new teachers.
• Teacher leaders are identified, supported, and provided opportunities to develop.
• Personnel records reveal the leader hires and retains effective personnel.
• Standardized interview processes and/or protocols are utilized.
• Nondiscriminatory hiring practices are evident.
• Personnel records document that support systems are utilized to ensure personnel meet their goals.
• Teachers can describe their progress on their pedagogical growth goals.
• Staff members demonstrate continuous growth in their area of responsibility.
• Personnel can share documented examples of how reflection has improved their craft.

A Scenario for Domain 3, Element 1

Dr. Smith is the principal of Metfork Lakes High School, a Title I school. During the past five years, Dr. Smith has continued to see high turnover in the school's teaching staff. Many teachers leave after one year to take positions in more affluent schools. At the beginning of the school year, Dr. Smith meets with teachers to present current school performance data. He tells staff that, this year, they must focus on improving instruction. He then reviews the process for creating yearly growth plans, and he schedules department meetings to help teachers complete their plans.

In department meetings, Dr. Smith provides teachers with the achievement data of their students and a copy of the instructional model. He encourages teachers in the department to select organizing students in groups as one goal and to develop action steps to help meet the goal. He also sends teachers a deadline to submit their plans.

After reviewing and accepting the teacher growth plans, he meets with the school's leadership team to create an evaluation schedule. Together, they decide who will supervise each department. Dr. Smith determines that teachers' growth plans will be measured during the formal observation process. He informs the leadership team that prior to each teacher's evaluation, teams should send communications to the teacher announcing the expectation that observers should see evidence of the growth goal, organizing students in groups, being practiced or implemented during instruction.

At the end of the year, when formal evaluations are complete, Dr. Smith signs off that growth plans are complete.

Rating: Beginning

Feedback

In this scenario, Dr. Smith has teachers provide written pedagogical growth plans. The implementation of the plans, however, falls short of supporting teacher growth and reflection. Providing teachers with student achievement and evaluation data is a good start. The data provided are meant to help teachers reflect and determine an area of pedagogical weakness.

Nevertheless, pieces of the element are missing. Without a plan to provide ongoing feedback and support, the likelihood that teachers will improve their practice is slim. The goal of the leader and leadership team is to support teachers as they implement and practice their stated growth goals. For growth to happen, teachers will need multiple opportunities to learn, to apply learning to instruction, to receive and reflect on feedback, and then to make adjustments. Dr. Smith and his team do not provide evidence of a viable plan to support teachers.

To move to the Developing or Applying level, Dr. Smith would need to evaluate his observation and feedback systems. He should establish a baseline rating for each teacher related to his or her individual growth goal and then provide the teacher with multiple opportunities to receive feedback and time to reflect. Teachers would then use this process to show continuous improvement. Perhaps, Dr. Smith and the leadership team should meet periodically to discuss teacher progress and determine which teachers, if any, are not making progress. Additional support could then be provided to the identified teachers to ensure they make progress toward their goals.

Growth and Reflection Questions for Domain 3, Element 1

- Why is it important for a school leader to continually develop each person who works at the school?
- What hiring practices could be implemented to help identify personnel who want to keep getting better at their job?
- How do teachers identify areas of pedagogical weakness? How do other personnel—e.g., clerical, media specialists, school psychologists—identify growth goals?
- How do you provide ongoing feedback to teachers targeted at improving identified areas of weakness?
- What is the plan and process for providing teachers feedback?
- What additional supports would a leader need to provide teachers and other personnel who are not demonstrating progress toward written growth goals?

Domain 3, Element 2: Conducting Ongoing Evaluations

The school leader uses multiple sources of data to provide teachers with ongoing evaluations of their pedagogical strengths and weaknesses that are consistent with student achievement data.

Desired Effect: Teacher observation/evaluation data are consistent with student achievement data.

Knowing trends in instructional practices is a starting point, but school leaders are charged with giving each teacher accurate feedback about his or her pedagogical strengths and weaknesses. Note that the scales and evidences for Element 2 (figure 3.3) contain multiple embedded constructs:

- Teachers are provided with clear, ongoing evaluations of their teaching strengths and weaknesses.
- Evaluations are based on multiple sources of data.
- Evaluation data are consistent with student achievement data.

We would urge school leaders to consider if one yearly observation serves as a mechanism for changing a teacher's instructional practice. Most states require only one annual evaluation observation for teachers with more than three years of teaching experience. For teachers with one to three years of teaching experience, most states recommend up to four observations annually. We propose that *if* the purpose of evaluation is to refine and improve teachers' instructional practices through targeted feedback consistent with student achievement data, then one evaluation per year will not suffice. The challenge we must confront is: do we ensure that teachers are provided *ongoing* evaluations of their performance?

A single point of measurement does not paint a complete picture of a teacher's performance, nor does it allow a teacher to demonstrate growth. Obtaining a true score representing a teacher's instructional practice would basically require a commitment for an observer to be in the classroom daily.

Thus, to achieve the fairest picture of a teacher's performance, evaluation systems should use multiple measures to determine whether teachers have met performance expectations.

In TNTP's 2010 paper, "Teacher Evaluation 2.0," the authors argue that, whenever possible,

> [multiple measures] should include objective measures of student academic growth, such as value-added models that connect students' progress on standardized assessments to individual teachers while controlling for important factors such as students' academic history. Other possible measures include performance on districtwide or teacher-generated assessments, and classroom observations centered on evidence of student learning. (p. 6)

In addition to observation data, we advise that evaluators draw on multiple data sources, which might include student survey data, teacher self-evaluated videos, peer feedback, and student artifacts. If the true measure of teacher effect is student outcomes, Element 2 says that there should be a relationship between a teacher's instructional practice evaluations and the achievement of the students in that teacher's classroom.

The process does not have to be complex. If a teacher consistently earns the highest rating for instructional practice, it follows logically that the students in that classroom benefit from the instruction and their achievement should show steady improvement. Thomas Kane and Stephen Cantrell in the Measures of Effective Teaching Project, a three-year project published in 2013, suggest that strong teacher performance positively impacts student learning and may in fact be the best predictor of student achievement.

A Test Case: Pilot Project Using Multiple Measures in a Large Urban School District

In 2012–2013, Learning Sciences International conducted a pilot project with a large urban school district to test the use of multiple measures for accurate teacher performance assessment. Regardless of the process utilized for considering multiple data sources to assess teacher proficiency, it's not possible to achieve an improvement in teacher pedagogy without multiple layers of coaching and support. Participants in the pilot can attest to the level of commitment necessary to positively impact student achievement.

This pilot relied on formal observation data to determine its effectiveness. But in reality, the designers of the pilot were aware that it would be extremely difficult to formally observe all teachers in the district four times per year (a challenge many school districts must confront). Therefore, multiple measures of teacher proficiency and growth were deliberately built into the pilot: student surveys, informal walk-throughs by instructional coaches, instructional data chats, and student artifacts.

A novel measure for teachers in the pilot was the use of student surveys. Students were asked to rate the effectiveness of their teacher's learning goals and accompanying scales. Additionally, students were asked to describe the current unit scale and address their perception of their most recent achievement along the scale. Many teachers were concerned that students wouldn't give accurate accounts of their understanding of the scales. To address these concerns, the leader's formal observation data was compared to student perceptions as a check for possible student bias or inaccuracy. In addition to student survey data, instructional coaches routinely conducted informal, nonevaluative walk-throughs to determine teacher proficiency. The focus of the walk-throughs was centered on the use of learning goals and scales and tracking student progress, Elements 1 and 2 of the 2014 Marzano Teacher Evaluation Model. Student artifacts and results from instructional data chats were also used to measure teacher proficiency.

Data chats can be defined this way: conversations centered around student achievement based on formative and summative assessment data. These routinely scheduled data chats were useful in determining how well teachers taught critical information from their shared lesson plans.

Data chats were conducted during scheduled weekly PLC meetings made up of grade- and subject-level teams, for example, sixth-grade math teams. During the PLC meetings, in addition to time devoted to common planning, conversations were scheduled to discuss data from common student formative and summative assessments. Information from data chats was used to assist observers in determining the effectiveness of the agreed-on instructional strategies that teachers were using and to impact planned instruction.

Teachers were able to determine if adaptations to future lesson plans and remediation would be needed before progressing to the next planned unit. Information from the chats was also used to identify students who could benefit from planned interventions, such as pull-out groups and after-school tutoring.

If teacher behavior is the leading indicator for the lagging indicator of student achievement, we might ask why most reform initiatives have goals to improve student achievement without an accompanying focus on improving teacher pedagogy. No Child Left Behind, for example, focused on improving achievement of subgroups and meeting proficiency targets but lacked an emphasis on how to improve teacher effectiveness.

However, the federal Race to the Top initiative included a focus on building great teachers and leaders as a major element of its reform project. The Marzano Focused School Leader Evaluation Model builds on and reinforces those efforts.

Technology-Based Platforms Can Simplify Data Collection

Technology platforms are now available to simplify data collection for evaluation, to provide immediate feedback, and to track teacher growth. Although there are a number of such platforms available, we focus in this section on the platform developed by Learning Sciences International, iObservation, to illustrate the role such platforms play in providing formative feedback and tracking teacher growth as part of the evaluation process.

Platforms such as iObservation allow unprecedented access to resource libraries, virtual communication and conferencing, video examples of classroom strategies, and other digitized documents to help both teachers and school leaders. iObservation reports real-time data from classroom walk-throughs, teacher observations, school leader observations, confidential self-assessments, instructional rounds, and evaluations conducted by school leaders or the supervisors of school leaders. Such electronic tools and professional development resources enable users to focus on instructional leadership while maintaining compliance with state and district requirements. Technology platforms like iObservation allow observers to send feedback to teachers or school leaders immediately following a classroom or school visit for a transparent and effective process.

A supervisor may, for example, use the platform to inform school leaders of upcoming observations and preconference meetings and to share relevant resources for preconference review. Digitized protocols with scales, evidences, and desired effects for each domain are loaded into the platform for easy reference.

The Scales and Evidences for Domain 3, Element 2

Figure 3.3: **The scales and evidences for Domain 3, Element 2.**

Scale Value	Description
Innovating (4)	The school leader ensures that teacher evaluation processes are updated regularly to ensure the results are consistent with student achievement data.
Applying (3)	The school leader uses multiple sources of data to provide teachers with ongoing evaluations of their pedagogical strengths and weaknesses that are consistent with student achievement data AND monitors the extent to which teacher evaluations are consistent with student achievement data.
Developing (2)	The school leader uses multiple sources of data to provide teachers with ongoing evaluations of their pedagogical strengths and weaknesses that are consistent with student achievement data.
Beginning (1)	The school leader attempts to use multiple sources of data to provide teachers with ongoing evaluations of their pedagogical strengths and weaknesses that are consistent with student achievement data but does not complete the task or is not successful.
Not Using (0)	The school leader does not attempt to use multiple sources of data to provide teachers with ongoing evaluations of their pedagogical strengths and weaknesses that are consistent with student achievement data.

Sample Evidences for Element 2 of Domain 3
• Specific evaluation scales are in place to provide teachers accurate feedback on their pedagogical strengths and weaknesses.
• Teacher feedback and evaluation data are based on multiple sources of information including but not limited to direct observation, teacher self-report, analysis of teacher performance as captured on video, student reports on teacher effectiveness, and peer feedback to teachers.
• A schedule of teacher observations is in place to ensure all observations are completed in the designated time frame.
• Teacher evaluation data are regularly used as the subject of conversation between school leaders and teachers.
• Data show the school leader provides frequent observations and meaningful feedback to teachers.
• Data are available to support that teacher evaluations are consistent with student achievement data.
• Achievement data from classroom formative, benchmark, and/or summative/end-of-year assessments are consistent with teacher evaluation feedback.
• Teachers can describe how the implementation of specific instructional strategies affects student achievement.

> - When observation data are not consistent with student achievement data, the leader works to update accuracy in assigning observational feedback.
> - When observation data reveal inconsistencies with student achievement data, the leader provides teachers with appropriate support and interventions.

A Scenario for Domain 3, Element 2

Mrs. Franks has been principal of Fairview Elementary School for the past six years and has focused on establishing a common language of instruction as well as implementing effective data systems. At the beginning of the year, Mrs. Franks schedules data chats with each teacher to discuss state performance data for past and current students, and reviews the teacher's final evaluation results.

During the data chats, she discusses with each teacher what pedagogical strengths and weaknesses might be evident in the student data. After Mrs. Franks completes observations and evaluations, she has one-on-one conferences with teachers to review student formative data as compared to observation and evaluation data. She meets with each teacher three times during the year and reviews observation and evaluation scores with student performance data. She carefully plans guiding questions to facilitate the conversation that would help teachers connect their classroom performance to student learning.

In addition, Mrs. Franks makes sure to participate in PLCs so she can observe teachers talking about their instructional practices. She believes engaging in this work with teachers gives her additional insight into teacher performance and whether teachers are meeting the needs of students. Often, she shares student performance data from recent common assessments and asks teachers who have students showing growth to share their successful instructional practices.

Rating: Applying

Feedback

When the principal supervisor looked at the leadership actions taken by Mrs. Franks, it was agreed that she has solid systems in place to provide teachers with multiple data sources aligning pedagogy and student achievement. The evidence and data tracked from evaluation, student assessments, and PLC interactions demonstrate her ability to monitor whether instructional practices are resulting in desired student outcomes. Feedback to assist Mrs. Franks to move to Innovating should revolve around what happens when a discrepancy is identified between the scoring in observations/evaluations and student achievement data. The school leader needs to determine what additional feedback or support is needed for individual teachers or to personally reflect on additional support she may need in providing accurate and effective observation/evaluation feedback that is aligned with student achievement.

Growth and Reflection Questions for Domain 3, Element 2

- How do you manage your schedule to allow maximum opportunities to observe teaching?
- What data sources do you use to compare teacher evaluation data with student achievement data?
- What are different ways that you provide teachers ongoing feedback as part of their evaluation?
- What different data sources can be used to determine instructional effectiveness?
- How often should a leader examine the relationship between evaluation/observation performance and student achievement data with teachers?
- What other opportunities, outside of instruction, exist for a leader to provide teachers with pedagogical data and feedback?

Domain 3, Element 3: Providing Job-Embedded Professional Development

The school leader ensures that teachers and staff are provided with job-embedded professional development to optimize professional capacity and support their growth goals.

Desired Effect: Teachers and staff improve their skills as a result of attending professional development.

Element 3 should be the culmination of continuous improvement. The emphasis on teacher and staff development implies the associated need for professional development directly related to teachers' or staff members' areas of weakness. Element 3 asks the school leader to ensure that teachers are provided with differentiated PD that will demonstrably help them achieve their instructional growth goals (figure 3.4).

Numerous studies have examined the link between professional development and improved student achievement. For example, a 2007 review of 1,300 studies conducted by the Regional Education Laboratory (REL) Southwest found that teachers who received an average of forty-nine hours of professional development improved their student achievement scores by twenty-one percentile points (Yoon, 2007). Unfortunately, other studies have found no statistically significant difference in the test scores of students whose teachers received professional development versus student scores of teachers who received none. Most studies do, however, tend to measure *quantity* of professional development rather than *quality*. Researchers note, for example, that types of professional development can vary from school to school and district to district. These studies would indicate that not all professional development is created equal. A 2015 TNTP report recommends that "states and districts should develop systems for school leaders and teachers that provide a curated list of vetted learning opportunities aligned to individual evaluation feedback. States or districts could empower high-performing teachers with more choice, while requiring struggling teachers to engage in activities identified by evaluators as targeting areas for improvement" (Tooley, 2015).

We recommend utilizing professional development that specifically addresses areas of pedagogical weakness as identified in teacher or staff growth plans or identified as the leader analyzes observation trends and evaluation data. Teacher evaluation systems like the Marzano Focused Teacher Evaluation Model allow teachers to hone in on specific strategies for improvement and provide the most opportunities for targeted professional development.

The Scales and Evidences for Domain 3, Element 3

Figure 3.4: **Scales and evidences for Domain 3, Element 3.**

Scale Value	Description
Innovating (4)	The school leader continually reevaluates the professional development program to ensure that it remains job-embedded and focused on instructional growth goals and intervenes with personnel who are not making sufficient progress toward achieving growth goals.
Applying (3)	The school leader ensures that teachers and staff are provided with job-embedded professional development to optimize professional capacity and support their growth goals AND monitors the extent to which teachers and staff improve their skills.
Developing (2)	The school leader ensures that teachers and staff are provided with job-embedded professional development to optimize professional capacity and support their growth goals.
Beginning (1)	The school leader attempts to ensure that teachers and staff are provided with job-embedded professional development to optimize professional capacity and support their growth goals but does not complete the task or is not successful.
Not Using (0)	The school leader does not attempt to ensure that teachers and staff are provided with job-embedded professional development to optimize professional capacity and support their growth goals.

Sample Evidences for Element 3 of Domain 3
• Teachers and staff have ongoing opportunities to participate in job-embedded professional development or training.
• Online professional development courses and resources are available to teachers and staff regarding their growth goals.
• Teacher and staff participation in professional development activities is recorded and tracked.
• Teacher-led professional development is available to teachers regarding their instructional growth goals.
• Instructional coaching is available to teachers to help them achieve their instructional growth goals.
• Data are collected linking the effectiveness of professional development/training to the improvement of teacher and/or staff practices.
• Data are available documenting how deliberate practice is improving teacher performance.
• Teachers and staff can describe how professional development supports attainment of growth goals.
• Teachers and staff implement new strategies after attending professional development.
• Interventions are documented for staff who do not utilize professional development opportunities.
• Interventions are in place to support personnel who do not continue to grow in their area of responsibility.

A Scenario for Domain 3, Element 3

At the end of the school year, Principal Norwald sent a survey to teachers asking them to think about their growth goals and to rank professional learning topics for the next school year. She used the results of the survey in combination with observation trends to determine a specific area of focus for next year's professional learning days. She determined the data collected supported her decision to focus on effective small-group instruction. Over the summer, the principal researched strategies, engaged in collaboration with district content experts, and created a professional learning calendar that included face-to-face sessions presented by experts and teachers, PLCs, coaching cycles, and common planning.

When the new school year begins, Principal Norwald presents teachers with schoolwide and individual student achievement data, as well as the professional learning focus for the year. She then reviews with teachers how to generate individual growth plans and indicates that this year's plans should be connected to the schoolwide professional learning focus.

As the year progresses, teachers have access to multiple learning opportunities and supports. All teachers engage in at least one coaching cycle, and the majority of PLC and professional development time is focused on planning for and improving small-group instruction. Over the course of the year, teachers are provided with opportunities to share success stories, observe peers during small-group instruction, work with district literacy specialists, and/or have coaches model effective small-group strategies. Prior to school ending, Mrs. Norwald sends out another survey asking teachers to provide feedback on the year's professional learning focus and to rank-order potential topics for the following year.

Rating: Developing

Feedback

While Principal Norwald has provided teachers with job-embedded professional development, her next step is to collect evidence and monitor the extent to which the professional learning has resulted in improved teacher performance and student achievement outcomes.

Growth and Reflection Questions for Domain 3, Element 3

- What process is in place to help determine the professional learning focus for each teacher?
- How does a leader ensure that staff other than teachers are supported through professional development and that it results in improved job performance?
- How can a leader utilize the instructional strengths of teachers and coaches to support others in their professional growth?
- What evidence will show whether the provided professional learning opportunities result in improved teacher and student performance?
- Is there a plan to scaffold support for teachers as they make progress toward growth goals?

Conclusion

Teaching is not a static occupation. The demands of the twenty-first century require that we continually strive to improve our practice for the benefit of our students. The PISA report of 2012 has set a recent challenge for American students, who currently rank twenty-sixth in math, twenty-first in science, and seventeenth in reading (Programme for International Student Assessment, 2012), findings that former United States education secretary Arne Duncan has called "a picture of educational stagnation" (Duncan, 2013). Rapid technological advances put further pressure on teachers, and whole schools, to continuously improve. From the newest first-year teacher to the seasoned veteran, becoming better educators must be a nonnegotiable goal.

The good news is that educational research and innovations in systems and technology are giving us better knowledge and tools to meet those challenges. We know more than ever about how collaborative cultures can work to meet school goals, how performance evaluations can function as an integrated aspect of a model of instruction, and how the cycle of deliberate practice can be a major component of building pedagogical expertise.

The primary purpose of the school leader evaluation model outlined here, and certainly the focus of Domain 3, is to foster a *culture of continuous improvement*, one "that shatters the norms of isolation and autonomy . . . thus leading to the establishment of an 'educational practice' that trumps the notion of teaching as an art, a craft, or a style" (City, Elmore, Fiarman, & Teitel, 2009, p. xi). We are seeing a definitive trend away from islands of excellence toward a comprehensive landscape where *all* educators are connected in a common project to improve public education and raise the achievement of our students. Evaluation systems have an important role to play in fostering and supporting educator growth.

Domain 3 is a new domain with an expanded focus on continuous improvement of *all* personnel in a school, rather than teachers only (the elements have been adapted from Domain 2 of the previous model). This domain also represents the beginning of a shift for the school leader from the role of instructional leadership to that of organizational leadership. As we discussed earlier in this chapter, the organizational behaviors of the leader in Domain 3 focus on the big picture of hiring the best people, providing feedback, then helping everyone in the school continuously improve their practice. Improvement is guided by a plan to accelerate growth while providing support and job-appropriate learning experiences.

So far, we have been focusing on principal behaviors that foster continuous, whole-school improvement with the ultimate goal of improving student achievement. In the next chapter, we will turn to another aspect of organizational leadership in Domain 4, Community of Care and Collaboration, to look at how creating a collaborative culture, empowering teachers and staff, and committing to equity and celebrating the diversity of all students supports the goal of enhancing instruction and creating a supportive community to improve student achievement.

CHAPTER 4

Domain 4: Community of Care and Collaboration

If everyone is moving forward together, then success takes care of itself.
—Henry Ford

Figure 4.1: **The four elements of Domain 4 support a collaborative culture and equity for all students.**

Community of Care and Collaboration

Element 1:
The school leader ensures that teachers work in collaborative groups to plan and discuss effective instruction, curriculum, assessments, and the achievement of each student.

Element 2:
The school leader ensures a workplace where teachers have roles in the decision-making process regarding school planning, initiatives, and procedures to maximize the effectiveness of the school.

Element 3:
The school leader ensures equity in a child-centered school with input from staff, students, parents, and the community.

Element 4:
The school leader acknowledges the successes of the school and celebrates the diversity and culture of each student.

Domain 4, Community of Care and Collaboration, retains its emphasis from the Domain 4 (Cooperation and Collaboration) of the previous model, with a slight shift in focus. The aim is to promote a more inclusive way of thinking about the school leader's role in establishing a culture that reflects a community of care, a collaborative workplace, the celebration of diversity, and an emphasis on collaborative teamwork for teachers to plan effective instruction. Domain 4 addresses the way a school does its work, looking at how staff forms a unified, transparent, and collaborative environment so that the school functions at optimal levels. This domain emphasizes organizational management, and now contains four elements, rather than the five elements from the previous model.

What Do We Mean by a Community of Care?

The school leader must ensure that the school culture and climate foster a rich and collective sense of a shared enterprise among all stakeholders in the system. Indeed, the updated PSEL standards for school leaders, released in 2015, place increased emphasis on the leader's role as a community builder. The PSEL standards say that effective leaders "create and sustain a school environment in which each student is known, accepted and valued, trusted and respected, cared for, and encouraged to be an active and responsible member of the school community" (National Policy Board for Education Administration, 2015, p. 13). The authors of the revised standards call this environment a "Community of Care and Support for Students."

This focus on the cultivation of positive school and community environments is threaded throughout the 2015 PSEL standards. The earlier 2014 ISLLC Standards for School Leaders also emphasized the school leader's community building role. In his paper discussing the foundations of the ISLLC standards, Joseph Murphy (2014) references three "distinct but related dimensions" of the school leader as community builder. The first is the *extended school environment*, where the school leader honors the voices of parents and members of the larger community, reflected in Element 3 of Domain 4. In the second sphere, the school leader acts as guardian of *communities of learning* for teachers and staff, reflected in Element 1 of Domain 4. And in the third, he or she builds and safeguards *caring learning environments* for students, which is the overall focus of Domain 4.

What Do We Mean by Collaboration?

A great deal has been written about the need for cooperation and collaboration as a means to improve schools and student learning outcomes. But how is *collaboration* within the K–12 environment both similar to and different from the kinds of collaboration called for in other professions and industries? And what might we learn from them?

Most school systems have programs and structures in place to foster collaboration throughout the entire network of participants. PLCs encourage collaboration among teachers. School board meetings ideally foster collaboration among parents, the community, and school administrators (Center for Public Education, 2011; Office of Superintendent of Public Instruction, 2004). Conferences between teachers and parents build connections. Celebrations, games, and sports set a foundation for cooperation and goodwill among students, teachers, parents, administrators, and the community at large. The purpose of all these activities and interactions is to build a vibrant, cohesive, and productive school culture—a culture that sets in motion widening spheres of influence that impact the larger community.

Clearly collaboration in the school environment goes far beyond just "getting along." The ultimate goal is to develop what Philip C. Schlechty and others have called "civic capacity." Civic capacity, Schlechty (2009) notes in *Leading for Learning*, "refers to the ability of business leaders, union leaders, civic leaders, educational leaders, and leaders of other significant organizations to work together on behalf of common goals" (p. 187). Developing such civic capacity builds trust, a common identity, and the willingness to work with a shared purpose for the success of the school or schools within the system.

Writing on the connection between teacher and administrator relationships and student learning in the *Stanford Social Innovation Review*, Carrie Leana (2011) notes, "When the relationships among teachers in a school are characterized by high trust and frequent interaction—that is, when social capital is strong—student achievement scores improve."

Another way of looking at such a flourishing school community is what Marzano has called a "purposeful community." In *School Leadership That Works*, Marzano, Waters, and McNulty (2005) define the purposeful community as "one with the collective efficacy and capability to develop and use assets to accomplish goals that matter to all community members through an agreed-upon process" (p. 99). Marzano et al. go on to elaborate on the four concepts embedded in this definition:

1. *Collective efficacy.* Collective efficacy occurs when group members share the perception or belief that they can dramatically enhance the effectiveness of an organization—in other words, that they can make a difference. This sense of collective efficacy has been correlated to student achievement.

2. *Development and use of all available assets.* Available assets include both tangible assets, such as financial and physical resources, the talent of the school's personnel, and technology, but also intangible assets such as the shared ideals and beliefs about the school's core mission.

3. *Accomplishment of goals that matter to the community members.* The school functions as a community created for a specific purpose with specific goals to meet that purpose. Sergiovanni (2004) has called such groups "communities of hope."
4. *Agreed-on process.* An agreed-on process enhances communication among community members, provides efficient reconciliation of disagreements, and keeps members attuned to the status of the community.

Domain 4 of the Marzano Focused School Leader Evaluation Model supports the school leader's capacity to develop such a community of purpose. Marzano et al. (2005) identified nine primary responsibilities of the school leader that help the leader move toward that goal. Those responsibilities include the capacity for the leader to be an *optimizer* (an inspiration and driving force), who practices *affirmation* (recognizing and celebrating school accomplishments), and who clearly articulates *ideals* and *beliefs*. The leader is a person of high *visibility*, with a similarly high degree of *situational awareness* (the ability to honestly appraise the state of the organization), who cultivates *relationships*; hones effective *communication*; creates a strong, cohesive culture; and cultivates and invites teacher, student, and community *input*.

Marzano et al. (2005) also found the following behaviors were associated with "the responsibility of Culture":

- Promoting cohesion among staff
- Promoting a sense of well-being among staff
- Developing an understanding of purpose among staff
- Developing a shared vision of what the school could be like

These responsibilities are reflected in Elements 1 and 2 of Domain 4.

In previous chapters, we have focused primarily on the impact that individual leaders, and by extension individual teachers, can have on student achievement. But as DuFour and Marzano (2011) note in *Leaders of Learning*:

> The research has concluded that focusing on individual development does not develop the interdependence, collaboration, and collective effort essential to improving results (Carroll, 2009; Kruse et al., 1995; Little, 2006; McCauley & Van Velsor, 2003). (p. 66)

DuFour and Marzano (2011) go on to note that Newmann and Wehlage (1995) also found many schools that had competent individual teachers lacked the organizational capacity to raise student achievement because meeting that challenge "is beyond the skills of individual staff" and requires instead the organization of "human, technical, and social resources into an effective collective effort" (pp. 29–30). More recently, Fullan (2010a) has argued emphatically that strategies that focus solely on improving individuals will fail to improve schools because meeting that challenge requires building collective capacity. (p. 66)

In other words, as we have discussed, an effective school leader must have a strong vision of his or her purpose and goals for the school. But the individual visionary is not enough. The effective school leader relies on the support of an extended team of teachers and community members to accomplish those goals—as Henry Ford put it, *moving forward together*.

A study conducted by the University of Chicago Consortium on Chicago School Research, led by Anthony S. Bryk (2010) identified a high degree of "relational trust" in the most effective schools. In her *Washington Post* column summarizing this research, Valerie Strauss (2013) notes that "using advanced statistical methods, the consortium identified, with a high degree of reliability, the organizational traits and processes that can predict whether a school is likely to show above-average improvement in student outcomes."

Four of these aspects of cooperation and collaboration are aligned to Domain 4 and are reflected in the elements (italicized below). As summarized by Strauss (2013), they are:

- A coherent instructional guidance system, in which the curriculum, study materials, and assessments are coordinated within and across grades with meaningful teacher involvement *[reflected in Element 1]*
- Strong parent-community-school ties, with an integrated support network for students *[Element 3]*
- A student-centered learning climate that identifies and responds to difficulties any child may be experiencing *[Element 3]*
- Leadership focused on cultivating teachers, parents, and community members so that they become invested in sharing overall responsibility for the school's improvement *[Element 3]*

Domain 4 of the Marzano Focused School Leader Evaluation Model offers research-based strategies to meet the challenge to build a community of care and collaboration. The actions and behaviors in this domain help ensure that teachers, staff, students, and parents engage in a collaborative process to ensure the optimal functioning of the school and operate as a cohesive, caring team.

Creating a Social Space for Collaboration to Flourish

In *The Answer to How Is Yes: Acting on What Matters*, the philosopher Peter Block (2003) suggests that asking *how* questions too early in the change process undermines the power of dialogue and potentially encourages early closure that could derail solutions. As Marzano et al. (2005) note in *School Leadership That Works*:

> Block suggests that effective leaders are social architects who create a "social space" that enhances the effectiveness of an organization. The ideal social space is one conducive to solving even the most perplexing of organizational problems. For Block, critical leadership skills include convening critical discussions, naming the question, focusing the discussion on learning as opposed to premature closure on solutions, and using strategies for participative design of solutions. (pp. 19–20)

In our consultations with schools across the United States, we have identified a number of factors working within the social space that help ensure effective collaboration in schools. We will delve into these in detail later in this chapter, but it may be helpful to introduce and summarize them here.

- Effective school collaboration means teachers are interacting with other teachers around the subject of effective instruction. Teachers may be participating in instructional rounds or PLCs, conducting lesson studies where they are modeling planned instructional strategies, discussing planned interventions, and generally modeling *learning in action.*
- Effective school instruction means that teachers have a say in decisions important to the school. They are aware of new initiatives and participate in planning for those initiatives. Formal processes are in place to ensure that teachers have a way to voice concerns and provide other input.
- The school also has in place formal structures for becoming an effective learning organization. These structures might include systems for collective decision making, implementation of a research-based instructional model, establishment of key roles for leadership, thoughtful allocation of resources, attention to the social needs of the group, and so on.
- There is evidence of shared leadership. *Shared leadership* is a term often used in school effectiveness literature. In a nutshell, shared leadership means that the school leader has been able to identify teachers and nonclassroom personnel who have the ability to build capacity

within the school and the larger community and that the school leader is secure enough in his or her role to encourage this to happen.

Learning Organization or Learning Community?

In *Leading for Learning*, Phillip C. Schlechty (2009) makes a distinction between a "learning community" and a "learning organization" that sharpens the focus on this sense of *purposefulness* identified by Marzano. Schlechty defines *learning organizations* as the larger organizational structure inside of which learning communities flourish. Learning organizations are

> formal social organizations that purposefully create, support, and use learning communities and communities of learners as the primary means of inducting new members; creating, developing, importing, and exporting knowledge; assigning tasks and evaluating performances; and establishing goals and maintaining direction. Learning organizations create and maintain networks of learning communities and use these networks as the primary means by which the work of the organization is accomplished. (p. 115)

Schlechty (2009) emphasizes that it is the learning organization that lends legitimacy to the learning community or communities, such as PLCs, under its larger umbrella. Bureaucracies are the enemies of learning communities (and learning organizations) because bureaucracies do not assume either participatory decision making or open dialogue between leaders and followers. "In bureaucracies, the key questions are 'What is the rule?' and 'Who is in charge?' In a learning organization the key questions are 'What is the problem?' and 'Who is likely to know what to do about it?'" (p. 117)

Schlechty concurs with Marzano in naming the necessary conditions to support a successful learning organization, to create the social space Marzano has identified. There must be "sufficient cohesion within the school and district so that cooperation with others does not needlessly threaten the internal integrity of the system" (Schlechty, 2009, pp. 237–238). Shared authority is crucial, he says, but that does not mean the abandonment of authority.

Secondly, school leaders must shed their identities as managers and become leaders who encourage and support varied interactions among members so that the social space becomes "permeable." And lastly, all members must have a clear sense of the school's mission and vision.

With these characteristics in place, the school leader can create a culture that "drives out fear, encourages responsible risk taking, separates unsuccessful tries from punishment." He adds, "Only organizations that have clear beliefs to which most members are committed can collaborate without fear of compromising their mission and their integrity" (Schlechty, 2009,

p. 238). Schlechty emphasizes that collaboration is necessary for the "disruptive innovations needed to ensure a healthy future for public education in America" (p. 237).

Effective Communication Breaks Down Isolation

The assumption is that in order to foster such a social space or to build civic capacity, the school leader must be an excellent communicator. In the absence of communication, the school leader will not be able to establish a collaborative environment that builds shared leadership and will be unable to develop a coherent succession plan for new school leaders and instructional leaders. Because teaching has, in the past, been such an isolated profession (Lortie, 1975; Scholastic & The Gates Foundation, 2012), it will be up to the school leader to help teachers build the bridges they need to become effective collaborators.

Successful leaders will see that teachers get out of their own classrooms to observe other teachers, participate in study and planning groups, and otherwise become aware and engaged in what is happening throughout the entire building. Communication in this sense involves the entire school community, not just top-down communication from the school leader.

A school leader we know shared a story that sheds some light on the importance of schoolwide communication. She was working to get the teachers in her high school to leave their classrooms and explore and learn from their peers. Many of the teachers in this high school were seasoned veterans with fifteen to thirty years' experience. But a large number of veteran teachers were using ineffective instructional strategies. The school leader encouraged peer observations or instructional rounds, with the focus of pairing some seasoned veterans with more novice teachers who were using student-centered strategies and getting good results.

The veteran teachers were initially hesitant. It was the first time a school leader had suggested peer observations, and many were afraid that their peer data would be used against them in some way. To curtail these fears, the school leader met with the more vocal of these hesitant teachers and took their suggestions. She didn't shy away from having these conversations.

Based on their feedback, the first change she made was the term *instructional rounds*. She renamed the observation practice "Watch and Grow." She also changed the form for discourse to a simple yellow smiley-face Post-it note, and the reflection form to a green smiley-face Post-it. Instead of *requiring* that teachers share peer suggestions with administrators, it was just strongly suggested. Finally, the school leader created a contest as an incentive. The teacher with the most smiley-face Post-its and the teacher with the most reflective evidence won a prize: an assistant leader would cover his or her assigned duty for a week. Because she had welcomed open dialogue and made crucial changes to the original plan, the collegial process of learning from peers and sharing effective instructional practices was a success. The peer observation process has now been successfully integrated into the school's culture for half a decade.

We always recommend that teachers have structured opportunities to observe other teachers so as to assess their practice against the teaching strategies of their peers. The school leader's job is to facilitate and encourage those interactions. The school leader who fails to do this will, in the long run, be inhibiting the growth of teachers, who will remain isolated.

Building Evidence of Cooperation and Collaboration

The central question the school leader will ask in Domain 4 is this: do I honestly have *evidence* that I have built a Community of Care and Collaboration?

Let's take a look at the four elements of Domain 4. These elements focus on collaboration around effective teaching, participation in decision making, team building for issues around curriculum and assessment, and formal ways for staff to provide input about schoolwide policies and procedures. The elements also address the need for students, parents, and the wider community to be positively engaged by providing input, and lastly, for the school leader to acknowledge success and celebrate diversity.

Domain 4, Element 1

The school leader ensures that teachers work in collaborative groups to plan and discuss effective instruction, curriculum, assessments, and the achievement of each student.

Desired Effect: Teachers working in collaborative groups enhance instruction and student achievement.

Moving from Isolation to Collaboration

Element 1 of Domain 4 is focused on ensuring that teachers are fully engaged in the conversation about effective teaching: what it looks like in the classroom, how to plan for it, and the effect of specific strategies in specific lessons for specific results.

Teachers do collaborate. They just don't get to collaborate as much as they would like to. The MetLife *Survey of the American Teacher* published in 2009 reported that on average, teachers spend just 2.7 hours per week in structured collaboration with other teachers and school leaders. And less than one-third spent time observing other classroom teachers and providing feedback:

> By far, the least common collaborative activity is teachers observing each other in the classroom and providing feedback to each other. Much fewer teachers (22%) and leaders (32%) report it occurring always or often, with 44% of teachers and 26% of leaders saying it happens rarely or never. However, new teachers are more likely than other teachers to report teacher observation and feedback at their school (32% vs. 20%). (p. 10)

Furthermore, 67 percent of teachers and 78 percent of leaders responded that greater collaboration among teachers and school leaders would have a major impact on improving student achievement. In schools with high levels of collaboration, teachers and leaders held markedly different attitudes about the role of collaboration and collective responsibility.

> Teachers and leaders in schools with higher levels of collaboration are more likely than others to strongly agree that teachers in a school share responsibility for the achievement of all students and that greater collaboration among teachers and school leaders would have a major impact on improving student achievement.... Most striking is the higher level of trust in more collaborative schools. [Schools with] higher levels of collaboration are more likely to strongly agree that this level of trust exists (teachers: 69% vs. 42%; leaders: 78% vs. 60%). Furthermore, teachers in schools with higher levels of collaboration are more likely to be very satisfied with teaching as a career (68% vs. 54%). (p. 11)

The Gates Foundation supports this view, reporting that nearly 90 percent of US teachers believe that collaboration with colleagues is crucial to retaining good teachers (Scholastic & the Gates Foundation, 2012).

Marzano (2013) identifies a number of leading indicators for effective classroom instruction. One of these is that teachers have opportunities to observe and discuss effective teaching—for example, by engaging in instructional rounds, virtual discussions, and other forms of collaboration (p. 28).

Another way of looking at this element, as we have noted, is that the school leader is working against the tendency of teachers to isolate themselves. Dan Lortie, in his classic 1975 book *Schoolteacher*, proposed that without a solution to this tendency for teachers to work behind closed doors, it would be virtually impossible for schools to improve. Historically, the teacher "spent his teaching day isolated from other adults; the initial pattern of school distribution represented a series of 'cells' which were construed as self-sufficient" (p. 14).

One middle school leader we know shared her experience with creating such a culture. As part of the PLC process, she made sure to create opportunities for teachers to visit other classrooms. Teachers reported that they were often surprised that even the best teachers in the school were not consistently using what were agreed to be highly effective practices, such as having students elaborate on new content. The purpose was certainly not to be critical of the teachers observed; instead, the sixth-grade teachers internally devised a system, which they titled "Teachers Teaching Teachers," where they scheduled hours devoted to sharing their practice with other teachers, in facilitated discussions of effective teaching. Although the sixth-grade teachers initiated this practice independently with support from the leader, it was so successful that it eventually spread from grade to grade.

Building Evidence of Collaboration

School leaders must create structured periodic opportunities for teachers to meet, either as a whole or in small groups, to discuss the implementation of effective instructional strategies. As teachers propose classroom strategies they would like to try, the leader's role is to provide examples of such effective strategies, either through classroom observation or other coaching. The key is that the school leader must be deliberate and intentional in planning and allocating resources to allow teachers to actively engage in these professional collaborative conversations and to define and set expectations. It's important that the pedagogical examples provided are consistent with the critical needs of students.

The desired effect would be evidence of ongoing collaborative meetings and classroom visits. Over time, there should also be evidence that pedagogy throughout the school continues to improve. To measure the desired effect, the school leader would set up a system to facilitate participation, to provide data about the outcome, and to ensure full accountability.

The Role of PLCs

Element 1 helps create an environment where teachers routinely come together, in communities of practice, to discuss curriculum, to build units, and to examine and share practices that build student achievement. Because teachers don't have the autonomy to change their schedules, the school leader must build time into the schedule for teachers to have these supportive, collaborative opportunities and to prioritize these sessions so they are guarded from intrusions.

The school leader should not only make time for PLCs but should provide direction, set expectations, and monitor the results of what happens during these community meetings. This is the time and place for teachers and leaders together to address assessments and draw on student data to gauge how well students are meeting their goals. This information allows teachers to adjust instructional strategies and build units and lessons to directly meet the needs of individual students.

The Role of Collaboration in a PLC

In *Leaders of Learning*, DuFour and Marzano (2011) emphasize that they believe PLCs are crucial to developing a school's collective capacity:

> The best strategy for improving schools and districts is developing the collective capacity of educators to function as members of a professional learning community (PLC)—a concept based on the premise that if students are to learn at higher levels, processes are in place to ensure the ongoing, job-embedded learning of the adults who serve them. (p. 21)

The PLC concept, as DuFour et al. have defined it, represents "an ongoing process in which educators work collaboratively in recurring cycles of collective inquiry and active research to achieve better results for the students they serve" (DuFour, DuFour, Eaker, & Many, 2010, p. 11).

DuFour and Marzano (2011) elaborate, "It is not a program to be purchased, it is a process to be pursued but never quite perfected" (p. 22), and Sparks (2004) says it's "an ethos that infuses every single aspect of a school's operation" (p. 48).

DuFour and Marzano (2011) identify three big ideas that drive the PLC process:

1. The fundamental purpose of our school is to ensure that all students learn at high levels.
2. If we are to help all students learn, it will require us to work collaboratively in a collective effort to meet the needs of each student.
3. Educators must create a results orientation in order to know if students are learning and use that evidence to drive continuous improvement of the PLC process. (p. 24)

What conditions are necessary to make a PLC effective? What are the challenges a school leader may expect to face in setting up, supporting, and monitoring the PLC?

Let us offer an example. To help ensure that PLCs were faithfully implemented, one school district gave teachers an hour of early release time each Monday afternoon so staff could participate in focused collaborative groups. Setting up early release time throughout the county was no simple task. It required careful coordination: buses had to come early, some parents had to arrange childcare, an after-school program had to be put in place, and a host of other administrative decisions had to be made. But by doing so, the county very clearly signaled that time for collaborative PLCs was a priority for teachers. Teachers responded by taking and using the time seriously.

The focus statement for this element contains multiple constructs. The first construct focuses on the school leader ensuring that teachers work in collaborative groups, but it also gives direction for what the group should be accomplishing. As part of the PLC process, effective instruction is discussed in terms of what is working in lessons, what is not working, and what corrective actions should be taken. Another part of the construct says the PLC works together to plan and discuss curriculum, which is directly related to Domain 2, Elements 4 and 5. These elements say the leader ensures that teachers focus on essential standards and that each student has equal opportunity to learn the critical content of the curriculum. The final constructs of this element reinforce the concept that the PLC should be developing assessments and constantly keeping an eye on the achievement of each student.

To determine the desired effect of this element one can think about the results expected from the multiple constructs of the element. Consequently, the desired effect is that teachers working in collaborative groups enhance instruction and student achievement.

Scales and Evidences for Domain 4, Element 1

Figure 4.2: **The scales and evidences for Domain 4, Element 1.**

Scale Value	Description
Innovating (4)	The school leader continually reevaluates that teachers work in collaborative groups to enhance instruction and student achievement and intervenes with groups who are not enhancing instruction and student achievement.
Applying (3)	The school leader ensures that teachers work in collaborative groups to plan and discuss effective instruction, curriculum, assessments, and the achievement of each student AND monitors the extent to which working in collaborative groups enhances instruction and student achievement.
Developing (2)	The school leader ensures that teachers work in collaborative groups to plan and discuss effective instruction, curriculum, assessments, and the achievement of each student.
Beginning (1)	The school leader attempts to ensure that teachers work in collaborative groups to discuss and plan effective instruction, curriculum, assessment, and the achievement of each student but does not complete the task or is not successful.
Not Using (0)	The school leader does not attempt to ensure that teachers work in collaborative groups to discuss and plan effective instruction, curriculum, assessment, and the achievement of each student.

Sample Evidences for Element 1 of Domain 4
• Professional learning communities (PLCs) are in place and meet regularly.
• PLCs have written goals.
• Progress of PLCs toward their goals is regularly examined by the school leader.
• Classroom assessments are created by PLCs.
• Formative student achievement and growth data are analyzed by PLCs.
• Teachers have opportunities to observe other teachers.
• Teachers work collaboratively to write standards-based unit plans and assessments.
• Teachers unpack standards and write learning targets demonstrating a progression of knowledge.
• Teachers routinely examine student work for alignment to standards.
• Progress of each PLC team toward reaching its goals is regularly reviewed.
• To maintain a focus on student achievement, the school leader collects and reviews minutes, notes, and goals from PLC meetings.
• Teachers can explain how being a member of a PLC has helped them grow their pedagogy.
• Teachers can explain the process the PLC uses to analyze data to identify appropriate instructional practices.
• PLCs that are working effectively or ineffectively are identified by the school leader
• Ongoing interventions are in place for teams or teachers who do not work as a PLC.
• Student data reveal that PLCs are enhancing student achievement.

A Scenario for Domain 4, Element 1

Principal Ally leads a staff of forty elementary teachers and support staff. She is invested in the PLC process and has personally attended numerous trainings on how to lead effective PLCs. When meeting with her supervisor, Principal Ally provides a master calendar that includes meeting dates for all the various PLC teams. Also included in the calendar is a schedule of teacher walk-throughs, where teachers actually visit other classes as part of their own growth and reflective practice process. Agendas and notes demonstrate the teams consistently focus on examining student work, planning upcoming units, and designing common assessments. They have developed their own version of lesson study, in which they compare notes about what has worked and what hasn't worked instructionally by looking at student work. Principal Ally shows her supervisor that in the grade levels where the teams are consistent and committed to the PLC process, teacher observation data and student achievement data, confirmed by recent benchmark tests, has consistently shown greater growth than before PLCs were implemented.

Score: Applying

Feedback

Ms. Ally and her supervisor review the documents she provided and note that the focus statement of this element has been achieved. Collaborative groups are in place, all teachers participate, and the teams are focused on achievement and instruction. In addition, Principal Ally has monitored the groups, not just for attendance and participation, but also for whether the teams have data to confirm improved instruction and student achievement. To move to the next level of Innovating, the principal would need to look at the current process to determine if any adaptions or changes could be made to the PLC process so it better supports curriculum, assessment, and instruction.

Growth and Reflection Questions for Domain 4, Element 1

- How and when do PLCs analyze their own results? What structures and supports can be put in place to help PLCs with this process?
- Is there a formal process for PLCs to follow, or does each team use its own process?
- What role does goal setting play in the PLC process?
- How can PLCs help future leaders build leadership capacity?
- What is the process for monitoring the effectiveness and the outcomes of PLCs?
- How can the PLC team be used to develop a community of care and collaboration?
- When data reveals that a PLC is not operating effectively, what interventions could be implemented to help improve their process and the results?

Domain 4, Element 2

The school leader ensures a workplace where teachers have roles in the decision-making process regarding school planning, initiatives, and procedures to maximize the effectiveness of the school.

Desired Effect: Through shared decision making the school continues to improve its overall effectiveness.

Element 2 addresses the various formal roles teachers play in making decisions at the school. Many schools struggle with the number of initiatives that are meted out by the district, but the key is to involve teachers in the decision making about how those initiatives will be implemented at their school.

In his 8-Step Process for Leading Change, John Kotter (2012) emphasizes the importance of clearly communicating a vision for any new initiative that facilitates stakeholder buy-in. Kotter maintains that most organizations undercommunicate their vision of large-scale change efforts by at least a factor of ten. An effective leader will work tirelessly to communicate an essential vision and strategy in a way that is simple, vivid, repeatable (the message can be spread by anyone to anyone), and invitational (opening avenues for two-way communication).

Element 2 helps ensure that the school faculty is involved in constructive conversations about important school issues, including academic initiatives like scheduling, placement of students, or college and career readiness standards. The key here is to define initiatives clearly and to continue to articulate the message often.

In order to initiate the growth of a culture where decisions are made collectively more often than they are delivered from the top down, it is critical that teacher leaders play important roles in implementing, planning, and monitoring new projects.

This element also focuses on ways that the school leader involves teachers in the design and implementation of important decisions and policies. In addition to ensuring teacher input, the school leader must delegate authority, create a succession plan, and ensure that the right staff is in the right leadership seat.

Shared or Distributed Leadership

Some research, such as Silins, Mulford, and Zarins (2002), has suggested that school effectiveness is proportional to the extent that teachers participate in all aspects of the school's functioning, not only in instructional and curricular decisions but also in school policy decisions and review. Such participation is necessary to foster a coherent sense of direction and understanding of the wider school community.

When a school leader actively seeks staff input, formal processes for collecting input data might include teacher surveys, formal committee recommendations, school advisory committees, and the like. Decisions require collective conversations that may, for example, result in formal resolutions. School advisory committees must become not just a matter of compliance but important drivers of collective efficacy.

In this element, transparency of decision making is paramount. Responsibilities are distributed, and there is evidence that leadership is shared throughout the school.

We have identified at least five possible steps for achieving shared leadership in your school:

- Develop a strong school leadership team.
- Distribute responsibilities throughout the leadership team.
- Select the right work.
- Identify the order of magnitude implied.
- Match management style to the order of magnitude of the change.

Another aspect of this element is that the school leader identifies future leaders and continues to build leadership capacity. The school leader must, as business writer Jim Collins (2001) has often repeated, place "the right people on the bus in the right seats"; in other words, the leader must delegate responsibility appropriately. The school leader who delegates responsibility effectively is doing far more than just handing out projects to key team members. He or she will be providing growth opportunities for teachers who aspire to be leaders. The leader will be designing a succession plan and building capacity for leadership within the school. The overarching idea is that the school becomes self-functioning—in other words, the school will continue to operate at a high level under successive generations of leaders. If the leader provides clear guidance—articulating a vision and ensuring that teacher leaders are motivated toward promotion opportunities—the school culture built on such a solid foundation will carry on for many years. One former school leader we know reports that many of the policies and procedures she put in place at her elementary school twenty years ago are still operating today—and that the vision she and her team established is still strong.

All of the actions in Element 2 should create the desired effect that through shared decision making, the school continues to improve its overall effectiveness.

Scales and Evidences for Domain 4, Element 2

Figure 4.3: **The scales and evidences for Domain 4, Element 2.**

Scale Value	Description
Innovating (4)	The school leader continually seeks new venues for teacher input regarding important decisions and the effectiveness of the school.
Applying (3)	The school leader ensures a workplace where teachers have roles in the decision-making process regarding school planning, initiatives, and procedures to maximize the effectiveness of the school AND monitors the extent to which the decision-making process improves the effectiveness of the school.

(Continued)

Developing (2)	The school leader ensures a workplace where teachers have roles in the decision-making process regarding school planning, initiatives, and procedures to maximize the effectiveness of the school.
Beginning (1)	The school leader attempts to ensure a workplace where teachers have roles in the decision-making process regarding school planning, initiatives, and procedures to maximize the effectiveness of the school but does not complete the task or is not successful.
Not Using (0)	The school leader does not attempt to ensure a workplace where teachers have roles in the decision-making process regarding school planning, initiatives, and procedures to maximize the effectiveness of the school.

Sample Evidences for Element 2 of Domain 4

- Teachers are made aware of the specific types of decisions in which they will have direct input.
- Data-gathering techniques are in place to collect information from teachers.
- Notes and reports are in place that describe how teacher input was used when making specific decisions or changes.
- Virtual tools are utilized to collect and report teacher opinions regarding specific decisions (e.g., online surveys).
- Groups of teachers are selected and utilized to provide input regarding specific decisions.
- Teacher leaders are enabled to proactively initiate, plan, implement, and monitor projects.
- The school leadership team has critical roles in facilitating school initiatives.
- Data are available to show how input is used by the school leader.
- Teachers report that their input is valued and taken into consideration by the school leader.
- Data are available to reveal the school improves its overall effectiveness through a shared decision-making process.
- The school leader can describe the systematic processes in place to solicit teacher input.
- Initiatives are analyzed to evaluate their effect on teaching and learning.

A Scenario for Domain 4, Element 2

At the beginning of each school year, teachers and other staff at Kensly High School sign up to participate in a number of committees that the principal has established to give teachers a voice and to allow them active participation in making decisions that affect the school. Each department elects a lead teacher to serve as their representative on the school leadership team.

When the principal meets with her supervisor, she is able to show evidence that demonstrates that the

- Leadership team has representation from all departments and meets regularly to review data and give input about curriculum and operation issues at the school
- Leadership team regularly surveys school staff for input about building-level decisions
- Leaders of different school committees have used staff input to plan and implement a building Science Fair and Invention Convention, a staff lounge upgrade to include technology devices, and an updated parent communication network

The principal shares one specific example from an operational committee, the Safety Team: The team gathered information from outside agencies like the fire department and police department, as well as from all staff members and parents, and used that information to recommend some changes regarding school safety procedures, including a change in arrival and dismissal practices as well as new signage that was needed outside the school building. These changes were implemented and recently reviewed by local safety personnel. They found that the changes had increased the school's safety rating using district standards, and feedback from the community was extremely positive.

Score: Applying

Feedback

The supervisor of the principal reviews the documentation and notes that the principal has fulfilled the requirements of this element at the Developing level by ensuring that all teachers have a voice and participate in decision making and planning. In addition, the supervisor notes multiple pieces of evidence that the principal has reviewed decisions made by different committee teams and uses a shared decision-making approach. The evidence presented clearly indicates that the decisions and projects have improved the overall effectiveness of the school.

Growth and Reflection Questions for Domain 4, Element 2

- What is the process for involving staff members in key decisions regarding new initiatives in the building?
- What evidence indicates the desired results have been achieved?
- What personnel could help gather evidence that the shared decision making is improving the effectiveness of the school?

- What additional ways can a leader or aspiring leader get input from teachers to ensure all voices are part of the decision-making process in the school?
- If there are teachers who are reluctant to serve on committees, how can a leader get them involved?
- What is the school leader's process for identifying future leaders?
- What growth opportunities does the school leader provide for future leaders?
- How does the school leader determine which responsibilities to delegate and which must be made only by the school leader?
- What evidence would demonstrate that a school leader has moved to the Innovating level?

Domain 4, Element 3

The school leader ensures equity in a child-centered school with input from staff, students, parents, and the community.

Desired Effect: Equity is evident for each student.

Another aspect of a community of care and collaboration is found in Element 3, where the school leader is focused on ensuring equity in a child-centered school with input from students, staff, parents, and the community. This element is closely aligned to PSEL Standard 3, Equity and Cultural Responsiveness, and Standard 8, Meaningful Engagement of Families and Community.

Writing about equity, Blankstein, Nogera, and Kelly (2016) have noted that:

> In most schools throughout the United States, a child's race, socioeconomic status, and zip code continues to predict not only how well he or she will do in school but also the quality of school he or she will attend. While it is certainly good to reward talent and effort, it is also important to recognize that some children are denied the opportunity to have their talents developed because their families lack the time and resources to invest in them, and the schools they attend are often unable to develop their latent abilities. Too many students possess talents and potential that are unrecognized in school, especially when their parents lack the ability to advocate for their educational needs. The current approach to educating children has left us with millions who leave school disinterested in learning and unprepared for work, college, or the challenges of life in the 21st century.

This becomes the challenge for school leaders: how do we then ensure that we are able to create equity?

We believe that equity in education recognizes that some populations, based on race, ethnicity, zip code, and gender, may face obstacles to achieving a fair and optimal education. In a child-centered school, these obstacles are removed so that each student is able to reach his or her educational potential.

Most schools have at least a rudimentary process for involving students, parents, and the community in school initiatives. However, the process is often not focused on ensuring equity. This construct of Element 3 represents a shift from the original model, which focused solely on obtaining input. Now the goal is that the school leader continues to obtain input while ensuring equity.

As Marzano (2003) has noted in *What Works in Schools*, parental and community involvement has been identified in most attempts to synthesize the research on effective schooling. Research has shown that positive involvement from family and community is correlated with higher grades, better attendance, more positive attitudes toward school, higher graduation rates, and greater enrollment in college (Henderson & Berla, 1994). Parental involvement has been associated with a .26 effect size, which translates into a gain of 10 percent in student achievement. Marzano has identified three features that define effective parental and community involvement: communication, participation, and governance.

Communicating with Parents and Community

Strong two-way channels of *communication* are a defining feature of effective parent and community involvement (Antunez, 2000). In other words, the medium of communication will be most effective if it allows for parents and community members to participate and respond. Technology has made two-way communication much easier to achieve in recent years. Many schools rely on social media (blogs, Twitter, Facebook, etc.) in addition to traditional avenues of communication such as bulletins, newsletters, and flyers.

These two-way channels of communication should naturally lead to increased *participation* and community involvement in the day-to-day running of the school. As Marzano (2003) has noted: "Involved parents sense that the school values and welcomes not only their ideas but also their physical participation" (p. 48). As an added benefit, parent and community involvement can significantly add to a school's resource base (Tangri & Moles, 1987, cited in Marzano, 2003), which can include access to expertise, community contacts, financial contributions, and donation of equipment.

In addition to communication and participation, *governance* allows parents and community to participate in key school decisions. Marzano notes that a 1982 survey of parents in six southwestern states (Stallworth & Williams, 1982) found that parents were very interested in decisions regarding programs and practices that bore directly on the achievement of their children, which is just as relevant today. Therefore, to ensure equity in a child-centered school, the leader must have a process to continually seek input from staff, students, parents, and the broader school community.

In building a positive relationship with the larger community, the school leader will not only put workable communication and feedback systems in place and make transparency a priority but also will carefully consider that the community is a diverse place. The leader will have implemented formal ways to cross any cultural or language barriers, for example, and processes to get all parents engaged in school initiatives and policies. The leader might hold physical or virtual town hall meetings, set up interactive websites, hold focus groups, and speak at community events.

It's crucial that the school leader is known to the community. He or she must be active in making opportunities to connect with parents, students, business leaders, and the public. Strong participation in noneducation-related community meetings helps connect with business leaders for potential partnerships; the school leader can also invite community members in for face-to-face chats, set up parent advisory committees, and survey local organizations for useful feedback.

The desired result is that inputs from the community result in increased equity for each student. The community feels that they are valued, participatory members in decision making. This process helps the community feel more connected, which may have multiple positive results: increased participation in parent activities, increased student attendance, increased support for school initiatives, and a general sense that the school is performing well and that people want to be part of the school community.

The Role of Student Participation

So far, we have discussed ensuring teacher, parent, and community input, but it's important to understand that students, too, can play critical roles in giving feedback. Students, after all, are usually the members most affected by new policies and procedures. The school leader will need to develop ways to get input on important policies from *each* student, for example, by creating a student advisory committee. In the absence of such a committee, only the most vocal students usually have a voice.

Our interviews with multiple school leaders have found scant evidence that student input is either routinely gathered or used to influence decisions. But a truly cooperative environment includes *all* stakeholders. The fact is, students can make or break initiatives. Without student buy-in, many new policies will have a tough time taking root. And when students are the last to know, it's likely their reactions will be similar to those of adults who have been left out of a process—particularly when the issues affect them directly. Student voice and self-advocacy can play a large role in ensuring equity.

Scales and Evidences for Domain 4, Element 3

Figure 4.4: **The scales and evidences for Domain 4, Element 3.**

Scale Value	Description
Innovating (4)	The school leader intervenes and seeks assistance if the school does not provide equity for each student.
Applying (3)	The school leader ensures equity in a child-centered school with input from staff, students, parents, and the community AND monitors the extent to which the input creates equity for each student.
Developing (2)	The school leader ensures equity in a child-centered school with input from staff, students, parents, and the community.
Beginning (1)	The school leader attempts to ensure equity in a child-centered school with input from staff, students, parents, and the community but does not complete the task or is not successful.
Not Using (0)	The school leader does not attempt to ensure equity in a child-centered school with input from staff, students, parents, and the community.

Sample Evidences for Element 3 of Domain 4
• Data collection systems are in place to collect opinion data from staff, students, parents, and community regarding equity for each student.
• Use of input data is made transparent.
• Examples of how equity is ensured are available.
• Data are available to show that input from the school's diverse population is valued and used.
• Use of interactive or social media is provided for staff, students, parents, and community to provide input.
• An inclusive culture is evident (e.g., student engagement in school-sponsored activities, attendance, behavior data, enrollment patterns).
• Focus group meetings with students and parents are routinely scheduled.
• The school leader hosts and/or speaks at community/business events.

(Continued)

- Examples of how input from the school community results in change and improvements are available.
- Processes are made available for how data gathered from subpopulations at the school are incorporated in school planning.
- Survey data indicate that the school is perceived as a child-centered school where equity is evident.
- Staff, students, parents, and community members report that their input is valued and used by the school leader to improve the functioning of the school.

A Scenario for Domain 4, Element 3

Ms. Joans and her supervisor meet to review her evaluation as leader of Northstar Elementary. As they look at this element, Ms. Joans states that equity in her building has been difficult to address, as they have a very diverse student population. Students of many ethnic and socioeconomic backgrounds attend the school, and there are more students arriving every day. Ms. Joans shares that it has been difficult for her staff to meet the needs of so many students with different cultural backgrounds and that many of the teachers have stated that "these students need to learn our culture, rather than us learning theirs." She disagrees with that position and has sent teachers emails encouraging them to be more culturally responsive. She also shows her supervisor the emails she sent to all parents regarding parent meetings scheduled during teacher work hours to provide opportunities for parents to come see their children's work.

Score: Beginning

Feedback

The supervisor and Ms. Joans review the constructs of the element and decide that her actions are steps in the right direction, but they do not meet the constructs of the element. While she has sent communications to her staff about equity, this does not ensure that teachers follow up on the requests. In addition, sending emails to diverse communities of parents falls short of ensuring a process to collect input from those groups and to ensure equity for each student. As a result of unpacking the element, Ms. Joans states that she now has a better understanding of the steps she needs to take to provide more inclusive opportunities for the parents and students. She plans to have a committee work on inclusive and culturally responsive practices. She makes a plan to include parent representatives from each cultural group represented in the school community on the school improvement team and to meet with them once a month to gather their insights and feedback about the school. She recognizes there is still a lot of work to be done, but she is developing a plan.

Growth and Reflection Questions

- How can members of the school leadership team assist in developing a plan and collecting information and input from the school communities?
- Does the school have a clear definition of equity and a plan for ensuring equity for each student?
- What evidence would show that a school is valuing and instituting an equitable environment for each student?
- What is the process for collecting input data from teachers, staff, students, parents, and community?
- How is the community informed about the use of input data?
- How are inclusive practices to promote equity shared throughout the school?
- What evidence would the school leader collect to document that achieving the desired effect for this element has been achieved?

Domain 4, Element 4

The school leader acknowledges the successes of the school and celebrates the diversity and culture of each student.

Desired Effect: Each member of the school feels valued and honored.

Element 4 focuses on ways to cultivate a collective sense of belonging, specifically by planning and implementing ways to celebrate the success of both the school as a whole and the diversity and culture of the individuals within it. Effective leaders set goals and plan celebrations to mark accomplishments.

In their 2004 report from the Wallace Foundation, *How Leadership Affects Student Learning*, authors Kenneth Leithwood, Karen Seashore-Louis, Stephen Anderson, and Kyla Wahlstrom (2004) discuss the relationship between what they call "affective bonds" and the sense of school community:

> The creation of a widely shared sense of community among all of a school's stakeholders is important for several reasons. First, the affective bonds between students and teachers associated with a sense of community are crucial in engaging and motivating students to learn in schools of any type. A widely shared sense of community is also important as an antidote to the unstable, sometimes threatening and often insecure world inhabited by a significant proportion of the families and children by especially challenging schools.

A collective sense of belonging for those living with these circumstances provides psychological identity with, and commitment to, others (Beck and Foster, 1999). Individuals who feel secure and purposeful as a result of these connections, identities and commitments are, in turn, less susceptible to the mindset of fatalism and disempowerment which often arises from repeated episodes of loss. Success at school depends on having goals for the academic, personal and vocational strands of one's life, as well as a sense of self-efficacy about the achievement of those goals. (pp. 53–54)

In the original School Leader Evaluation Model, Element 4 was Element 6 of Domain 5, which focused on formally celebrating the success of the school and the individuals within it. In the Focused Model, we have broadened the element so that a school leader must plan and implement ways to also celebrate the diversity and culture of each student. By adding this construct to the element, we shift the focus so that each student feels that he or she is part of a caring and collaborative community.

What kind of data might the school leader gather as evidence of success with Element 4? For one thing, the school leader might gather evidence of student, teacher, and parent participation in a variety of activities: for example, school events, open houses, course curriculum nights, award ceremonies, sports activities, and other events which draw family, students, faculty, and community together. Within the building, the school leader might also help set up grade-level teams to articulate goals and celebrate formative accomplishments. Other data for use in celebrating success might include college acceptances, improved attendance, and graduation rates. Whole-school assemblies, newsletters, and other forms of communication can also be used to celebrate success.

But this is not enough. The challenge for the school leader is to analyze these typical celebrations and activities to determine if they are culturally responsive and how they might be avenues for celebrating the diversity and culture of each student in the school.

For example, when analyzing the celebration of the athletes of the year, it is incumbent on the leader to dig deep to ensure that no students were overlooked based on their gender, culture, or ethnicity. School leaders should employ the same sensitivity and perspective any time students are recognized in awards ceremonies, family nights, and other celebratory events.

In thinking about celebrating school success, we need to remember that celebrations can include anything from public "employee of the year" celebrations for teachers or noninstructional staff all the way down to notes left on teacher or staff member desks acknowledging their hard work. The same can be said for celebrating student success: It's not always about the large public recognitions. Stickers, notes, mentorships, and other signs of caring and affection will make students feel valued and included. Celebration plays a major role in how the school feels about itself. Do we have a school where we recognize members not just for major accomplishments but for the many contributions they make to the school's successful functioning?

A school leader who takes the time to recognize and celebrate many different forms of accomplishment will go a long way to creating a community of care and collaboration. Element 4 of Domain 4 is a culminating element; it pulls together all the recognitions, large and small, that we find in schools to achieve the desired result: teachers and students feel valued and honored. We believe school personnel and students who go without recognition are like flowers that wither on the vine. Celebration is the water that allows the school to flourish in a diverse community.

Scales and Evidences for Domain 4, Element 4

Figure 4.5: **The scales and evidences for Domain 4, Element 4.**

Scale Value	Description
Innovating (4)	The school leader actively seeks a variety of methods for acknowledging individual and schoolwide successes that meet the unique needs of faculty and staff.
Applying (3)	The school leader acknowledges the successes of the school and celebrates the diversity and culture of each student AND monitors the extent to which people feel honored for their contributions.
Developing (2)	The school leader acknowledges the successes of the school and celebrates the diversity and culture of each student.
Beginning (1)	The school leader attempts to acknowledge the successes of the school and celebrate the diversity and culture of each student but does not complete the task or is not successful.
Not Using (0)	The school leader does not attempt to acknowledge the successes of the school or celebrate the diversity and culture of each student.

Sample Evidences for Element 4 of Domain 4
• Accomplishments of individual teachers, teams of teachers, and the whole school are celebrated in a variety of ways (e.g., faculty celebrations, newsletters to parents, announcements, websites, social media).
• Incremental successes of students and teachers are routinely recognized.
• Successes of the diverse school community are celebrated.
• Faculty and staff report that accomplishments of the school and their individual accomplishments have been adequately acknowledged and celebrated.

(Continued)

- Perception inventories and other feedback data document that each member of the school feels valued and honored.
- Adaptations to current practices are made after analysis of feedback data.
- Staff, students, parents, and community report that their accomplishments are adequately acknowledged and celebrated.
- Actions of the school leader demonstrate that the leader accepts responsibility for the success of each student.
- Celebrations demonstrate understanding of the cultures represented in the school.

A Scenario for Domain 4, Element 4

The leadership team at Central Middle School has developed a number of ways to encourage and celebrate the successes of their staff and students. Principal Ray provides his supervisor a list of how the school acknowledges and celebrates everyone who is part of the school. The list includes:

- Success Night at the end of the year. Each student creates a portfolio of his or her best work and accomplishments during the year and then shares it with parents and teachers during student-led conferences. This year, Principal Ray collected the parent sign-in sheets and reviewed them to determine if parents from students of diverse cultural and ethnic backgrounds attended the Success Night. When he noted that a small subpopulation of students had no parent representation, he personally communicated with each student's family to talk about how proud he was of their child, and he encouraged them to ask their child to share their portfolio of best work with them.
- School performance evenings. Students demonstrate accomplishments in the arts that include performances and displays that celebrate the many cultures of the students at Central.
- The school's marquee, school newsletters, and social media postings are used to recognize and celebrate athletic accomplishments, academic awards, and special community accomplishments.
- The Parent Teacher Association provides lunches, dinners, and other recognitions for teachers who have reached milestones such as degree programs, teacher awards, etc.

Score: Developing

Feedback

The principal supervisor congratulates Mr. Ray on having so many different ways to celebrate the successes of students and staff. Together, they review the desired effect of this element and note that in the Success Night example, the principal started the monitoring process but did not complete it. The supervisor asks whether analyzing attendance and discipline data shows that students and staff feel valued and honored at the school. Mr. Ray responds that he thinks all of these celebrations should make everyone feel valued. But an analysis of the data shows that attendance rates have declined while discipline incidents have been soaring, so perhaps the celebrations have not been achieving the desired results. Mr. Ray commits to developing a plan to survey the school community to gain a better understanding of what celebrations and acknowledgments students and teachers see as valuable and meaningful for them. He commits to using this information to redesign how students and teachers are recognized at the school.

Growth and Reflection Questions for Domain 4, Element 4

- How can it be determined if current celebrations result in students and staff feeling valued?
- What students, staff members, or school committees can assist in planning and implementing celebrations to celebrate the diversity and culture of each student?
- What data would provide evidence that the school's current celebrations capture the multiple and/or different accomplishments of students and staff?
- Is there a process in place to ensure that each student has the opportunity for recognition?
- Is there a process in place to recognize students for formative (incremental) progress as well as summative progress?
- What evidence would show that the community is aware of the positive things happening in the school?

Conclusion

In a 2018 *New York Times* op-ed, David Brooks outlines the recent research on how good leaders make good schools and how the culture a principal builds in a school can have profound impacts on student success:

> What do principals do? They build a culture. Researchers from McKinsey studied test scores from half a million students in 72 countries. They found that students' mind-sets were twice as powerful in predicting scores as home environment and demographics were. How do students feel about their schooling? How do they understand motivation? Do they have a growth mind-set to understand their own development?

These attitudes are powerfully and subtly influenced by school culture, by the liturgies of practice that govern the school day: the rituals for welcoming members into the community; the way you decorate walls to display school values; the distribution of power across the community; the celebrations of accomplishment and the quality of trusting relationships.

Principals set the culture by their very behavior—the message is the person. (Brooks, 2018)

The elements in Domain 4 work together to collectively create a community of care and collaboration. Element 1, often referenced as the PLC element (previously Element 3 in Domain 4), remains largely the same. The updated Element 2 combined Elements 2 and 4 of the original model, with a focus on shared decision making resulting in maximizing the effectiveness of the school. The updated Element 3 in the Focused Model aligns with Element 5 in the original model, but now the school leader gathers input with the goal of creating equity in a child-centered school. The final Element 4 was previously found in Domain 5, Element 6. The rationale for moving it to Domain 4 was to include it in the domain focused on the culture of the school, now titled A Community of Care and Collaboration.

In conclusion, not every school leader is fortunate enough to inherit a school with a culture that represents a community of care and collaboration. But the good news is that it is possible to create this culture, where each stakeholder feels valued and wants to be a part of the school.

CHAPTER 5

Domain 5: Core Values

Figure 5.1: **The three elements of Domain 5 focus on the leader's communication of the school's core values.**

Core Values

Element 1:
The school leader is transparent, communicates effectively, and continues to demonstrate professional growth.

Element 2:
The school leader has the trust of the staff and school community that all decisions are guided by what is best for each student.

Element 3:
The school leader ensures that the school is perceived as safe and culturally responsive.

Domain 5, Core Values, represents a shift from the domain name of the previous model, School Climate, to broader ways of thinking about the values that the school leader is committed to: transparency, trust, cultural responsiveness, and safety. These are the values that the school leader instills in the school so that the values create the climate as perceived by all stakeholders. Domain 5 is based on the understanding that what the school leader values and models influences the community's perception of the school and how it feels to be a part of the school. The three elements that comprise Domain 5 are drawn from the original Domain 5 and are related to organizational responsibilities.

Core values are reflected in multiple indicators of PSEL standards. In fact, they are central to the first standard of PSEL. Standard 1, Vision, Mission, and Core Values, emphasizes that "effective educational leaders develop, advocate, and enact a shared mission, vision, and core values of high-quality education and academic success and well-being of each student." Part C of PSEL Standard 1 states that effective leaders "articulate, advocate, and cultivate core values that define the school's culture and stress the imperative of child-centered education; high expectations and student support; equity, inclusiveness, and social justice; openness, caring, and trust; and continuous improvement. Part F of PSEL emphasizes commitment to those core values in that leaders "develop shared understanding of and commitment to mission, vision, and core values within the school and the community," and part G states, "Model and pursue the school's mission, vision, and core values in all aspects of leadership."

As noted above, the three elements of Domain 5 are centered on the values of *transparency, trust, cultural responsiveness,* and *safety*. These areas of focus help create school climate, and school climate, in turn, has an indirect impact on student achievement. The authors of *The School Climate Challenge* (National School Climate Center, 2007) cautioned that we still have much to learn about how school climate affects student achievement, but they summarized the relationship this way:

> We are still learning why positive school climate leads to academic achievement and positive youth development. In broad strokes, it seems a positive school climate leads to greater focus and attunement to what students need to learn and teachers need to teach. (p. 7)

Furthermore, a positive climate contributes to building precisely the kind of learning environment conducive to new college and career readiness standards focused on twenty-first century skills (Partnership for 21st Century Skills, 2002). Transparency (in communication), trust (among staff and students), and cultural responsiveness and safety (for all) are related to the social-emotional skills the CCR standards emphasize for twenty-first century learning:

> When students, in partnership with educators and parents, work to improve school climate, they promote essential learning skills (e.g., creativity and innovation skills, critical thinking and problem solving skills, communication and collaborative skills) as well as life and career skills (e.g., flexibility and adaptability, initiative, social and cross culture skills, productivity and accountability, leadership and responsibility) that provide the foundation for 21st century learning. (p. 6)

ASCD's (n.d.) *A Lexicon of Learning* defines *school climate* as: "The sum of the values, cultures, safety practices, and organizational structures within a school that cause it to function and react in particular ways." We might begin by rephrasing this with a simple definition of *positive school climate*: a positive school climate is defined by *the extent to which a school creates an atmosphere that students perceive as supportive, safe, and culturally responsive.*

In a 2004 best practices brief, *School Climate and Learning*, produced by University Community Partnerships at Michigan State University, the authors defined school climate as follows:

> School climate reflects the physical and psychological aspects of the school that are more susceptible to change in that they provide the preconditions necessary for teaching and learning to take place. . . . School climate . . . is evident in the feelings and attitudes about a school expressed by students, teachers, staff, and parents—the way students and staff "feel" about being at school each day. (p. 2)

It should come as no surprise that students who feel safe and valued are likely to do better academically. Research has added to our understanding of the long-term impact of school climate. A positive school climate correlates with students attending school regularly and staying in school longer, creating lower dropout rates. Students who stay in school are more likely to have better lifelong health and higher incomes (Kolata, 2007).

It's important to note that school climate as generally understood by educators refers to the *subjective experience* of the school, rather than the *actual* state of the school, which is our understanding of school *culture*. This is an important distinction. Boisterous classroom activity, for example, might be one aspect of a school's culture—but how people *feel* about it ("the kids are running wild" versus "students here are full of energy and enthusiasm") reflects the school climate.

Closely related to school climate is school culture, which we think of as simply "the way things are done"—e.g., norms and traditions, whether the environment is closed or open, collaborative (as we discussed in Domain 4) or not. Climate is the way it feels, usually as the result of the culture at a school. Do people feel safe? Valued? Is the school inviting? Most perceptions are a result of the way things are done at a school. All of these characteristics reflect the core values established by the school leader.

Building Evidence of a Positive School Climate

As we have suggested, school climate is related to how the school *feels* and how staff, faculty, and community perceive the school: Is it safe? Is it open? Is it accepting? A place where actions can be trusted? A place where diverse cultures are accepted and supported?

The central question the school leader will ask in Domain 5 is this: do I honestly have *evidence* that I have taken specific actions to foster transparency, trust, safety, and cultural responsiveness?

Thus, the school leader's role is to model the values and positive behavior emphasized in Domain 5 through a process that Burns (1978), Bass (1985), and Bass and Avolio (1994) have identified as *idealized influence*. As Marzano, Waters, and McNulty (2005) explain in *School Leadership That Works*, "idealized influence is characterized by modeling behavior through exemplary personal achievements, character, and behavior" (p. 14).

As we can see, each of the four previous domains includes areas of focus that impact the perception of core values. Students, teachers, and parents perceive that there is a strong focus on school improvement driven by data (Domain 1); there is support for a common vision of instruction and a viable and guaranteed curriculum for all students (Domain 2); teachers and staff perceive themselves as professionals who continuously build expertise (Domain 3); and a community of care and collaboration is established (Domain 4). A safe, transparent, and responsive environment allows these components to function optimally. Regular opportunities to acknowledge the success of all these functioning parts contribute to a community whose core values are clear and a staff who model those values every day.

The unstated but important premise that underlies Domain 5 is that the school leader has a profound influence on the way every member of the system—teachers, students, parents, and support staff—perceive the values of the school, a perception which in turn impacts the performance of teachers and students.

Domain 5, Element 1

The school leader is transparent, communicates effectively, and continues to demonstrate professional growth.

Desired Effect: The school leader is recognized in the school community as a leader who continues to enhance his or her leadership skills.

General Colin Powell famously defined leadership as "creating the conditions of trust": "The longer I have been in public service and the more people have asked me about leadership over the years, leadership ultimately comes down to creating conditions of trust within an organization. Good leaders are people who are trusted by followers. They will follow you into the darkest night, down into the deepest valley, up the highest hill, if they trust you."

One aspect of building organizational trust is to become a model of the kinds of behavior one would expect of others, which include the elements of transparency, clarity of communication, and the commitment to continually improve professional practice. The school leader must continuously demonstrate improvement in his or her own professional practice by seeking out mentors and professional development and building leadership capacity.

Discussing transparency in continuous professional growth, Lisa Freeman, principal of Pinellas Park Elementary, shares that when she was assigned to a high-needs school, she recognized that she needed to grow as a leader. She says, "I took it to heart and to head. And it was so hard. I had to try not to beat myself up in the process. But I would share with my teachers how important it is to have a mindset about growth. I even shared my own evaluation with my staff so they could see how I was using it to grow as a leader" (Freeman, 2018).

In *Mentoring Principals: Frameworks, Agendas, Tips, and Case Stories for Mentors and Mentees*, Paul Young and Jeffrey Sheets (2005) acknowledge that for school leaders, developing mentor relationships is crucial:

> Research has provided a fairly reliable body of knowledge about how adults learn. From review of the literature, one can gather that adults learn best when they are goal oriented and self-directed. They seek out experiences when facing life-changing events. New principals' success when facing the steep learning curve during the first critical years of service depends on their ability to meet external expectations, develop interpersonal relationships, turn obstacles or barriers into goals and positive outcomes, and maintain their self-esteem and sense of pleasure in the work they do. Mentors need to be attuned to the factors that impact their mentee's motivation to learn. They must also help their mentee visualize how to apply these basic concepts to the job-embedded situations they face. Guiding the mutual reflection on experiences and new learning within a standards-based framework is important work for the mentor. (p. 4)

The mentor/mentee relationship is to some extent built into the Focused Model. The evaluator functions as a potential mentor for the school leader in that he or she provides focused performance feedback in this and other domains. Just as supervisors of principals mentor principals, principals also mentor assistant principals and aspiring leaders. But mentoring is not limited to the relationships between leaders and supervisors; all leaders as they grow and develop should look for other leaders to serve as mentors. As Brown, Collins, and Duguid (1989) note, mentorship is a crucial factor in professional growth:

> Participation with others, especially members of the field of practice who are more expert in some areas (perhaps a more experienced leader), substantially extends the potential for individual leadership development. (as cited by Leithwood et al., 2004, p. 69)

Developing relationships with mentors, participating in professional networking, and continuously improving practice is only one facet of this element. The second area of focus is that these practices should enhance the perception of teachers, staff, students, and parents; that the school leader is a person who takes seriously his or her responsibility to continually develop professional practice; and that he or she is a responsible leader in whom the community may place its confidence.

In the updated model, the focus of Element 1 includes leadership characteristics of transparency and communication. In other words, the actions and deeds of the school leader are perceived as not having hidden agendas, but are transparent. Communication, which is a key to sharing your vision, your mission, and the way your school operates, is also emphasized in this updated element. For Element 1, then, the desired outcome is that the school leader is recognized in the school community as a person who continues to enhance his or her leadership skills. Note that on the following scale, at the Applying level, the school leader continues to pursue professional growth but also strives to ensure that his or her commitment to professional growth is *perceived* by the faculty and staff.

How would a leader know how he or she is perceived by faculty and staff? In addition to the possible evidences in the following protocol, the school leader may also draw on district-provided staff and teacher surveys, or school climate surveys, that include questions related to the school leader's visibility and communication skills or that identify levels of trust or perceptions of leadership. In other words, evidence should demonstrate that the school leader is recognized as a transparent leader: data should show that teachers and the school community support his or her initiatives and that there is a shared perception that the leader is actively working to continuously improve leadership skills, which should ultimately translate into continuous improvement for the school.

Scales and Evidences for Domain 5, Element 1

Figure 5.2: **The scales and evidences for Domain 5, Element 1.**

Scale Value	Description
Innovating (4)	The school leader actively seeks expertise/mentors for validation and feedback to enhance leadership skills.
Applying (3)	The school leader is transparent, communicates effectively, and continues to demonstrate professional growth AND monitors the extent to which the school community perceives that the leader continues to enhance his or her leadership skills.

Developing (2)	The school leader is transparent, communicates effectively, and continues to demonstrate professional growth.
Beginning (1)	The school leader attempts to be transparent, communicate effectively, and continue to demonstrate professional growth but does not complete the task or is not successful.
Not Using (0)	The school leader does not attempt to be transparent, communicate effectively, and continue to demonstrate professional growth.

Sample Evidences for Element 1 of Domain 5
• Core values of the school are modeled by the school leader.
• Goals, mission, and vision of the school are clearly communicated.
• A published annual growth plan is in place to address how the school leader will address strengths and weaknesses.
• Professional development activities consistent with the leader's growth plan have been identified.
• Evidence of leadership initiatives is available.
• Problem-solving and decision-making skills are demonstrated.
• Regular interactions with an identified mentor are documented.
• Communication is clear and accurate.
• Multiple media sources are utilized to communicate with staff and community.
• Faculty and staff identify the school administrator as the leader of the school.
• Faculty and staff describe the school leader as uncompromising regarding raising student achievement.
• Data indicate that school and community members perceive the leader as visible, welcoming, and approachable.
• Faculty and staff describe the school leader as an effective communicator of nonnegotiable factors that have an impact on student achievement.

A Scenario for Domain 5, Element 1

Dr. Edwards is highly visible on campus. He starts each day by greeting teachers before they reach their classrooms. He uses this time to get quick updates about what is happening with students. He sends out weekly newsletters to teachers and staff that include upcoming events and other dates for their calendars. Dr. Edwards also includes updates about the instructional model and reminders about any school policies or practices. The newsletter is sent by email and includes a space for teachers to respond with a note or a question. Every newsletter includes a statement reminding everyone of the school's most critical goals and notes about progress toward those goals. He often provides updates about district initiatives and works diligently with the leadership team to seek new ways to communicate with staff and parents. In staff meetings, Dr. Edwards shares his own professional development goals and action steps and how they align to support teachers in their growth goals. He frequently sends teachers articles or video clips related to what he is learning.

Score: Developing

Feedback

When Dr. Edwards meets with his supervisor, they review the focus statement for the element and the large body of evidence provided. Together, they decide that all of the parts of the focus statement have been met. Dr. Edwards demonstrates multiple ways of communicating with teachers. He is transparent about school and district initiatives. He provides evidence of his own professional growth. As they review the criteria for the Applying level, Dr. Edwards recognizes that although he is doing many of the behaviors associated with this element, he has not taken the step to ask if members of the school community perceive him as a leader who continues to enhance his leadership skills.

Growth and Reflection Questions for Domain 5, Element 1

- What evidence would confirm the staff and school community's perceptions of the school leader, and how could that information be used by the school leader?
- How is transparency measured?
- What evidence indicates the leader is an effective communicator?
- How does a leader change the school community's perceptions about his or her leadership?
- How does a school leader identify a potential mentor? Cite examples of how a mentor could assist in a leader's professional growth.
- How does the leader make the staff aware of his or her professional growth goals?
- Does the leader have a written professional growth plan that identifies specific actions that will help improve practice?
- How does the leader measure the effectiveness or impact of professional growth activities in his or her practice?
- From whom does the leader receive coaching and feedback?
- How does the leader communicate leadership initiatives to staff?

Domain 5, Element 2

The school leader has the trust of the staff and school community that all decisions are guided by what is best for each student.

Desired Effect: All decisions are measured by how they impact students.

The Perception of Integrity

Element 2 is related to Element 1 in that the school leader continues to model behavior, but in this case, the behavior is related to cultivating trust and acting as an example of ethical decision making, specifically decision making related to serving the best interests of students. Element 2, in a nutshell, is about the perception of the school leader's integrity. This element gauges the school leader's ability to make tough decisions that never fail to put students first. Those decisions may not always be popular with teachers and/or parents. But every decision must be measured by its impact on students. The school leader's ability to continuously make such difficult decisions with a focus on student outcomes will contribute to the perception that students are valued at the school and that the leader's integrity is uncompromised. This element is aligned to Standard 2 of the PSEL, which focuses on ethics and professional norms: "Effective educational leaders act ethically and according to professional norms to promote *each* student's academic success and well-being."

In their 2009 paper, *Why Does Leader Integrity Matter to Followers? An Uncertainty Management-Based Explanation*, Robert H. Moorman and Stephen Grover examine how leadership integrity can affect followers' perceptions of risk. The authors suggest that the perception of integrity, or the link between a leader's words and actions, is one of the primary ways that followers make decisions about whether to commit to cooperation with the leader. And although the perception of integrity and trustworthiness may at first glance appear to be highly subjective, recent research sheds some light on the perception of trustworthiness between teachers and school leaders.

A 2011 study conducted by Monica Kathleen Makiewicz for a dissertation at the University of California, for example, examined this question in relation to three factors that strongly influence teacher perception of principal trustworthiness: *ability, benevolence,* and *integrity* (p. 11). Makiewicz noted that although teachers, like all humans, exhibit individual propensities to trust or not trust other adults, there was a strong correlation between teacher trust in a school leader and frequency of specific principal and teacher interactions. Put most simply, a highly visible and engaged school leader will be able to mitigate or modify a personal propensity on the part of individual teachers toward mistrust.

Why is trust between faculty and administrators important? Makiewicz cites several studies that have found correlations between trust among administrators and teachers and student achievement (Bryk, Easton, Rollow, & Sebring, 1994):

> In schools that reported high levels of trust among faculty members, researchers have found gains in student performance—predominantly on standardized tests (Bryk & Schneider, 2002). Studies have also found that these schools have fewer discipline issues and higher attendance rates. (Makiewicz, 2011, p. 2)

Element 2, as we have said, also addresses a very specific area of trust: the faculty trusts that the school leader makes decisions that are *in the best interests of each student*. The desired effect of Element 2 is that all decisions are measured by how they impact students.

With Element 2, the leader is striving to improve the perception of trustworthiness, follow-through, integrity, and the best interests of each student—a perception that will in turn improve the unity and cohesiveness of the school and should positively impact student achievement.

An Example

Let us look at an example of how one school leader provided evidence of being a leader willing to take on tough issues, whose actions are guided by what is best for each student, and who works to build trust among staff and community.

A secondary school principal in a large urban middle school noted that, in studying the school's discipline incidents, certain patterns emerged. The majority of the discipline incidents were occurring during class changes, before school, and after school on the bus ramp. During these times, the students were moving around campus with minimal supervision. The principal asked teachers to station themselves at their doors during class changes, to greet students and supervise what was happening in the area around their classes. Other personnel were assigned to monitor areas where some of the prior discipline incidents had occurred.

Then the principal took an even more drastic step. He asked teachers to walk with their students to the cafeteria and to share the responsibility of walking with students to the bus ramp. Because it was a large school, with more than thirty school buses, a large number of unsupervised students were headed to the buses at the same time. Although at first teachers were unhappy about the added responsibilities, they knew that discipline incidents were extremely high in their school when students were unsupervised during transitions. They trusted their principal and supported the initiatives. Within the first quarter, disciplinary referrals were reduced by more than 30 percent.

In time, faculty and staff feedback revealed that although at first they were reluctant to change their routines and perform extra supervision, reduction in major infractions quickly convinced teachers that the principal's initiatives were sound. The principal followed through in the face of some resistance and made the tough decision to require everyone to take responsibility for maintaining a safe and orderly environment, demonstrating that the decision was in the best interests of students. In time, as problem incidents declined, the school was able to relax the policy, as students had developed a higher level of self-discipline.

This element begins with a leader establishing trust and making decisions that may not be popular, and may even be somewhat painful in the short term but that ultimately help establish the core value that the school leader makes decisions guided by what is best for each student. The school leader who makes decisions with student outcomes foremost in mind will eventually come to be seen as a transparent and fair leader.

> "A school that has a positive climate rooted in clear expectations, and supported with recognition and respect, leads to students and staff making decisions that are in the best interest of not only the school but also themselves." (Patchin, 2012a)
>
> Preliminary research conducted by Justin W. Patchin (2012b) for the CyberBullying Research Center tested the hypothesis that positive school climate could serve a protective function in "reducing cyberbullying, sexting, and other high-tech misbehaviors that largely occur *away from school*." In a random sample of approximately 4,400 middle and high school students from thirty-three schools in a large US school district, the research found that the better the climate of the school, the less likely students were to report experiencing either cyberbullying or sexting incidents. The Cyberbullying Research Center also suggests that there is greater efficacy in improving school climate than in merely banning technological devices such as cell phones and laptops outright. This is yet another example of how building a community of care and collaboration has profound influences that radiate far beyond the school walls.

Domain Scales and Evidences for Domain 5, Element 2

Figure 5.3: **The scales and evidences for Domain 5, Element 2.**

Scale Value	Description
Innovating (4)	The school leader actively seeks validation and feedback from multiple sources regarding perception in the school community.
Applying (3)	The school leader has the trust of the staff and school community that all decisions are guided by what is best for each student AND monitors how decisions impact students.
Developing (2)	The school leader has the trust of the staff and school community that all decisions are guided by what is best for each student.
Beginning (1)	The school leader attempts to have the trust of the staff and school community that all decisions are guided by what is best for each student but does not complete the task or is not successful.
Not Using (0)	The school leader does not attempt to have the trust of the staff and school community that all decisions are guided by what is best for each student.

Sample Evidences for Element 2 of Domain 5
• Perception inventories and/or other data indicate that the school leader is recognized by the school community as one who is willing to take on tough issues.
• Ethical decisions and practices are evident in all aspects of the work performed by the leader.
• Student policies and procedures are fair, unbiased, and culturally responsive.
• Perception inventories and/or other data show that the school leader performs with integrity and in the best interests of each student.
• Data reveal that the school leader acknowledges when school goals have not been met or initiatives have failed and revises the plan to ensure success for each student.
• Faculty and staff describe the school leader as an individual whose actions are guided by a desire to ensure the well-being of each student and to help each student learn.
• Faculty and staff describe the school leader as an individual who will follow through with his or her initiatives.
• Faculty and staff describe the school leader as one whose actions support his or her talk and expectations.
• Positive relationships are developed with staff, faculty, students, parents, and community.

A Scenario for Domain 5, Element 2

Stonewall Middle School has had the same student handbook for about ten years. The principal has been there for thirteen years. The demographics of the student body have changed significantly during this time. Most of the staff has left to go to other schools. When the leadership team meets with the principal and asks about changing some of the policies and procedures that affect students, such as the policy of "no cell phones on campus," the principal tells them that these procedures have worked so far and should continue working for the current students. The determined teachers make lists of suggestions and gather input from their students about how to make the school more responsive to student needs. The principal commits to implementing some of the suggested changes but emphasizes that retirement is just around the corner and that someone else can make these decisions.

Score: Not Using

Feedback

When the principal meets with her supervisor, she is questioned about how her decisions are in the best interests of students. When the principal cannot provide a reasonable answer, the supervisor suggests they develop an action plan focused on how to make decisions in the best interests of students, not because of a decade-old policy that is currently in place. The action is developed based on the list of suggestions and other input from teachers and staff about what needs to happen to make the school more student-friendly. The principal in this case makes a decision to not move forward and decides to retire.

Growth and Reflection Questions

- How do the decisions of a school leader demonstrate his or her core values?
- How can a leader determine if students and staff perceive that decisions are made in the best interests of students?
- What steps can a leader take to build staff, student, and parent trust in why certain decisions are made regarding students?
- How does a leader monitor for growth or changes in perception in this element?
- If action is required to change perception about how a leader makes decisions, how does a leader take corrective action?
- What evidences would support that a school leader has the trust of a faculty?
- How would the school leader move from Applying to Innovating in this element?

Domain 5, Element 3

The school leader ensures that the school is perceived as safe and culturally responsive.

Desired Effect: The school is safe and inclusive of each student.

A safe environment has a measurable effect on student achievement and whole-school effectiveness. Effective Schools Research (Levine & Lezotte, 1995) identifies a safe and orderly school as one of six correlates of effective schools. Lezotte notes that the first-generation correlate describes a school where students are free from psychological and physical harm. We suggest that a second-generation, or next step for Element 3, would increase emphasis on not only eliminating undesirable behaviors, such as bullying, but also cultivating desirable behaviors, such as tolerance and self-advocacy.

Element 3 has been updated from the original model to broaden the concept of safe and orderly. The updated model expands on *safety* to mean that the school is physically, emotionally, and academically safe. For example, Element 3 addresses physical bullying, cyberbullying, and emotional bullying. It also includes academic safety, which refers to a climate where students feel free to take academic risks, such as taking accelerated courses, or free to appropriately challenge teachers and peers during academic discussions. We would assert that for a school to be truly safe for students, it must respond to the cultural needs of each student, so that every student feels safe regardless of his or her ethnicity, gender, sexuality, or abilities.

In *What Works in Schools*, Marzano (2003) notes that safety and order are addressed in many studies on school effectiveness. A safe and orderly environment is critical to academic achievement (Chubb & Moe, 1990; Mayer, Mullins, Moore, & Ralph, 2000). At the federal level, Goals 2000: Educate America Act articulated a goal that by the year 2000, every school "will offer a disciplined environment conducive to learning" (National Education Goals Panel, 1994, p. 13).

However, our definition of what constitutes *safe* has changed a great deal since the events at Columbine and as a result of recent tragedies on school grounds in the United States and elsewhere. Previously, the concept of a safe environment focused primarily on classroom management, on mutual respect between teachers and students, and on maintaining order throughout the school. Post-Columbine, public schools are required to maintain and test crisis management systems and to ensure that both students and faculty are practiced in crisis management procedures. Schools may have installed metal detectors, utilized drug- or weapons-sniffing dogs, or even, more recently, discussed allowing security guards or school staff to carry firearms.

In this context, securing a safe environment becomes even more complex. It requires a focused effort on the part of all members of the school community.

A school principal shared a decision she made as a new principal that was initially unpopular with parents and students, but student safety was an issue. Before her tenure, parents and members of the public freely walked on campus and delivered outside or restaurant food to the high school students during the four lunch periods. For a three-hour period, anyone could be on campus. At its worst, students would routinely walk out the school's front door to meet their parents bringing lunch. During lunch hours, to thwart these visits, the new principal immediately posted school personnel by the front doors and in the parking lot. All school doors were also locked from the inside, and parents were escorted into the building to sign into the office before walking into the school cafeteria. It wasn't a popular decision. At times, school personnel had to manage very vocal and irate parents and students, but over time, the decision to increase security and schoolwide safety measures was understood as a necessary change, both locally and nationally. As a measure of goodwill toward the students, the principal did survey students about their concerns with school lunch and was able to provide more healthy and tasty school lunch options.

Potential actions the school leader might take, as outlined by Marzano (2005) in *What Works in Schools*, include (1) establishing rules and procedures for behavioral problems that might be caused by the school's physical characteristics or the school's routines, (2) establishing clear schoolwide rules and procedures for general behavior, (3) establishing and enforcing appropriate consequences for violations of rules and procedures, (4) establishing a program that teaches self-discipline and responsibility to students, and (5) establishing a system that allows for the early detection of students who have high potential for violence and extreme behaviors.

Community Perceptions of Safety and Cultural Responsiveness

According to Tolerance.org, "Being culturally responsive recognizes the importance of including students' cultural references in all aspects of learning, enriching classroom experiences, and keeping students engaged" (Teaching Tolerance, n.d.). As Mathew Lynch (2012) has written in the *Huffington Post*, "A culturally responsive school helps students develop a sense of wellbeing about a student's cultural place in the world."

We look at culture to not only include ethnicity, but in a broader scope, to include socioeconomic status, gender, sexuality, and abilities. In our current educational environment, it is generally accepted that cultural responsiveness motivates students to learn. More and more districts are requiring schools to incorporate culturally sensitive indicators and standards within their curricula. For example, the state of Alaska requires Alaska Cultural Standards for Educators; frequently, urban districts require cultural standards to reflect the diversity of their districts.

There are many reasons public perception of safety and cultural responsiveness is crucial. Schools often function as the heart of a community. The school's effect spreads far beyond the walls of the school itself. A school perceived as safe and culturally responsive can have a profound impact—through school programs, after-school activities, volunteer opportunities, civic organizations, and local business involvement. Note that parents may avoid sending their children to schools perceived as unsafe or schools that are not culturally responsive.

The business community will not support unsafe schools. Attendance at school and at school activities will suffer. Property values may decline. In this way, the perception of school safety may have a positive or negative impact on entire communities.

An aggressive school safety plan might include interactive ways to survey students, parents, and community members on their perceptions of school safety. A leader should endeavor to address issues, correct misconceptions, and build a positive image regarding the school's safety record, including consistent communications about safety and emergency procedures, discipline policies, bullying awareness campaigns, and other safety measures. An effective school leader will develop accessible media outlets so that stakeholders may have input into policies and procedures having to do with school safety. And finally, the school leader will develop an ongoing schedule to revisit the policies and procedures related to school safety. Safety is not a static process but requires constant attention and mindfulness.

It is important to note that this element is about perception of safety and cultural responsiveness. Some schools face challenges that occur in their communities. A principal can be assigned to a building where there are incidents of gang violence in the neighborhood, high levels of crime, and other adverse conditions. The principal must take proactive and reactive steps to manage perception that the environment is safe and orderly.

The effective school leader clearly communicates the positive actions he or she is taking. Safe and culturally responsive schools often have an open-door policy for parents, for example, so that parents feel welcome. However, to ensure a safe school, it is critical to have safety measures in place to screen visitors to campus.

There are many informal ways a school leader can monitor the perception of safety and cultural responsiveness. Social media is an extremely effective tool for monitoring and communicating initiatives related to safety.

The authors of *School Climate and Learning* (Michigan State University, 2004) offer a number of approaches for promoting a safe environment. These include but are not limited to: (1) maintaining buildings in good physical condition; (2) rewarding students for appropriate behavior; (3) enforcing consequences for inappropriate behavior; (4) using contracts for students to reinforce behavioral expectations; (5) posting behavioral policies on bulletin boards and periodically announcing them over the public address system; (6) initiating antibullying, conflict resolution, and peer mediation programs; and (7) engaging students, staff, and parents in planning school safety activities.

The desired effect for this element is that students feel the school is safe and inclusive of each student. In order for this to happen, processes are put in place so that the students and the community feel connected across a multicultural spectrum. These processes may have multiple positive results: increased participation in parent and community activities, increased student attendance, increased support for school initiatives, and a general sense that the school is performing well and that people want to be part of a diverse, multicultural, and inclusive school community.

Scales and Evidences for Domain 5, Element 3

Figure 5.4: **The scales and evidences for Domain 5, Element 3.**

Scale Value	Description
Innovating (4)	The school leader ensures that rules and procedures are regularly reviewed and updated as necessary to ensure a safe and culturally responsive environment.
Applying (3)	The school leader ensures that the school is perceived as safe and culturally responsive AND monitors the extent to which the school is safe and inclusive of each student.
Developing (2)	The school leader ensures that the school is perceived as safe and culturally responsive.
Beginning (1)	The school leader attempts to ensure that the school is perceived as safe and culturally responsive but does not complete the task or is not successful.
Not Using (0)	The school leader does not attempt to ensure that the school is perceived as safe and culturally responsive.

Sample Evidences for Element 3 of Domain 5
- Each student is treated respectfully.
- Institutional practices are regularly analyzed to safeguard against any bias relating to individuality, culture, and/or diversity.
- Decision making reflects cultural considerations and responsiveness.
- Clear and specific rules and procedures are in place.
- Faculty and staff are provided the means to communicate about the safety of the school.
- Emergency management procedures for specific incidents are practiced.
- Updates and communication to the faculty and staff regarding emergency management plans are available.
- Faculty and the school community describe the school as a safe and orderly place.
- Faculty and the school community describe the school as inclusive and focused on supporting learning.
- Social media is utilized so that students may anonymously report potential incidents.
- Students have choice, work in groups, feel empowered, and demonstrate self-efficacy.
- Systems are in place for mass communication to parents (e.g., a call out system, mass texting).
- Teachers foster positive relationships with students and the community.
- Coordination with local law enforcement agencies regarding school safety issues is a routine event.
- Students, parents, and the community provide input regarding issues of school safety.

A Scenario for Domain 5, Element 3

As part of back-to-school procedures, Ms. Main asks the leadership team to convene to work on an update of the school's safety procedures and student handbook. As part of that work, they review a parent, student, and staff end-of-year survey regarding safety and another survey that elicits whether students feel the environment is inclusive of each student. Survey results indicate students, parents, and staff feel safe at the school and believe the school has a good balance of safety drills, procedures, and policies that creates a safe school without being in a lockdown mode.

The survey also reveals that some parents don't think specific procedures are working, and the leadership team is tasked to study those concerns and make recommendations. The second survey finds that students feel safe, but they do not always feel like staff understand their cultural nuances.

When the leadership team reviews the current student code of conduct and safety procedures for student checkout, they quickly determine that some new procedures are needed to meet the concerns expressed.

For example, they identify a need for an update to student check-in and checkout procedures. It appears that school staff do not always follow the same procedures for each student. After input from multiple stakeholder groups, the policies are revised and school personnel are trained to use the same procedure for each student.

Based on feedback, the leadership team also determines that communication from school to home needs to be translated into multiple languages and that more parent meetings for subgroup populations are needed. The team and principal quickly develop a plan to meet these specific needs. They also add a link on their school website for parents, staff, and students to provide input on how these changes are working.

Score: Innovating

Feedback

The principal's supervisor notes that Ms. Main has fulfilled the criteria set out in the focus statement for this element by taking actions to ensure a safe and culturally responsive school and by monitoring the school community for its perceptions of safety and cultural responsiveness. Together, they review the process of the team. Ms. Main took the initiative to review and revise procedures to meet the needs of the school's population and to ensure all parties perceive the school as safe and responsive. Since Ms. Main also implemented a process to give each person an opportunity to provide input about how the changes were working, she was assigned the score of Innovating.

Growth and Reflection Questions for Domain 5, Element 3

- How does a leader define school safety? Cultural responsiveness?
- Which members of a school community could participate on a committee or team to regularly review the feedback on a website or from other social media?
- How does a leader institutionalize changes in safety processes and procedures?
- What evidence demonstrates that a school is culturally responsive? If the evidence is not apparent, how does one ensure this becomes a core value?
- How does a leader constantly analyze decisions and policies to ensure that they are responsive to the students represented in the school?

Conclusion

In their "Guide to Developing and Implementing Core Values, Beliefs, and Learning Expectations," the New England Association of Schools and Colleges (2016) writes:

> Once the school has established its core values, beliefs, and learning expectations it can take steps to ensure they are actively reflected in the culture of the school and drive curriculum, instruction, and assessment practices in every classroom. As well, the school should use the core values, beliefs, and learning expectations to guide the school's policies, procedures, decisions, and resource allocations. As part of the school's reflective and growth processes, the school will also regularly review and revise its core values, beliefs, and 21st century learning expectations based on research, multiple data sources, as well as district and other school priorities. (p. 3)

The school leader communicates core values through every decision, action, and policy established at the school. These core values create the climate or perception of what the school values and respects. Domain 5 of the Focused Model renames the domain from School Climate to Core Values to more closely align with national leadership standards and to clearly state that what a leader values creates the climate of the school. Domain 5 compacts the number of elements from six to three critical indicators of the school leader's core values, beginning with transparency and communication, establishing trust, and finally ensuring the school is perceived as safe and culturally responsive.

In the following chapter, please note that the multiple constructs of Element 5 in the original model have been unpacked to create a new Domain 6, Resource Management. The three elements in this new domain clearly delineate the multiple tasks a school leader faces in meeting compliance measures required by district, state, and federal rules and regulations.

CHAPTER 6

Domain 6: Resource Management

Resources are to a complex organization what food is to the body. Resources important to a school extend well beyond books and materials.
—From *School Leadership That Works* (Marzano, Walters, & McNulty, 2005)

Figure 6.1: **The new Domain 6 recognizes the critical importance of operational management.**

Resource Management

Element 1:
The school leader ensures that management of the fiscal, technological, and physical resources of the school supports effective instruction and achievement of each student.

Element 2:
The school leader utilizes systematic processes to engage district and external entities in support of school improvement.

Element 3:
The school leader ensures compliance to district, state, and federal rules and regulations to support effective instruction and achievement of each student.

Domain 6, Resource Management, is a new domain, created from a single element to focus on the comprehensive task of *operational management* required of a school leader. This domain closely aligns to the PSEL standard Operations and Management. In the day-to-day business of operating a school, it is sometimes the management pieces that can essentially create a path for success. Conversely, ineffective management of the many resources required to keep a school moving forward can create a bumpy road. Even in a twenty-first century schoolhouse, careful attention to budgets and technology to support teaching and learning requires highly efficient resource management by a school leader.

As we noted in the introduction to this book, the school leader's resource management duties outlined in Domain 6 contribute to the larger vision of the school in his or her specific and targeted support of the other five domains within the model: school improvement, instruction and curriculum, continuous development of teachers and staff, collaboration and care, and core values. The three elements of Domain 6 specifically emphasize this focus on teaching and student achievement. The authors of the 2018 Marzano Focused School Leader Evaluation Model have conceptualized school management of resources and operations as evidence of effective organizational leadership.

In this domain, we explore how a steady hand on the fiscal stewardship of the school helps create a positive climate in which student achievement can flourish. The school leader:

- Develops, submits, and implements detailed budgets with the capacity to implement a variety of resources focused on building student achievement
- Utilizes systematic processes to engage other entities in support of school improvement
- Complies with district, state, and federal mandates to support instruction and achievement

In other words, within Domain 6, the school leader is *managing resources to create the optimal climate for teaching and learning*. These resources may include fiscal resources, curriculum materials, and human resources such as the use of staff and schedules created to maximize the human capital in the building, as well as community resources.

In *School Leadership That Works*, Marzano (2005) cites the work of Deering, Dilts, and Russell (2003) for a broad definition of the concept of *resources*. The authors note that successful organizations will be fluid enough to respond quickly to new circumstances. "This involves the alignment of several levels of resources," Marzano notes, "necessary to analyze, plan, and take action in response to opportunities and threats that the future brings" (p. 34). Resources, as we have emphasized, include materials, equipment, space, time, technology, and access to new ideas and expertise (Fullan, 2001).

The overall desired effect of the elements in Domain 6 is that resource management should support effective instruction and the achievement of each student.

Domain 6, Element 1

The school leader ensures that management of the fiscal, technological, and physical resources of the school supports effective instruction and the achievement of each student.

Desired Effect: Management of fiscal, technological, and physical resources support instruction and student achievement.

From a look at the history of American schooling, we know that principals were originally drawn from the ranks of head teachers. At the beginning of the twentieth century, these "principal teachers" gradually became full-time administrators. Early principals were most often building managers, dealing with fiscal operations, scheduling, and implementing school policy, among other operational duties. More recently, under increasing pressures for accountability in public education, principals have been called on to become instructional leaders. Today, principals must balance instructional leadership with organizational leadership. The Focused Model, as we have noted, restores the balance of organizational leadership to its essential role in school operations.

The constructs of Element 1 drill down to the management of the fiscal, technological, and physical resources of the school. However, the management of these resources is not just for the sake of management but to ensure that all of these resources support instruction and the achievement of each student. So it is with a careful lens that a leader must balance this operational management to support the role of instructional leadership.

The Scales and Evidences for Domain 6, Element 1

Figure 6.2: **The scales and evidences for Domain 6, Element 1.**

Scale Value	Description
Innovating (4)	The school leader ensures adjustments are made or new strategies are created so that all fiscal, technological, and physical resources support effective instruction and student achievement.
Applying (3)	The school leader ensures that management of the fiscal, technological, and physical resources of the school supports effective instruction and the achievement of each student AND monitors the extent to which fiscal resources support effective instruction and student achievement.
Developing (2)	The school leader ensures that management of the fiscal, technological, and physical resources of the school supports effective instruction and the achievement of each student.

(Continued)

Scale Value	Description
Beginning (1)	The school leader attempts to ensure that management of the fiscal, technological, and physical resources of the school supports effective instruction and the achievement of each student but does not complete the task or is not successful.
Not Using (0)	The school leader does not attempt to ensure that management of the fiscal, technological, and physical resources of the school supports effective instruction and the achievement of each student.

Sample Evidences for Element 1 of Domain 6
• Budgets are clearly aligned and prioritized to support instruction and achievement. • Resources and materials reflect the cultural assets and interests of students in the community. • Effective management of human resources that provide support for instruction and achievement (i.e., support staff) is documented by the school leader. • Faculty and staff report that they have adequate materials to teach effectively. • Faculty and staff report that they have adequate time to plan, teach, and incorporate appropriate resources. • Student achievement can be linked to effective use of resources. • Technology improves the quality and efficiency of operational management. • Analysis of utilized technology confirms how it supports effective teaching and improved learning.

A Scenario for Domain 6, Element 1

Principal Jones makes sure teachers have all the copy paper that they need. They have the newest textbooks, as the principal does not like students using tattered textbooks. Manipulatives and classroom resources are abundant. When the principal supervisor visits Mr. Jones's school and observes several classrooms, she notices that most classrooms appear to be using traditional resources, such as textbooks and workbooks, with little evidence of any technology present. Mr. Jones shares that he would like his teachers to use more technology with students but that he had to spend most of his budget on textbooks, paper, and on replacing the gym floor. Very little money is left to purchase the latest technology devices. When questioned, he isn't sure how much money was allocated for technology in the budget because he delegates budget matters to his assistant principal. Mr. Jones also reports that they still have two classroom support positions for hire and he has been planning to get the positions filled but hasn't had time to review the resumes that HR sent to him. The supervisor says she has been fielding calls from staff because of the impact of open positions. The two review the master schedule and discover that there are adjustments that could be made to ensure the appropriate support is available for teachers, even with the two open positions. They also discuss how management of physical resources could be impacting the support of instruction.

Score: Beginning

Feedback

The supervisor asks Mr. Jones to identify the critical parts of the focus statement for this element. He notes that management of three parts (fiscal, technological, and physical resources) is required but so is ensuring that these resources support effective instruction and the achievement of students. They discuss how the lack of technology could potentially impact required online testing, rob students of opportunities to use online resources, and ultimately impact student achievement. The supervisor points out the key word *ensures* and agrees that Mr. Jones certainly can delegate key functions of the school but is also tasked with ensuring implementation and required action. Together, they work on an action plan with timelines to help Mr. Jones focus on the required details of this element.

Reflection and Growth Questions for Domain 6, Element 1

- What is the process to align budget allocation and implementation to meet the critical needs of the school?
- How does a leader determine if resources are positively impacting student achievement?
- What is the plan to ensure follow-through on delegated responsibilities?
- What actions does the school leader need to take to move this element to the next level?
- How does a leader develop a budget to ensure that teachers have adequate resources for teaching?
- What is the process to evaluate instructional technology to determine if it is up to date and if teachers are actually using the technology available to them?
- What procedures are in place for obtaining feedback from teachers and students about the availability of resources and any specific needs they may have for particular resources?

Domain 6, Element 2

The school leader utilizes systematic processes to engage school district and external entities in support of school improvement.

Desired Effect: Data confirm that the use of resources supports school improvement.

Element 2 looks at expanding the leader's role in resource management by exploring the systems in place to engage district resources that may be available to support the school. This element also evaluates the leader's processes for engaging external entities or partners in support of school improvement. In PSEL Standard 9, Operations and Management, the standards emphasize that effective school leaders "develop and manage productive relationships with the central office and school board" (9k), "manage governance processes and internal and external politics toward achieving the school's mission and vision" (9l), and "develop and maintain data and communication systems to deliver actionable information for classroom and school improvement" (9g). In our experience working with school districts and school leaders, it is sometimes evident that school leaders do not access the resources offered from the central office and create extra work for themselves and their teachers by not systematically using these free and available resources. For example, many districts offer curricula with unpacked standards and provide the basis for standards-based units, but many schools are still doing this work themselves. We find teachers spending much of their PLC time unpacking standards and developing units when in fact there are already many other resources available that have the work completed for them.

It is also the responsibility of the school leader to systematically and strategically seek and acquire support from external entities (e.g., foundations, state and federal grants, and local business partners) to improve the school. This task sometimes seems daunting for school leaders, but it provides opportunities for aspiring leaders and teacher leaders to help in obtaining support from external partners.

Scales and Evidences for Domain 6, Element 2

Figure 6.3: **The scales and evidences for Domain 6, Element 2.**

Scale Value	Description
Innovating (4)	The school leader continually examines and expands options for utilizing systematic processes to engage school district and external entities in support of school improvement.
Applying (3)	The school leader utilizes systematic processes to engage school district and external entities in support of school improvement AND monitors data to determine if the resources support school improvement.

Domain 6: Resource Management

Developing (2)	The school leader utilizes systematic processes to engage school district and external entities in support of school improvement.
Beginning (1)	The school leader attempts to utilize systematic processes to engage school district and external entities in support of school improvement but does not complete the task or is not successful.
Not Using (0)	The school leader does not attempt to utilize systematic processes to engage school district and external entities in support of school improvement.

Sample Evidences for Element 2 of Domain 6
• Success with accessing and leveraging a variety of resources (e.g., grants and local, state, and federal funds) is evident.
• Budgets and projects, with plans and objectives, are organized in such a way that the focus on instruction is maintained.
• District resources are utilized to maximize improvement of the school (e.g., academic/curriculum support).
• University partnerships are utilized to provide support for the school.
• Processes used by the leader to improve the school are evident and readily explained.
• Partnerships with external entities are actively pursued.
• Partnerships are monitored to determine how they impact the school.
• Documentation of how outside resources support school improvement is available.

A Scenario for Domain 6, Element 2

Principal Jacob works in a small rural district, and at first glance, she thought this standard would be difficult to achieve. After reading the element statement and reviewing the sample evidences, Principal Jacob began to compile a list of all the local businesses and resources that could be available to Tamlin Middle. This was her second year at the school, and there were no records of prior leaders engaging the school community in support of the school. She thoughtfully crafted a survey asking students and teachers to give input regarding anything they thought would improve the school. After collecting the results, she noted that a walking trail around the perimeter of the school was a much-noted item. She worked with district personnel to learn all the requirements for installing a walking trail. The district told her there was no money in the budget for a walking trail, but they would support her in providing guidance and oversight. Next, she began working to get community support. She talked to the parents on the school improvement team, sent out an appeal in the school newsletter asking for volunteers to come to a meeting to discuss using their equipment, donating fencing, and then having Saturday workdays to build the walking trail. Much to her amazement, the information session was packed; multiple parents and local farmers showed up offering equipment and their services. The plan and timeline were formulated, and within a few weeks, students and teachers were found walking the trail. The principal continually asked teachers how having the trail was impacting their classes, and their feedback confirmed that students were motivated to complete their work to earn time on the trail. Also, teachers shared that the opening of the trail afforded opportunities to share life lessons about healthy choices and the benefits of physical activity. At first, a few teachers seemed reluctant to take their students outside, but when Ms. Jacob shared that attendance in the classes that were using the trail had increased by several percentage points, the reluctant teachers had their students walking the trail. The success of this effort led Ms. Jacob to develop a standing team of teachers and community leaders to identify school needs and community resources that might meet those needs.

Score: Innovating

Feedback

The supervisor uses the protocol and scale for this element to demonstrate that Ms. Jacob is at the Innovating level. All parts of the element statement were evident, and the principal was able to use attendance results to help other teachers see the value of using the trail with their students. The other evidences noted were that the principal had developed and implemented a systematic plan in a district with limited resources.

Growth and Reflection Questions

- Who are the business partners at a school? How does a leader identify and engage community resources in support of the school?
- How does a leader know what grants or other resources may be available to the school?
- How might a leader include community members in the process of accessing external funding and identifying key programs?
- Does the school partner with local and/or regional universities to help accomplish school goals? Can these partnerships be virtual? What are the benefits of partnering with colleges and universities?
- How does a leader begin the process of engaging partners outside the immediate school community or district?
- Can the leader cite examples of ways he or she has secured funds outside of local funding sources, for example, community grants, state grants, or federal grants?

- What evidence indicates whether resource management supports effective instruction and achievement?
- What evidences would demonstrate that using resources from the district or external partners actually supports school improvement?

Domain 6, Element 3

The school leader ensures compliance to district, state, and federal rules and regulations to support effective instruction and the achievement of each student.

Desired Effect: The compliance to rules and regulations supports effective instruction and student achievement.

In the realm of school leadership, it is a well-known fact that noncompliance to federal, state, and local requirements can quickly undermine a leader's effectiveness. If budgets, student individualized education plans, resource allocation documents, or even time allocated for instruction are out of compliance, it can affect the overall performance of the school. For example, if the school leader charges a budget item such as copy paper to the budget for professional development, it could cause the school to be out of compliance with budgetary procedures. Therefore, having detailed knowledge of the rules and regulations for budgeting sources is essential in resource management and compliance.

When it comes to management of student individualized educational plans, there may be guidelines at the local, state, and even federal levels that the school leader must have knowledge of. The school leader may not directly perform the acts of compliance, but nonetheless, it is the leader's responsibility to ensure that appropriate personnel provide evidence of compliance in their area of responsibility to meet the required rules and regulations. The leader is responsible for constant monitoring for compliance. This element closely aligns with PSEL Standard 9h, which states that the leader "know, comply with, and help the school community understand local, state, and federal laws, rights, policies, and regulations so as to promote student success."

The Scales and Evidences for Domain 6, Element 3

Figure 6.4: **The scales and evidences for Domain 6, Element 3.**

Scale Value	Description
Innovating (4)	The school leader continually examines for compliance to district, state, and federal rules and regulations and implements interventions when compliance is not working to support effective instruction and the achievement of each student.

(Continued)

Scale Value	Description
Applying (3)	The school leader ensures compliance to district, state, and federal rules and regulations to support effective instruction and the achievement of each student AND monitors the extent to which compliance to rules and regulations supports effective instruction and student achievement.
Developing (2)	The school leader ensures compliance to district, state, and federal rules and regulations to support effective instruction and the achievement of each student.
Beginning (1)	The school leader attempts to ensure compliance to district, state, and federal rules and regulations to support effective instruction and the achievement of each student but does not complete the task or is not successful.
Not Using (0)	The school leader does not attempt to ensure compliance to district, state, and federal rules and regulations to support effective instruction and the achievement of each student.

Sample Evidences for Element 3 of Domain 6
• Deadlines are managed to enhance overall instructional effectiveness.
• Operations and facility resources are managed effectively to provide support for instruction.
• Curriculum materials and other resources meet district, state, or federal specifications.
• Data reveal how compliance to rules and regulations supports instruction and student achievement.
• Adherence to district and state policies and procedures is evident.
• Compliance documents are available for each auditable department (e.g., Title funds, grants, special education).
• When compliance to rules and regulations is not evident, interventions are put in place.

A Scenario for Domain 6, Element 3

Mr. Masterson is the director of a large career and technical center where funding is paramount to accurate record keeping. As a new director, he was told that in the past, the center had lost funding and that if he wants to keep his job he must be in compliance with all local, state, and federal regulations. He knows it is a big task, so he begins by working with the bookkeeper to review the system that is currently in place and quickly notes several areas where additional safeguards are needed to ensure that timelines and requirements are met. He develops a timeline for all compliance documents. He delegates enrollment details to an assistant principal with directions for follow-up. He prepares checklists for teachers who must keep daily attendance logs and track the progress of each student toward getting a certification or mastery-level documentation. He develops a spreadsheet to help him track the large number of courses and their individual certification requirements. He implements a calendar with alerts to help him track the different due dates for each program. When he meets with his supervisor, he presents the multiple tracking systems generated to ensure compliance.

Score: Developing

Feedback

Mr. Masterson has evidence of accomplishing all the parts of the element statement. He developed multiple systems to help ensure compliance at the local, state, and federal levels. He presents evidence of keeping appropriate records in adherence to established policy. However, at this point, Mr. Masterson has not monitored to determine if there is a relationship between compliance and an impact on instruction and student achievement.

Growth and Reflection Questions for Domain 6, Element 3

- How can a leader measure whether compliance with local, state, and federal requirements is having a positive effect on instruction and learning?
- In what ways can a leader involve staff in meeting compliance requirements?
- How can aspiring leaders learn about compliance requirements?

Conclusion

In his 2010 article, "The Principal and the School: What Do Principals Do?" Fred C. Lunenburg notes that:

> In analyzing the role of the principal, Marshall Sashkin and Gene Huddle (1986) identified thirteen major task dimensions of the principal's job. They divided these task dimensions into two major categories. One category includes managerial tasks normally associated with the role of the principal—creating and enforcing policies, rules, procedures, and authority relationships. (p. 8)

Sashikin and Huddle (1986) describe the tasks in "building bureaucratic linkages" to include "sound relationships with Central Office." They also identify other tasks as "managing financial resources, developing budgets, developing maintenance schedules and using general management policies and procedures." Although these bureaucratic linkages date back to the 1980s, they still remain a viable part of a school leader's responsibilities.

In the original model, the three elements now found in Domain 6 were captured in a single element, Element 5 of Domain 5 ("The school leader manages the fiscal, organizational, and technological resources of the school in a way that focuses on effective instruction and the achievement of all students"). As we have noted throughout this book, our emphasis in the Focused Model has been on striking the right balance between organizational and instructional duties. The three elements of Domain 6 clearly delineate in more specificity the multiple management responsibilities required of an effective school leader.

CHAPTER 7

Implementation and Scoring

We have long believed that formative feedback should be the primary purpose of leader evaluation. Historically, leader evaluation models have primarily used a summative measurement system that provides a score for one point in time, typically at the end of the year. We advocate a formative approach focused on school leader growth and less focused on meeting the compliance requirements of a district. In the Marzano Focused Model, supervisors and principals meet periodically throughout the year to discuss and give feedback on elements within the model. Growth and development of expertise should be the primary goal of implementing this growth and evaluation system.

Ideally, a formative model requires evaluators to have regular consultations with school leaders so that formative data are collected throughout the course of the school year. Such ongoing conferencing allows both the school leader and the evaluator to monitor progress, provide and receive feedback, reflect on practice, and identify areas for improvement. As we have noted throughout this book, this evaluation model also requires a constant feedback loop from many sources of data—teacher surveys; student assessments; communications with parents, students, and community; feedback from supervisors; and other sources. What this means is that both school leaders and their supervisors will have access to a steady stream of information about how both the leader and the school as a whole are doing.

Planning the Process of Implementation

Districts planning implementation of a new school leader growth and evaluation model should take one important preliminary step: it's vital to achieve buy-in for the need to move to an evaluation system focused on growth rather than merely compliance. Districts that have previously implemented growth-based *teacher* evaluation systems will often perceive the clear need to move their leader evaluation system toward a growth-based model. But the focus on continuous leader professional growth must be clearly communicated and understood throughout the district.

Typically, once a district has made the decision to use the Marzano Focused School Leader Evaluation Model, professional development is the vehicle to introduce the framework and deepen understanding of the model's domains, its elements, and any specific bodies of evidence applicable to the individual district. As part of this introductory plan, personnel who supervise principals need to be active participants along with principals and assistant principals.

Schools may choose to implement all twenty-one elements in their first year, or the implementation team may identify specific domains or elements on which to focus in year 1 and focus on the remainder in year 2. We often recommend that districts use a phase-in process to allow supervisors and school leaders time to establish what evidence documents that a leader is achieving the desired results of each element. Based on our experience, if a district uses the phase-in approach, we recommend phasing in Domains 1, 2, and 3 in year 1 and Domains 4 through 6 in year 2. After year 2, as we have noted, all twenty-one elements should be rated every year.

In a second, equally effective option, the committee selects a few elements from each of the six domains to focus on in year 1 and adds in the remaining elements in year 2.

We have found, for implementation to be effective, having a champion at the district level who shares this vision for a growth model ensures not only clear communication about the rationale for the model but also that training and planning for implementation is successful. Open, honest communication about the evaluation system should include everyone who will be impacted.

An example of one such champion of the Marzano School Leader Evaluation Model was Assistant Superintendent of Human Resources Dr. April Grace, formerly of Putnam City Oklahoma Schools and now superintendent of Shawnee Public Schools. Dr. Grace shared with us the importance of gathering and analyzing feedback around implementation. Although the process can be painful at times, it can also result in enormous shifts in practice that spur professional growth.

Grace noted that her former district chose to begin implementation by selecting elements of the model and evidences from each domain that they felt were critical for developing effective principals and assistant principals. She added:

> The leader model provided us with a laser-like focus, with more specificity for conversation about the principal's work. It provided more direction for principals and increased the depth of conversation between the district-level evaluator and the building-level leader, as well as between the building-level leader and the assistant principal. With regard to building-level leaders, this

forced specific leader-focused conversation with their assistant principals, where previously the conversation may have been more management-focused. Now we are seeing conversations that led to the further development of each assistant principal and the role they played in school improvement and climate. This made all stakeholders more accountable for the improvement efforts. There was more focus and a clearer base-line for conversation.

One of the greatest benefits has been the reflective pieces that the model offers to principals. This model asks them to examine goals, perceptions, feedback, and data from staff members through a variety of methods. We have seen leaders transformed by the feedback they received from their staff related to the work they were doing in their schools. (Grace, 2015)

With this evaluation model, the objective is for the school leader's supervisor to collect formative pieces of evidence so that by year's end, the formative evidence and data can be compiled for an end-of-year summative evaluation score. We believe the great benefit of this system is that *school leaders are empowered to make adjustments and refine their actions throughout the course of the year*, effectively taking control of their professional development as they increase their expertise.

Planning Support for Implementation

In planning for implementation, it is critical that both supervisors and school leaders understand that each element in the model has a desired result and that constant monitoring for the desired result is critical to the growth process. As part of implementing the model, a district may need to come to consensus regarding what evidence constitutes achievement of the desired result. This is an important factor in establishing a fair and equitable system of evaluation. We would say that all principals within a system should be held accountable for the same body of evidence.

The sample evidences provided in the Marzano Focused School Leader Evaluation Model are written in generic terms that represent large categories of behaviors but can be customized to meet the expectations of individual districts. In the absence of agreed-on bodies of evidence, the implementation will most likely remain at the compliance level. However, when the team, with the buy-in of school leaders, moves into identifying specific evidence of desired effects for each element, the model potentially becomes a growth model for development of expertise.

The Five Steps of the Evaluation Cycle

As figure 7.1 indicates, supervisors should plan to meet with each school leader during at least five designated points during the evaluation cycle.

Before the initial meeting, it's recommended that school leaders conduct self-assessments on each element in the model. (If the district uses the iObservation platform, there is a self-assessment form available to expedite this process. We discuss iObservation later in this chapter.)

Five designated meeting points are indicated in figure 7.1.

Figure 7.1: **The evaluation cycle.**

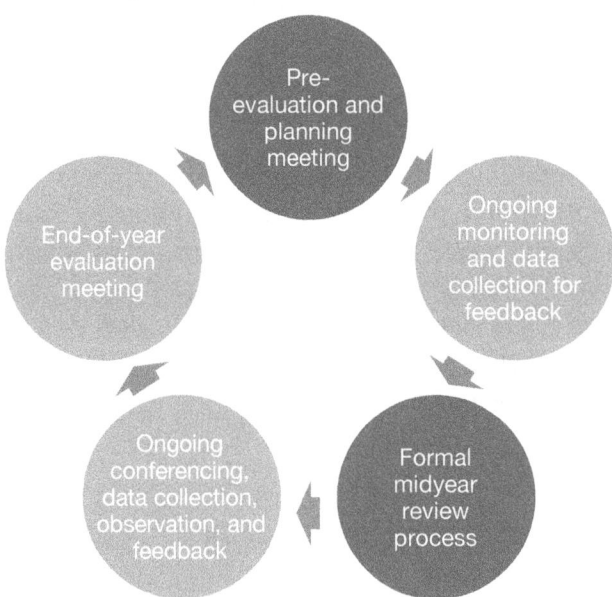

Step 1 in the evaluation cycle is the *pre-evaluation and planning meeting* between the supervisor and the school leader or between the school leader and his or her assistant principal. This meeting provides an opportunity for the leader who is being evaluated to share his or her goals and vision for the year and to identify potential growth areas. This meeting is also a good time for the supervisor to outline suggested goals for the school leader. In addition to goal setting, we recommend the development of a formal growth plan for each school leader. (An annual growth plan form is also available in iObservation.)

Step 2 of the cycle is a focus on *ongoing formative monitoring and data collection* so that the supervisor can provide feedback regarding the leader's growth plan. Such monitoring typically includes face-to-face visits with the school leader in the school building to discuss performance data, test data, surveys, and other evidence. These regular meetings, which provide a space for mentoring, collaboration, and feedback, are an important component of a growth model.

By midyear, in step 3, the supervisor will want to conduct the first *formal formative review* to ensure that the leader is on track for obtaining the desired results. This meeting continues a dynamic, ongoing process and, when conducted in a timely manner, allows the school leader to take corrective action as warranted.

We stress that supervisors and school leaders can and will prioritize certain elements to work on and discuss during each meeting in year 1 and year 2 of implementation. It is not necessary to conference about all twenty-one elements of the model in every meeting. The elements under discussion at the beginning of the year will likely differ from the elements focused on at the end. How the school leader and supervisor choose to prioritize the elements will depend on many factors: the specific needs of the school during different times of year, the growth areas of most concern to the leader and supervisor, and other factors specifically relevant to the school leader and the school.

The evaluation cycle continues, in step 4, with *ongoing monitoring and formative feedback*. Typically, observations of principal behavior include not only formal and informal school visits but other opportunities where the supervisor can witness the principal in action, for example, town hall meetings and community forums, conference presentations, school board meetings, and school celebrations.

The final step in the cycle is for the supervisor to conduct an *end-of-year summative evaluation meeting* to take all the formative pieces collected throughout the year and aggregate them to produce the final Leader Practice Score. (Scoring will be discussed in detail later in the chapter.)

Deliberate Practice as an Added Measure

Many districts use a deliberate practice score as an optional measure. As we noted in chapter 3, deliberate practice is a mindful, systematic, highly structured effort toward continuous improvement. School leaders can use deliberate practice to grow expertise in clearly identified elements through a series of planned activities, reflection, and collaboration. A leader working on a deliberate practice plan typically receives end-of-year scores reflecting growth on the selected elements in the plan. In some districts, these scores are calculated and added into the final Leader Practice Score as an additional measure. The purpose is to align and incentivize growth, professional development, reflection, and evaluation into a single process.

Scoring

The Marzano Focused School Leader Evaluation Model uses, in effect, a competency or standards-based scoring system. Each *element* functions as a standard, and leaders are scored on their competency relating to each element. A leader may well start the year at the Beginning level (1) in any one element, move to Developing (2) during the year, and finish the year at Innovating (4)—the leader's end score shows evidence of meeting competency in the element and thus becomes the final score for that element. More important, the leader's final summative score is based on evidence of meeting the *desired effect* or *result* of the standard. Because formative assessment is focused on growth, we do not recommend averaging at the element level, so that school leaders are not penalized in their early stages of development. In reality, Averaging is not compatible with our focus on demonstrating growth or competency.

It is our recommendation to weight each domain. See figure 7.2 for weighting of individual domains. Please note that Domain 2 carries significantly more weight than the other domains, as it captures the focus of instructional leadership—teaching and learning. However, districts may choose how to weight each domain based on the needs and goals of the individual district.

Figure 7.2: **Final Leader Practice Score example.**

Domain	Weight	Domain Score	Weighted Score
Domain 1	15%	3.3	0.50
Domain 2	30%	2.8	0.84
Domain 3	15%	3.3	0.50
Domain 4	15%	3.3	0.50
Domain 5	15%	3.0	0.45
Domain 6	10%	2.7	0.27
		Final Leader Practice Score:	3.05

To calculate a final Leader Practice Score, the weighted scores from each of the six domains are added together. Figure 7.3 is an example of how the element scores are averaged together to obtain a weighted score for Domain 1 and Domain 2 (other domains are calculated in the same manner). In the previous example, figure 7.2 shows the aggregated score of all six domains (3.05), which represents the school leader's final Leader Practice Score.

Figure 7.3: **Scoring example for Domains 1 and 2.**

Domain 1 Element	Most Recent Score
Element 1	Innovating (4)
Element 2	Applying (3)
Element 3	Applying (3)
Domain 1 Average:	3.3

Domain 2 Element	Most Recent Score
Element 1	Innovating (4)
Element 2	Applying (3)
Element 3	Applying (3)
Element 4	Developing (2)
Element 5	Developing (2)
Domain 2 Average:	2.8

The next step is to go to the proficiency scale (figure 7.4) and place the Leader Practice Score (in this case, 3.05) on the scale for the final score of Effective.

Figure 7.4: **Proficiency Scale for Final Leader Practice Status Rating**

Level	Range
Highly Effective (4)	3.50 to 4.00
Effective (3)	2.50 to 3.49
Developing (2)	1.50. to 2.49
Needs Improvement (1)	0.00 to 1.49

The descriptive indicators on the proficiency scale can be customized to meet the requirements of state language and scoring rules. For example, in some states the descriptor at Level 4 might be *Exceeds Expectations*, and at Level 3 the descriptor could be *Meets Expectations*. The range of scores can also be customized to meet state or district requirements. A virtual platform like iObservation makes all these conversions to meet state requirements.

Finally, the recommendation for weighting at the domain level allows for very specific feedback about areas of responsibility in which the leader may have strengths or weaknesses. Both the leader and the evaluator can drill down even further to the elements within the domain to look at the individual scores of the elements.

However, districts may choose not to weight the domains but take the final score for each element and then average the total of the twenty-one elements. For example, if the leader scored a three for all twenty-one elements to equal sixty-three total points, that total would be divided by twenty-one for a final Leader Practice Score of three, which would place the leader at the Effective level (figure 7.4).

As noted earlier, some districts may choose a two-year phase-in process, but it is our recommendation that by the end of year 2, the school leader should be rated on all twenty-one elements, as these elements represent research-based measures of a school leader's effectiveness. In other words, each of the twenty-one elements is critical to developing effective leadership and obtaining the desired results.

Using Parallel Models of Evaluation

Districts simultaneously using the Marzano Focused Teacher Evaluation Model with the Focused Leader Model will note that the scoring weights and processes between the two models are now similar. The two models both use formative and summative approaches to final evaluation; they both use sources of evidence and are focused on achieving the desired results. This close alignment of scoring furthers the goal of a shared, schoolwide understanding of evaluation procedures. Because the leader evaluation process mirrors the teacher evaluation process, teachers and leaders feel that they are in this together and that they share the same challenges, goals, and successes. In this way, aligned models help foster collegiality and collaboration. We will discuss aligned, hierarchical evaluation models later in this chapter.

Establishing Inter-rater Reliability

If a district has more than one supervisor who provides input to a school leader's evaluation, those supervisors must establish a degree of inter-rater reliability. Inter-rater reliability is achieved if multiple people observing the same body of evidence give the same or similar feedback based on the evidence. In a best-case scenario, they will score the leader identically on the element being evaluated. Beyond this, there is also a districtwide aspect to inter-rater reliability: all school leaders in the district should be held to the same measures for desired results. If the district establishes, from the first, a clear body of evidence to measure whether school leaders achieve desired results, evaluations are more likely to be objective and perceived as such. We believe establishing common evidence-based measures helps ensure objectivity, reliability, accuracy, and fairness, which are requirements of effective evaluation systems. Although each school has unique needs, the Marzano Focused Leader Model is a standards-based, evidence-based model that requires a consistent body of evidence to demonstrate meeting the expected outcomes.

If the district has multiple raters, we recommend that raters either achieve consensus or average their endpoint scores. Depending on their roles, supervisors may be providing feedback and scoring through different lenses when rating school leaders (for example, special education directors or curriculum leaders may look for different evidence of the school leader achieving the desired results). Ideally, all evaluators should demonstrate rater proficiency and understand how to use common sources of evidence.

Data Management and Feedback Systems with the Marzano Models

In *Teacher Evaluation That Makes a Difference*, Marzano and Toth (2013) discuss technology platforms that foster cooperation and sharing, optimize data management, and play a role in the feedback loop. The Marzano Focused School Leader Evaluation Model is available exclusively with the iObservation technology platform developed by Learning Sciences International. The platform allows school leaders and their evaluators to engage in private conferences, participate in discussions with other school leaders and professionals, view and share resources, and communicate best practices both within schools and across the district. The platform supports all school leaders within the district to share a common language and common goals and facilitates collaboration toward those ends. Evaluators may use the system to compile formative evidence throughout the year, to review data and supporting evidence before meetings or conferences, and to provide virtual monitoring and mentoring. Coaching from a supervisor can occur in real time, taking advantage of the resources embedded in the platform. iObservation also facilitates uploading and sharing of evidences directly to the principal supervisor.

About Hierarchical Evaluation

Research has established the interdependent relationships between teachers, school leaders, and district leaders (Leithwood et al., 2004). Increasingly, researchers and policy makers understand that the classroom behaviors of teachers, the behaviors of instructional support members, the vision and daily practices of principals and assistant principals, and the priorities of central office constitute a dynamic body of influence. The Marzano Hierarchical Evaluation Systems recognize that the role of district leaders is to support school leaders, school leaders to support teachers, and teachers to support their students. A misaligned system—one without mutual goals, clear focus, and a common language of instruction—may struggle to meet high standards for student performance.

In figure 7.5, we see how the aligned Marzano evaluation models for district leaders, school leaders, and teachers work to support and enhance one another by keeping everyone in the system focused on improving teaching and learning. A district leader, for example, is evaluated on how achievement data are used to provide appropriate support for improving student learning. Following the Cascading Domains of Influence, the school leader is then evaluated on how well he or she uses data to focus on school improvement. In other words, the six domains of the district leader model directly influence the equivalent domains of the school leader model, which in turn impact the domains of the teacher model. Together, the models foster a collaborative, collegial culture, in which a common language of instruction and ultimately a common language of evaluation tie the models together.

Figure 7.5: **Cascading Domains of Influence.**

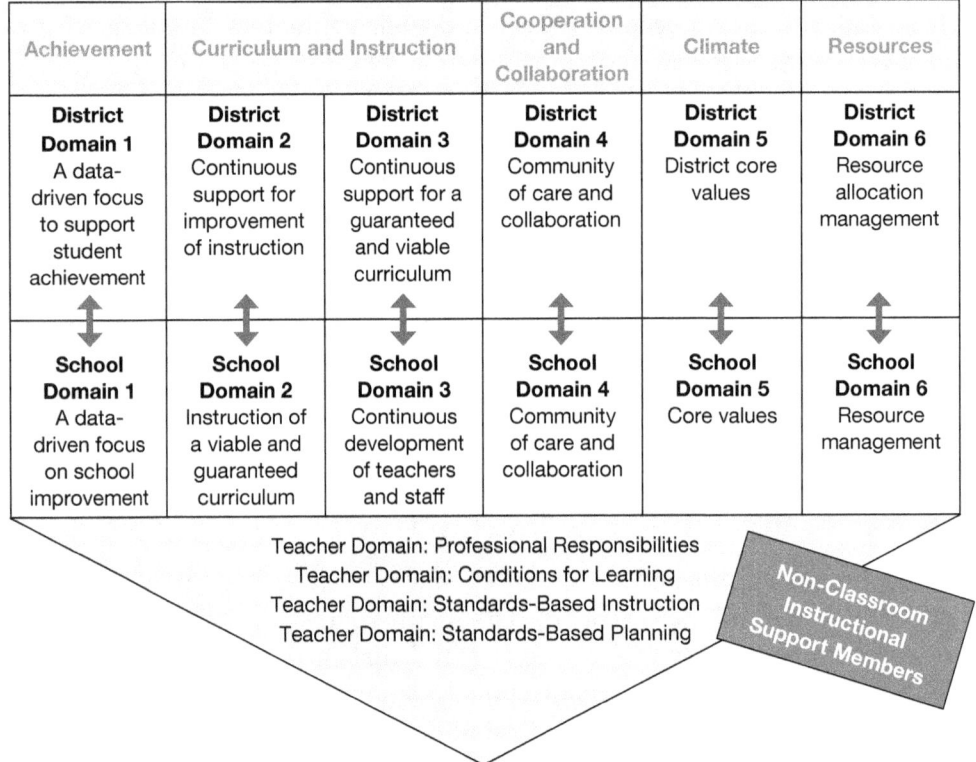

It seems most districts understand the benefits of a common language of instruction, even if they have not yet implemented a system that encourages it. A common language of instruction allows district leadership to focus on improving instruction and student achievement. Visionary district leadership (and school leadership) will use the implementation of a common language of instruction as a measure and criterion for all school- and district-level decisions, recognizing that teacher behavior and strategies are a leading indicator in predicting student achievement (US Department of Education, 2011; Gates Foundation, 2013; Marzano & Toth, 2013). Along these lines, Shannon and Bylsma (2004) write, "Effective leadership that focuses on all students' learning is at the core of improved school districts. Leadership is committed, persistent, proactive, and distributed through the system . . . and district vision and strategies must be sustained by educational leaders for significant change to occur" (p. 13). As such, district-level focus cascades down to principals and school leaders, who ought to receive the support they need to drive instructional improvement both for themselves and for their teachers, including instructional support members (or licensed non-classroom personnel).

Before entire districts can achieve alignment, however, some longstanding issues must be addressed. As we have outlined in this book, school leaders must build the instructional expertise to conduct more extensive, frequent, and rigorous teacher observations to help teachers develop their classroom practice. The National Association of Elementary School Principals (NAESP) found in a 2008 report, for example, that the average percentage of school time that principals allocated to their own professional development was just 2 percent (as quoted in Schacter, 2013). Ensuring that school leaders are able to build the instructional expertise they need to effectively mentor their teachers, then, should be a top priority.

Teachers facing more rigorous evaluations, too, want principals who are qualified instructional leaders. MetLife (2012) reported in the *29th Annual MetLife Survey of the American Teacher* that teachers rated experience as a classroom teacher as the most critical attribute for principals.

Conclusion

As we have noted in previous chapters, many elements in the Marzano Focused School Leader Evaluation Model are interrelated. We do not recommend a checklist approach to evaluation, but we recognize that evidences from one element may also be evidences listed in another element. A school leader who presents evidence for hiring and retaining the best teachers may, in some circumstances, provide that same evidence for ensuring a guaranteed curriculum. In sum, elements and evidences should never be considered in total isolation. This interconnected model facilitates the use of evidences in multiple elements and domains. The true focus is having evidence of achieving the desired result.

In *Teacher Evaluation That Makes a Difference*, Marzano and Toth (2013) outline a plan for implementing a teacher evaluation model that applies equally well to the implementation of the Marzano Focused School Leader Evaluation Model. Implementation is broken into five phases:

- Planning
- Initial implementation
- Fidelity
- Efficacy
- Sustainability and a human capital continuum

If planning is done well, succeeding phases of implementation should progress smoothly, given good communication, regular reporting, effective delegation of responsibilities, and recognition of best practices as they begin to emerge.

With faithful implementation and sustained effort and focus, even schools and districts in early phases of implementation may experience dramatic results. One Oklahoma district partnering with Learning Sciences Marzano Center shared the following experience:

> The Marzano Leader Evaluation Model has provided focus to our district leadership team. We have seen significant professional growth in our elementary principals as a result of the use of the evaluation tool. The example evidences provided for each element have spurred valuable conversation, which has challenged our principals to operate outside their comfort zone.
>
> We saw academic achievement growth in all eighteen elementary schools with significant growth in fifteen of the eighteen schools. We believe the Marzano Leader Evaluation tool has been instrumental in this growth.
>
> Principal feedback on the evaluation instrument has been positive. Principals feel the model is not only fair, but provides the necessary information to document yearly leadership growth.

The actions of the school leader serve as the leading indicator for teacher improvement within the school. Successful improvement in leadership capacity must be carefully planned and monitored, and the commitment to improvement must be sustained over many years, as such large-scale, second-order change takes time. In *How Leadership Influences Student Learning*, Leithwood et al. (2004) put it this way:

> The contribution of effective leadership is largest when it is needed the most: There are virtually no documented instances of troubled schools being turned around in the absence of intervention by talented leaders . . . leadership is the catalyst. (p. 17)

Good schools need good leaders. In this book, we have proposed that the silver bullet to develop and retain good leaders resides not necessarily in a program or a policy but is found within the capacity and motivation of every aspiring or current school leader to improve (Wallace Foundation, 2011) their practice. The Marzano Focused School Leader Evaluation Model was updated to serve as a road map to help focus and provide support for those leaders who believe they can get better and continue to fine-tune the skills necessary to lead.

We have developed this model, and written this book, to help every leader become the catalyst for school success.

APPENDIX A

The Map for the Marzano Focused School Leader Evaluation Model

The Six Domains of the Marzano Focused School Leader Evaluation Model

Marzano Focused School Leader Evaluation Model

 **A Data-Driven Focus on School Improvement**

Element 1:
The school leader ensures the appropriate use of data to develop critical goals focused on improving student achievement at the school.

Element 2:
The school leader ensures appropriate analysis and interpretation of data are used to monitor the progress of each student toward meeting achievement goals.

Element 3:
The school leader ensures the appropriate implementation of interventions and supportive practices to help each student meet achievement goals.

 **Instruction of a Viable and Guaranteed Curriculum**

Element 1:
The school leader provides a clear vision for how instruction should be addressed in the school.

Element 2:
The school leader uses knowledge of the predominant instructional practices in the school to improve teaching.

Element 3:
The school leader ensures that school curriculum and accompanying assessments align with state and district standards.

Element 4:
The school leader ensures that school curriculum is focused on essential standards so it can be taught in the time available to teachers.

Element 5:
The school leader ensures that each student has equal opportunity to learn the critical content of the curriculum.

 **Continuous Development of Teachers and Staff**

Element 1:
The school leader effectively hires, supports and retains personnel who continually demonstrate growth through reflection and growth plans.

Element 2:
The school leader uses multiple sources of data to provide teachers with ongoing evaluations of their pedagogical strengths and weaknesses that are consistent with student achievement data.

Element 3:
The school leader ensures that teachers and staff are provided with job-embedded professional development to optimize professional capacity and support their growth goals.

Marzano Focused School Leader Evaluation Model

 **Community of Care and Collaboration**

Element 1:
The school leader ensures that teachers work in collaborative groups to plan and discuss effective instruction, curriculum, assessments, and the achievement of each student.

Element 2:
The school leader ensures a workplace where teachers have roles in the decision-making process regarding school planning, initiatives, and procedures to maximize the effectiveness of the school.

Element 3:
The school leader ensures equity in a child-centered school with input from staff, students, parents, and the community.

Element 4:
The school leader acknowledges the successes of the school and celebrates the diversity and culture of each student.

 Core Values

Element 1:
The school leader is transparent, communicates effectively, and continues to demonstrate professional growth.

Element 2:
The school leader has the trust of the staff and school community that all decisions are guided by what is best for each student.

Element 3:
The school leader ensures that the school is perceived as safe and culturally responsive.

 Resource Management

Element 1:
The school leader ensures that management of the fiscal, technological, and physical resources of the school supports effective instruction and achievement of each student.

Element 2:
The school leader utilizes systematic processes to engage district and external entities in support of school improvement.

Element 3:
The school leader ensures compliance to district, state, and federal rules and regulations to support effective instruction and achievement of each student.

The Map for the Marzano Focused School Leader Evaluation Model

The Original 2014 Marzano School Leader Evaluation Model

Marzano School Leader Evaluation Model: *Learning Map*

Domain 1: A Data-Driven Focus on Student Achievement

Element 1: The school leader ensures clear and measurable goals are established and focused on critical needs regarding improving overall student achievement at the school level.

Element 2: The school leader ensures clear and measurable goals are established and focused on critical needs regarding improving achievement of individual students within the school.

Element 3: The school leader ensures that data are analyzed, interpreted, and used to regularly monitor progress toward school achievement goals.

Element 4: The school leader ensures that data are analyzed, interpreted, and used to regularly monitor progress toward achievement goals for individual students.

Element 5: The school leader ensures that appropriate school-level and classroom-level programs and practices are in place to help all students meet individual achievement goals when data indicate interventions are needed.

Domain 2: Continuous Improvement of Instruction

Element 1: The school leader provides a clear vision as to how instruction should be addressed in the school.

Element 2: The school leader effectively supports and retains teachers who continually enhance their pedagogical skills through reflection and professional growth plans.

Element 3: The school leader is aware of predominant instructional practices throughout the school.

Element 4: The school leader ensures that teachers are provided with clear, ongoing evaluations of their pedagogical strengths and weaknesses that are based on multiple sources of data and are consistent with student achievement data.

Element 5: The school leader ensures that teachers are provided with job-embedded professional development that is directly related to their instructional growth goals.

Domain 3: A Guaranteed and Viable Curriculum

Element 1: The school leader ensures that the school curriculum and accompanying assessments adhere to state and district standards.

Element 2: The school leader ensures that the school curriculum is focused enough that it can be adequately addressed in the time available to teachers.

Element 3: The school leader ensures that all students have the opportunity to learn the critical content of the curriculum.

(Continued)

Domain 4: Cooperation and Collaboration

Element 1: The school leader ensures that teachers have opportunities to observe and discuss effective teaching.

Element 2: The school leader ensures that teachers have formal roles in the decision-making process regarding school initiatives.

Element 3: The school leader ensures that teacher teams and collaborative groups regularly interact to address common issues regarding curriculum, assessment, instruction, and the achievement of all students.

Element 4: The school leader ensures that teachers and staff have formal ways to provide input regarding the optimal functioning of the school and delegates responsibilities appropriately.

Element 5: The school leader ensures that students, parents, and community have formal ways to provide input regarding the optimal functioning of the school.

Domain 5: School Climate

Element 1: The school administrator is recognized as the leader of the school who continually improves his or her professional practice.

Element 2: The school leader has the trust of the faculty and staff that his or her actions are guided by what is best for all student populations.

Element 3: The school leader ensures that faculty and staff perceive the school environment as safe and orderly.

Element 4: The school leader ensures that students, parents, and the community perceive the school environment as safe and orderly.

Element 5: The school leader manages the fiscal, operational, and technological resources of the school in a way that focuses on effective instruction and the achievement of all students.

Element 6: The school leader acknowledges the success of the whole school, as well as individuals within the school.

The Map for the Marzano Focused School Leader Evaluation Model

Crosswalk:
Marzano Focused School Leader Evaluation Model
& Marzano School Leader Evaluation Model

Marzano Focused School Leader Evaluation Model	Marzano School Leader Evaluation Model
Domain 1: A Data-Driven Focus on School Improvement	
Element 1	D1- E1, E2
Element 2	D1- E3, E4
Element 3	D1- E5
Domain 2: Instruction of a Viable and Guaranteed Curriculum	
Element 1	D2- E1
Element 2	D2- E3
Element 3	D3- E1
Element 4	D3- E2
Element 5	D3- E3
Domain 3: Continuous Development of Teachers and Staff	
Element 1	D2- E2
Element 2	D2- E4
Element 3	D2- E5
Domain 4: Community of Care and Collaboration	
Element 1	D4- E1, E3
Element 2	D4- E2, E4
Element 3	D4- E5
Element 4	D5- E6
Domain 5: Core Values	
Element 1	D5- E1
Element 2	D5- E2
Element 3	D5- E3, E4
Domain 6: Resource Management	
Element 1	D5- E5
Element 2	D5- E5
Element 3	D5- E5

APPENDIX B

The Protocols for the Marzano Focused School Leader Evaluation Model

Marzano Focused School Leader Evaluation Model

Domain 1: A Data-Driven Focus on School Improvement

1(1): The school leader ensures the appropriate use of data to develop critical goals focused on improving student achievement at the school.

Desired Effect: Everyone understands the school's most critical goals for improving student achievement.

Scale Value	Description
Innovating (4)	The school leader ensures adjustments are made or new methods are utilized so that all stakeholders sufficiently understand the critical goals.
Applying (3)	The school leader ensures the appropriate use of data to develop critical goals focused on improving student achievement at the school AND regularly monitors that everyone understands the critical goals for improving student achievement.
Developing (2)	The school leader ensures the appropriate use of data to develop critical goals focused on improving student achievement at the school.
Beginning (1)	The school leader attempts to use appropriate data to develop critical goals focused on improving student achievement at the school but does not complete the task or is not successful.
Not Using (0)	The school leader does not attempt to use appropriate data to develop critical goals focused on improving student achievement at the school.

Sample Evidences for Element 1 of Domain 1
• Published goals focus on a plan for eliminating the achievement gap for each student.
• Goals support the vision and mission of the school.
• School improvement goals are established as a percentage of students who will score at a proficient or higher level on state assessments or benchmark assessments.
• Multiple sources of data are used to develop critical goals.
• Schoolwide achievement goals are posted and discussed regularly at faculty and staff gatherings.
• Written goals address the most critical and severe achievement deficiencies.
• Written timelines contain specific benchmarks for each goal including who provides support for achieving the goal.
• A school improvement or strategic plan delineates the critical goals.
• Faculty and staff can explain how goals support and eliminate differences in achievement for students at different socioeconomic levels, English learners, and students with disabilities.
• Faculty and staff can describe why the identified schoolwide achievement goals are the most critical.
• Data are available to identify how the most critical achievement goals of the school are supported.

1(2): The school leader ensures appropriate analysis and interpretation of data are used to monitor the progress of each student toward meeting achievement goals.

Desired Effect: Data confirm students are making progress toward meeting their achievement goals.

Scale Value	Description
Innovating (4)	The school leader ensures that multiple sources of data are analyzed to provide the most relevant information and readdresses achievement goals using accrued achievement data.
Applying (3)	The school leader ensures appropriate analysis and interpretation of data are used to monitor the progress of each student toward meeting achievement goals AND monitors the extent to which student data are used to track progress toward goals.
Developing (2)	The school leader ensures appropriate analysis and interpretation of data are used to monitor the progress of each student toward meeting achievement goals.
Beginning (1)	The school leader attempts to ensure appropriate analysis and interpretation of data are used to monitor the progress of each student toward meeting achievement goals but does not complete the task or is not successful.
Not Using (0)	The school leader does not attempt to ensure appropriate analysis and interpretation of data are used to monitor the progress of each student toward meeting achievement goals.

Sample Evidences for Element 2 of Domain 1
• Reports, charts, graphs, and other relevant data for each student are available for tracking status and growth.
• Data are routinely analyzed for learning gaps.
• Individual student results from multiple types of assessments are regularly reported and used (e.g., classroom formative, benchmark, summative / end of year).
• Individual student reports, graphs, and charts are regularly updated to track the progress of each student.
• Teachers regularly meet to analyze school growth data for individual students.
• School leadership teams regularly meet to analyze individual student performance.
• Teachers utilize multiple sources of individual student data in planning to close achievement gaps.
• Teachers regularly analyze data of their individual students, including all subgroups.
• Students keep data logs regarding their individual goals and for tracking progress.
• Student-led conferences focus on the student's achievement goals.
• Parents have access to student achievement data systems to track student progress.
• Parent-teacher conferences focus on individual student goals and progress.
• Teacher plans address the learning goals of their students.
• Each student has recorded achievement goals for classroom formative, benchmark, and summative assessments.

1(3): The school leader ensures the appropriate implementation of interventions and supportive practices to help each student meet achievement goals.

Desired Effect: Data confirm interventions help each student meet achievement goals.

Scale Value	Description
Innovating (4)	The school leader continually examines and expands the options for individual students to make adequate progress toward meeting their achievement goals.
Applying (3)	The school leader ensures that appropriate interventions and supportive practices are implemented to help each student meet achievement goals AND monitors whether interventions help each student meet achievement goals.
Developing (2)	The school leader ensures the appropriate implementation of interventions and supportive practices to help each student meet achievement goals.

(Continued)

Scale Value	Description
Beginning (1)	The school leader attempts to ensure the appropriate implementation of interventions and supportive practices to help each student meet achievement goals but does not complete the task or is not successful.
Not Using (0)	The school leader does not attempt to ensure the appropriate implementation of interventions and supportive practices to help each student meet achievement goals.

Sample Evidences for Element 3 of Domain 1
• Processes are in place to identify students who need interventions.
• Interventions take place during the school day or in extended-day programs (e.g., Saturday school, summer school).
• Response to intervention measures and/or multitiered systems of support are in place and routinely measured for producing results.
• Enrichment programs are in place.
• Intervention, including enrichment, programs are constantly monitored to measure their effect on student achievement.
• Completion rates of programs designed to enhance academic achievement are monitored (e.g., gifted and talented, advanced placement, STEM).
• Processes for ongoing progress monitoring are used to appropriately place students and, when appropriate, redirect students into intervention support groups.
• Push-in or other in-class interventions are utilized when appropriate.
• Interventionist and classroom teachers regularly work together to track student progress.
• Teachers can explain how implemented interventions help individual students meet their goals.
• Students and/or parents can identify how interventions helped close their achievement gap.

Domain 2: Instruction of a Viable and Guaranteed Curriculum

2(1): The school leader provides a clear vision for how instruction should be addressed in the school.

Desired Effect: Teachers use the instructional model.

Scale Value	Description
Innovating (4)	The school leader continually examines and provides updates so that all teachers use the instructional model.
Applying (3)	The school leader provides a clear vision for how instruction should be addressed in the school AND monitors the extent to which the teachers use the instructional model.

The Protocols for the Marzano Focused School Leader Evaluation Model

Developing (2)	The school leader provides a clear vision for how instruction should be addressed in the school.
Beginning (1)	The school leader attempts to provide a clear vision for how instruction should be addressed in the school but does not complete the task or is not successful.
Not Using (0)	The school leader does not attempt to provide a clear vision for how instruction should be addressed in the school.

Sample Evidences for Element 1 of Domain 2
• A written document articulating the schoolwide model of instruction is in place.
• The schoolwide language of instruction is used regularly by faculty in their professional learning communities and in faculty and/or department meetings.
• The schoolwide language of instruction is used regularly by faculty in their informal conversations.
• Professional development opportunities are provided for new and experienced teachers regarding the schoolwide model of instruction.
• Implementation of the instructional model is evident in daily classroom instruction.
• Intentional planning to use the instructional model is evident in teacher lesson plans.
• New initiatives are prioritized and limited in number to support the instructional model.
• Teachers can describe the major components of the schoolwide model of instruction.
• Teachers can explain how strategies in the instructional framework promote learning for the school's diverse population.
• Data are available to support teacher implementation of the instructional model (e.g., lesson plans, observations, PLC notes).
• The vision for instruction is shared throughout the school and community.

2(2): The school leader uses knowledge of the predominant instructional practices in the school to improve teaching.

Desired Effect: Teachers improve instructional practices when the leader provides feedback regarding predominant instructional practices.

Scale Value	Description
Innovating (4)	The school leader regularly intervenes to ensure that ineffective instructional practices are corrected and effective instructional practices are implemented.
Applying (3)	The school leader uses knowledge of the predominant instructional practices in the school to improve teaching AND monitors the extent to which teachers improve their instructional practices.
Developing (2)	The school leader uses knowledge of the predominant instructional practices in the school to improve teaching.

(Continued)

Scale Value	Description
Beginning (1)	The school leader attempts to use knowledge of the predominant instructional practices in the school to improve teaching but does not complete the task or is not successful.
Not Using (0)	The school leader does not attempt to use knowledge of the predominant instructional practices in the school to improve teaching.

Sample Evidences for Element 2 of Domain 2
• Walk-through or other observation data are aggregated to disclose predominant instructional practices in the school.
• Accurate feedback is provided to each teacher regarding instructional practices.
• Systems are in place to monitor the effect of predominant instructional practices for each subgroup.
• Feedback is provided to each teacher regarding instructional practices needed to address learning gaps and diverse student populations.
• Predominant instructional practices and trends are documented and regularly shared with teachers.
• Effective instructional practices and problems of practice are accurately described by the school leader.
• Data show teachers implement new instructional strategies when provided feedback.
• Data regarding predominant instructional practices are used to inform professional development opportunities.
• Observation data confirm that teachers improve instructional practices.
• Student achievement data improve as teachers improve in the use of instructional strategies.
• Teachers can describe the predominant instructional practices used in the school and how they affect student achievement.

2(3): The school leader ensures that the school curriculum and accompanying assessments align with state and district standards.

Desired Effect: Assessments accurately measure student progress toward achieving the adopted standards.

Scale Value	Description
Innovating (4)	The school leader ensures that the assessment and reporting system focuses on state and district standards and intervenes with teachers who do not utilize the adopted standards.
Applying (3)	The school leader ensures that the school curriculum and accompanying assessments align with state and district standards AND monitors the extent to which the assessments accurately measure student progress toward achieving the adopted standards.

The Protocols for the Marzano Focused School Leader Evaluation Model

Developing (2)	The school leader ensures that the school curriculum and accompanying assessments align with state and district standards.
Beginning (1)	The school leader attempts to ensure that the school curriculum and accompanying assessments align with state and district standards but does not complete the task or is not successful.
Not Using (0)	The school leader does not attempt to ensure that the school curriculum and accompanying assessments align with state and district standards.

Sample Evidences for Element 3 of Domain 2
• An understanding of the alignment of curriculum and assessments is demonstrated by the school leader.
• Curriculum documents are in place that correlate the written curriculum to state and district standards.
• Resources to support the curriculum align to the standards.
• Rubrics or scales are in place that clearly delineate student levels of performance on essential standards.
• Classroom/formative, benchmark, and summative/end-of-year assessment data are consistently analyzed for alignment to the standards.
• School teams regularly analyze the relationship between the written curriculum/standards, the taught curriculum, and assessments and make adaptations when needed.
• Assessments accurately measure the adopted standards.
• Interventions are in place when standards are required and not incorporated.
• Implemented assessments reflect knowledge of child development and learning theories.
• Teachers can describe the essential standards for their subject area and/or grade level.

2(4): The school leader ensures that the school curriculum is focused on essential standards so it can be taught in the time available to teachers.

Desired Effect: Teachers have time to teach the core or essential standards.

Scale Value	Description
Innovating (4)	The school leader ensures that essential standards are regularly examined and revised to ensure teachers have time to teach the essential standards.
Applying (3)	The school leader ensures that the school curriculum is focused on essential standards so it can be taught in the time available to teachers AND monitors the extent to which the essential standards are few enough to allow adequate time for students to learn them.

(Continued)

Scale Value	Description
Developing (2)	The school leader ensures that the school curriculum is focused on essential standards so it can be taught in the time available to teachers.
Beginning (1)	The school leader attempts to ensure that the school curriculum is focused on essential standards so it can be taught in the time available to teachers but does not complete the task or is not successful.
Not Using (0)	The school leader does not attempt to ensure that the school curriculum is focused on essential standards so it can be taught in the time available to teachers.

Sample Evidences for Element 4 of Domain 2
• A written list of essential standards is in place and available to each teacher.
• The written curriculum has been unpacked in such a manner that essential elements/standards have been identified.
• A curriculum audit has been conducted that delineates how much time it would take to adequately address the essential standards.
• Teams regularly meet to discuss the progression and viability of documents that articulate essential content and timing of delivery (e.g., pacing guides, curriculum maps).
• Time available for specific classes and courses meets the state or district specifications for those classes and courses.
• Schedules are protected to allow teachers time to teach the essential curriculum/standards.
• A plan is in place to monitor that the essential curriculum is taught in the time available to teachers.
• Teachers can describe which elements are essential and can be taught in the scheduled time.
• Students report they have time to learn the essential curriculum/standards.
• Processes are implemented at the school to ensure teachers teach the essential curriculum/standards.
• Data are available to show that teachers teach the essential curriculum/standards.
• Technology systems support essential standards.

2(5): The school leader ensures that each student has equal opportunity to learn the critical content of the curriculum.

Desired Effect: Each teacher teaches the essential standards so every student has the opportunity to learn the essential standards.

The Protocols for the Marzano Focused School Leader Evaluation Model

Scale Value	Description
Innovating (4)	The school leader intervenes with teachers who do not teach essential standards that guarantee students have equal access to learning the critical content of the curriculum.
Applying (3)	The school leader ensures that each student has equal opportunity to learn the critical content of the curriculum AND monitors the extent to which each teacher teaches the essential standards to each student.
Developing (2)	The school leader ensures that each student has equal opportunity to learn the critical content of the curriculum.
Beginning (1)	The school leader attempts to ensure that each student has equal opportunity to learn the critical content of the curriculum but does not complete the task or is not successful.
Not Using (0)	The school leader does not attempt to ensure that each student has equal opportunity to learn the critical content of the curriculum.

Sample Evidences for Element 5 of Domain 2

- Tracking systems are in place that examine each student's access to the essential elements/standards of the curriculum.
- Parents are aware of their child's current access to the essential standards/elements of the curriculum.
- Each student has equal access to advanced placement or other rigorous courses.
- Each student has a prescribed program of study that documents access to appropriate courses.
- Data are available to show teachers have completed appropriate content area training in their subject area courses.
- Each student has equal access to courses that directly address the essential elements/standards of the required curriculum.
- Data are available to verify student achievement in critical content and standards.
- Teachers can describe the content strategies that result in the highest student learning for specific courses and topics.
- Student data/feedback reveal that they are given the opportunity to learn the critical content of the curriculum.
- Data are available to show that students are ready to be contributing members of society and participate in a global community (e.g., graduation rates, CTE certifications, post-graduation enrollment).
- Data are available to show that students are college and career ready.
- Appropriate technology is in place to support and enhance instruction and curriculum.
- The process in place to ensure that each student has an equal opportunity to learn the critical content/standards can be explained by the school leader.

Domain 3: Continuous Development of Teachers and Staff

3(1): The school leader effectively hires, supports, and retains personnel who continually demonstrate growth through reflection and growth plans.

Desired Effect: Teachers and staff continue to grow as they meet their growth goals.

Scale Value	Description
Innovating (4)	The school leader provides interventions and support for teachers and staff who are not meeting their growth goals.
Applying (3)	The school leader effectively hires, supports, and retains personnel who continually demonstrate growth through reflection and growth plans AND monitors the extent to which teachers and staff achieve their growth goals and continue to grow.
Developing (2)	The school leader effectively hires, supports, and retains personnel who continually demonstrate growth through reflection and growth plans.
Beginning (1)	The school leader attempts to effectively hire, support, and retain personnel who continually demonstrate growth through reflection and growth plans but does not complete the task or is not successful.
Not Using (0)	The school leader does not attempt to effectively hire, support, and retain personnel who continually demonstrate growth through reflection and growth plans.

Sample Evidences for Element 1 of Domain 3
• Each teacher provides written pedagogical growth goals. • Teachers regularly track their progress toward meeting pedagogical growth goals. • Evaluation results, growth plans, and interventions for struggling personnel are available. • Meetings are regularly scheduled with personnel regarding their growth goals and tracking progress. • A teacher induction program is in place to support new teachers. • Teacher leaders are identified, supported, and provided opportunities to develop. • Personnel records reveal the leader hires and retains effective personnel. • Standardized interview processes and/or protocols are utilized. • Nondiscriminatory hiring practices are evident. • Personnel records document that support systems are utilized to ensure personnel meet their goals. • Teachers can describe their progress on their pedagogical growth goals. • Staff members demonstrate continuous growth in their area of responsibility. • Personnel can share documented examples of how reflection has improved their craft.

3(2): The school leader uses multiple sources of data to provide teachers with ongoing evaluations of their pedagogical strengths and weaknesses that are consistent with student achievement data.

Desired Effect: Teacher observation/evaluation data are consistent with student achievement data.

Scale Value	Description
Innovating (4)	The school leader ensures that teacher evaluation processes are updated regularly to ensure the results are consistent with student achievement data.
Applying (3)	The school leader uses multiple sources of data to provide teachers with ongoing evaluations of their pedagogical strengths and weaknesses that are consistent with student achievement data AND monitors the extent to which teacher evaluations are consistent with student achievement data.
Developing (2)	The school leader uses multiple sources of data to provide teachers with ongoing evaluations of their pedagogical strengths and weaknesses that are consistent with student achievement data.
Beginning (1)	The school leader attempts to use multiple sources of data to provide teachers with ongoing evaluations of their pedagogical strengths and weaknesses that are consistent with student achievement data but does not complete the task or is not successful.
Not Using (0)	The school leader does not attempt to use multiple sources of data to provide teachers with ongoing evaluations of their pedagogical strengths and weaknesses that are consistent with student achievement data.

Sample Evidences for Element 2 of Domain 3
• Specific evaluation scales are in place to provide teachers accurate feedback on their pedagogical strengths and weaknesses. • Teacher feedback and evaluation data are based on multiple sources of information including but not limited to direct observation, teacher self-report, analysis of teacher performance as captured on video, student reports on teacher effectiveness, and peer feedback to teachers. • A schedule of teacher observations is in place to ensure all observations are completed in the designated timeframe. • Teacher evaluation data are regularly used as the subject of conversation between school leaders and teachers. • Data show the school leader provides frequent observations and meaningful feedback to teachers. • Data are available to support that teacher evaluations are consistent with student achievement data. • Achievement data from classroom formative, benchmark, and/or summative/end-of-year assessments are consistent with teacher evaluation feedback.

(Continued)

	Sample Evidences for Element 2 of Domain 3

- Teachers can describe how the implementation of specific instructional strategies affects student achievement.
- When observation data are not consistent with student achievement data, the leader works to update accuracy in assigning observational feedback.
- When observation data reveal inconsistencies with student achievement data, the leader provides teachers with appropriate support and interventions.

3(3): The school leader ensures that teachers and staff are provided with job-embedded professional development to optimize professional capacity and support their growth goals.

Desired Effect: Teachers and staff improve their skills as a result of attending professional development.

Scale Value	Description
Innovating (4)	The school leader continually reevaluates the professional development program to ensure that it remains job-embedded and focused on instructional growth goals and intervenes with personnel who are not making sufficient progress toward achieving growth goals.
Applying (3)	The school leader ensures that teachers and staff are provided with job-embedded professional development to optimize professional capacity and support their growth goals AND monitors the extent to which teachers and staff improve their skills.
Developing (2)	The school leader ensures that teachers and staff are provided with job-embedded professional development to optimize professional capacity and support their growth goals.
Beginning (1)	The school leader attempts to ensure that teachers and staff are provided with job-embedded professional development to optimize professional capacity and support their growth goals but does not complete the task or is not successful.
Not Using (0)	The school leader does not attempt to ensure that teachers and staff are provided with job-embedded professional development to optimize professional capacity and support their growth goals.

	Sample Evidences for Element 3 of Domain 3

- Teachers and staff have ongoing opportunities to participate in job-embedded professional development or training.
- Online professional development courses and resources are available to teachers and staff regarding their growth goals.
- Teacher and staff participation in professional development activities is recorded and tracked.
- Teacher-led professional development is available to teachers regarding their instructional growth goals.

- Instructional coaching is available to teachers to help them achieve their instructional growth goals.
- Data are collected linking the effectiveness of professional development/training to the improvement of teacher and/or staff practices.
- Data are available documenting how deliberate practice is improving teacher performance.
- Teachers and staff can describe how professional development supports attainment of growth goals.
- Teachers and staff implement new strategies after attending professional development.
- Interventions are documented for staff who do not utilize professional development opportunities.
- Interventions are in place to support personnel who do not continue to grow in their area of responsibility.

Domain 4: Community of Care and Collaboration

4(1): The school leader ensures that teachers work in collaborative groups to plan and discuss effective instruction, curriculum, assessments, and the achievement of each student.

Desired Effect: Teachers working in collaborative groups enhance instruction and student achievement.

Scale Value	Description
Innovating (4)	The school leader continually reevaluates that teachers work in collaborative groups to enhance instruction and student achievement and intervenes with groups who are not enhancing instruction and student achievement.
Applying (3)	The school leader ensures that teachers work in collaborative groups to plan and discuss effective instruction, curriculum, assessments, and the achievement of each student AND monitors the extent to which working in collaborative groups enhances instruction and student achievement.
Developing (2)	The school leader ensures that teachers work in collaborative groups to plan and discuss effective instruction, curriculum, assessments, and the achievement of each student.
Beginning (1)	The school leader attempts to ensure that teachers work in collaborative groups to discuss and plan effective instruction, curriculum, assessment, and the achievement of each student but does not complete the task or is not successful.
Not Using (0)	The school leader does not attempt to ensure that teachers work in collaborative groups to discuss and plan effective instruction, curriculum, assessment, and the achievement of each student.

Sample Evidences for Element 1 of Domain 4
• Professional learning communities (PLCs) are in place and meet regularly. • PLCs have written goals. • Progress of PLCs toward their goals is regularly examined by the school leader. • Classroom assessments are created by PLCs. • Formative student achievement and growth data are analyzed by PLCs. • Teachers have opportunities to observe other teachers. • Teachers work collaboratively to write standards-based unit plans and assessments. • Teachers unpack standards and write learning targets demonstrating a progression of knowledge. • Teachers routinely examine student work for alignment to standards. • Progress of each PLC team toward reaching its goals is regularly reviewed. • To maintain a focus on student achievement, the school leader collects and reviews minutes, notes, and goals from PLC meetings. • Teachers can explain how being a member of a PLC has helped them grow their pedagogy. • Teachers can explain the process the PLC uses to analyze data to identify appropriate instructional practices. • PLCs that are working effectively or ineffectively are identified by the school leader • Ongoing interventions are in place for teams or teachers who do not work as a PLC. • Student data reveal that PLCs are enhancing student achievement.

4(2): The school leader ensures a workplace where teachers have roles in the decision-making process regarding school planning, initiatives, and procedures to maximize the effectiveness of the school.

Desired Effect: Through shared decision making the school continues to improve its overall effectiveness.

Scale Value	Description
Innovating (4)	The school leader continually seeks new venues for teacher input regarding important decisions and the effectiveness of the school.
Applying (3)	The school leader ensures a workplace where teachers have roles in the decision-making process regarding school planning, initiatives, and procedures to maximize the effectiveness of the school AND monitors the extent to which the decision-making process improves the effectiveness of the school.
Developing (2)	The school leader ensures a workplace where teachers have roles in the decision-making process regarding school planning, initiatives, and procedures to maximize the effectiveness of the school.

The Protocols for the Marzano Focused School Leader Evaluation Model

Beginning (1)	The school leader attempts to ensure a workplace where teachers have roles in the decision-making process regarding school planning, initiatives, and procedures to maximize the effectiveness of the school but does not complete the task or is not successful.
Not Using (0)	The school leader does not attempt to ensure a workplace where teachers have roles in the decision-making process regarding school planning, initiatives, and procedures to maximize the effectiveness of the school.

Sample Evidences for Element 2 of Domain 4
- Teachers are made aware of the specific types of decisions in which they will have direct input.
- Data-gathering techniques are in place to collect information from teachers.
- Notes and reports are in place that describe how teacher input was used when making specific decisions or changes.
- Virtual tools are utilized to collect and report teacher opinions regarding specific decisions (e.g., online surveys).
- Groups of teachers are selected and utilized to provide input regarding specific decisions.
- Teacher leaders are enabled to proactively initiate, plan, implement, and monitor projects.
- The school leadership team has critical roles in facilitating school initiatives.
- Data are available to show how input is used by the school leader.
- Teachers report that their input is valued and taken into consideration by the school leader.
- Data are available to reveal the school improves its overall effectiveness through a shared decision-making process.
- The school leader can describe the systematic processes in place to solicit teacher input.
- Initiatives are analyzed to evaluate their effect on teaching and learning.

4(3): The school leader ensures equity in a child-centered school with input from staff, students, parents, and the community.

Desired Effect: Equity is evident for each student.

Scale Value	Description
Innovating (4)	The school leader intervenes and seeks assistance if the school does not provide equity for each student.
Applying (3)	The school leader ensures equity in a child-centered school with input from staff, students, parents, and the community AND monitors the extent to which the input creates equity for each student.

(Continued)

Scale Value	Description
Developing (2)	The school leader ensures equity in a child-centered school with input from staff, students, parents, and the community.
Beginning (1)	The school leader attempts to ensure equity in a child-centered school with input from staff, students, parents, and the community but does not complete the task or is not successful.
Not Using (0)	The school leader does not attempt to ensure equity in a child-centered school with input from staff, students, parents, and the community.

Sample Evidences for Element 3 of Domain 4
• Data collection systems are in place to collect opinion data from staff, students, parents, and community regarding equity for each student.
• Use of input data is made transparent.
• Examples of how equity is ensured are available.
• Data are available to show that input from the school's diverse population is valued and used.
• Use of interactive or social media is provided for staff, students, parents, and community to provide input.
• An inclusive culture is evident (e.g., student engagement in school-sponsored activities, attendance, behavior data, enrollment patterns).
• Focus group meetings with students and parents are routinely scheduled.
• The school leader hosts and/or speaks at community/business events.
• Examples of how input from the school community results in change and improvements are available.
• Processes are made available for how data gathered from subpopulations at the school are incorporated in school planning.
• Survey data indicate that the school is perceived as a child-centered school where equity is evident.
• Staff, students, parents, and community members report that their input is valued and used by the school leader to improve the functioning of the school.

4(4): The school leader acknowledges the successes of the school and celebrates the diversity and culture of each student.

Desired Effect: Each member of the school feels valued and honored.

Scale Value	Description
Innovating (4)	The school leader actively seeks a variety of methods for acknowledging individual and schoolwide successes that meet the unique needs of faculty and staff.
Applying (3)	The school leader acknowledges the successes of the school and celebrates the diversity and culture of each student AND monitors the extent to which people feel honored for their contributions.

Developing (2)	The school leader acknowledges the successes of the school and celebrates the diversity and culture of each student.
Beginning (1)	The school leader attempts to acknowledge the successes of the school and celebrate the diversity and culture of each student but does not complete the task or is not successful.
Not Using (0)	The school leader does not attempt to acknowledge the successes of the school or celebrate the diversity and culture of each student.

Sample Evidences for Element 4 of Domain 4
• Accomplishments of individual teachers, teams of teachers, and the whole school are celebrated in a variety of ways (e.g., faculty celebrations, newsletters to parents, announcements, websites, social media).
• Incremental successes of students and teachers are routinely recognized.
• Successes of the diverse school community are celebrated.
• Faculty and staff report that accomplishments of the school and their individual accomplishments have been adequately acknowledged and celebrated.
• Perception inventories and other feedback data document that each member of the school feels valued and honored.
• Adaptations to current practices are made after analysis of feedback data.
• Staff, students, parents, and community report that their accomplishments are adequately acknowledged and celebrated.
• Actions of the school leader demonstrate that the leader accepts responsibility for the success of each student.
• Celebrations demonstrate understanding of the cultures represented in the school.

Domain 5: Core Values

5(1): The school leader is transparent, communicates effectively, and continues to demonstrate professional growth.

Desired Effect: The school leader is recognized in the school community as a leader who continues to enhance his or her leadership skills.

Scale Value	Description
Innovating (4)	The school leader actively seeks expertise/mentors for validation and feedback to enhance leadership skills.
Applying (3)	The school leader is transparent, communicates effectively, and continues to demonstrate professional growth AND monitors the extent to which the school community perceives that the leader continues to enhance his or her leadership skills.
Developing (2)	The school leader is transparent, communicates effectively, and continues to demonstrate professional growth.

(Continued)

Scale Value	Description
Beginning (1)	The school leader attempts to be transparent, communicate effectively, and continue to demonstrate professional growth but does not complete the task or is not successful.
Not Using (0)	The school leader does not attempt to be transparent, communicate effectively, and continue to demonstrate professional growth.

Sample Evidences for Element 1 of Domain 5
• Core values of the school are modeled by the school leader.
• Goals, mission, and vision of the school are clearly communicated.
• A published annual growth plan is in place to address how the school leader will address strengths and weaknesses.
• Professional development activities consistent with the leader's growth plan have been identified.
• Evidence of leadership initiatives is available.
• Problem-solving and decision-making skills are demonstrated.
• Regular interactions with an identified mentor are documented.
• Communication is clear and accurate.
• Multiple media sources are utilized to communicate with staff and community.
• Faculty and staff identify the school administrator as the leader of the school.
• Faculty and staff describe the school leader as uncompromising regarding raising student achievement.
• Data indicate that school and community members perceive the leader as visible, welcoming, and approachable.
• Faculty and staff describe the school leader as an effective communicator of nonnegotiable factors that have an impact on student achievement.

5(2): The school leader has the trust of the staff and school community that all decisions are guided by what is best for each student.

Desired Effect: All decisions are measured by how they impact students.

Scale Value	Description
Innovating (4)	The school leader actively seeks validation and feedback from multiple sources regarding perception in the school community.
Applying (3)	The school leader has the trust of the staff and school community that all decisions are guided by what is best for each student AND monitors how decisions impact students.
Developing (2)	The school leader has the trust of the staff and school community that all decisions are guided by what is best for each student.

Beginning (1)	The school leader attempts to have the trust of the staff and school community that all decisions are guided by what is best for each student but does not complete the task or is not successful.
Not Using (0)	The school leader does not attempt to have the trust of the staff and school community that all decisions are guided by what is best for each student.

Sample Evidences for Element 2 of Domain 5
• Perception inventories and/or other data indicate that the school leader is recognized by the school community as one who is willing to take on tough issues.
• Ethical decisions and practices are evident in all aspects of the work performed by the leader.
• Student policies and procedures are fair, unbiased, and culturally responsive.
• Perception inventories and/or other data show that the school leader performs with integrity and in the best interests of each student.
• Data reveal that the school leader acknowledges when school goals have not been met or initiatives have failed and revises the plan to ensure success for each student.
• Faculty and staff describe the school leader as an individual whose actions are guided by a desire to ensure the well-being of each student and to help each student learn.
• Faculty and staff describe the school leader as an individual who will follow through with his or her initiatives.
• Faculty and staff describe the school leader as one whose actions support his or her talk and expectations.
• Positive relationships are developed with staff, faculty, students, parents, and community.

5(3): The school leader ensures that the school is perceived as safe and culturally responsive.

Desired Effect: The school is safe and inclusive of each student.

Scale Value	Description
Innovating (4)	The school leader ensures that rules and procedures are regularly reviewed and updated as necessary to ensure a safe and culturally responsive environment.
Applying (3)	The school leader ensures that the school is perceived as safe and culturally responsive AND monitors the extent to which the school is safe and inclusive of each student.
Developing (2)	The school leader ensures that the school is perceived as safe and culturally responsive.
Beginning (1)	The school leader attempts to ensure that the school is perceived as safe and culturally responsive but does not complete the task or is not successful.
Not Using (0)	The school leader does not attempt to ensure that the school is perceived as safe and culturally responsive.

Sample Evidences for Element 3 of Domain 5
• Each student is treated respectfully.
• Institutional practices are regularly analyzed to safeguard against any bias relating to individuality, culture, and/or diversity.
• Decision making reflects cultural considerations and responsiveness.
• Clear and specific rules and procedures are in place.
• Faculty and staff are provided the means to communicate about the safety of the school.
• Emergency management procedures for specific incidents are practiced.
• Updates and communication to the faculty and staff regarding emergency management plans are available.
• Faculty and the school community describe the school as a safe and orderly place.
• Faculty and the school community describe the school as inclusive and focused on supporting learning.
• Social media is utilized so that students may anonymously report potential incidents.
• Students have choice, work in groups, feel empowered, and demonstrate self-efficacy.
• Systems are in place for mass communication to parents (e.g., a call out system, mass texting).
• Teachers foster positive relationships with students and the community.
• Coordination with local law enforcement agencies regarding school safety issues is a routine event.
• Students, parents, and the community provide input regarding issues of school safety.

Domain 6: Resource Management

6(1): The school leader ensures that management of the fiscal, technological, and physical resources of the school supports effective instruction and the achievement of each student.

Desired Effect: Management of fiscal, technological, and physical resources support instruction and student achievement.

Scale Value	Description
Innovating (4)	The school leader ensures adjustments are made or new strategies are created so that all fiscal, technological, and physical resources support effective instruction and student achievement.
Applying (3)	The school leader ensures that management of the fiscal, technological, and physical resources of the school supports effective instruction and the achievement of each student AND monitors the extent to which fiscal resources support effective instruction and student achievement.
Developing (2)	The school leader ensures that management of the fiscal, technological, and physical resources of the school supports effective instruction and the achievement of each student.

Beginning (1)	The school leader attempts to ensure that management of the fiscal, technological, and physical resources of the school supports effective instruction and the achievement of each student but does not complete the task or is not successful.
Not Using (0)	The school leader does not attempt to ensure that management of the fiscal, technological, and physical resources of the school supports effective instruction and the achievement of each student.

Sample Evidences for Element 1 of Domain 6
• Budgets are clearly aligned and prioritized to support instruction and achievement.
• Resources and materials reflect the cultural assets and interests of students in the community.
• Effective management of human resources that provide support for instruction and achievement (i.e., support staff) is documented by the school leader.
• Faculty and staff report that they have adequate materials to teach effectively.
• Faculty and staff report that they have adequate time to plan, teach, and incorporate appropriate resources.
• Student achievement can be linked to effective use of resources.
• Technology improves the quality and efficiency of operational management.
• Analysis of utilized technology confirms how it supports effective teaching and improved learning.

6(2): The school leader utilizes systematic processes to engage school district and external entities in support of school improvement.

Desired Effect: Data confirm that the use of resources supports school improvement.

Scale Value	Description
Innovating (4)	The school leader continually examines and expands options for utilizing systematic processes to engage school district and external entities in support of school improvement.
Applying (3)	The school leader utilizes systematic processes to engage school district and external entities in support of school improvement AND monitors data to determine if the resources support school improvement.
Developing (2)	The school leader utilizes systematic processes to engage school district and external entities in support of school improvement.
Beginning (1)	The school leader attempts to utilize systematic processes to engage school district and external entities in support of school improvement but does not complete the task or is not successful.
Not Using (0)	The school leader does not attempt to utilize systematic processes to engage school district and external entities in support of school improvement.

Sample Evidences for Element 2 of Domain 6
• Success with accessing and leveraging a variety of resources (e.g., grants and local, state, and federal funds) is evident.
• Budgets and projects, with plans and objectives, are organized in such a way that the focus on instruction is maintained.
• District resources are utilized to maximize improvement of the school (e.g., academic/curriculum support).
• University partnerships are utilized to provide support for the school.
• Processes used by the leader to improve the school are evident and readily explained.
• Partnerships with external entities are actively pursued.
• Partnerships are monitored to determine how they impact the school.
• Documentation of how outside resources support school improvement is available.

6(3): The school leader ensures compliance to district, state, and federal rules and regulations to support effective instruction and the achievement of each student.

Desired Effect: The compliance to rules and regulations supports effective instruction and student achievement.

Scale Value	Description
Innovating (4)	The school leader continually examines for compliance to district, state, and federal rules and regulations and implements interventions when compliance is not working to support effective instruction and the achievement of each student.
Applying (3)	The school leader ensures compliance to district, state, and federal rules and regulations to support effective instruction and the achievement of each student AND monitors the extent to which compliance to rules and regulations supports effective instruction and student achievement.
Developing (2)	The school leader ensures compliance to district, state, and federal rules and regulations to support effective instruction and the achievement of each student.
Beginning (1)	The school leader attempts to ensure compliance to district, state, and federal rules and regulations to support effective instruction and the achievement of each student but does not complete the task or is not successful.
Not Using (0)	The school leader does not attempt to ensure compliance to district, state, and federal rules and regulations to support effective instruction and the achievement of each student.

Sample Evidences for Element 3 of Domain 6
· Deadlines are managed to enhance overall instructional effectiveness.
· Operations and facility resources are managed effectively to provide support for instruction.
· Curriculum materials and other resources meet district, state, or federal specifications.
· Data reveal how compliance to rules and regulations supports instruction and student achievement.
· Adherence to district and state policies and procedures is evident.
· Compliance documents are available for each auditable department (e.g., Title funds, grants, special education).
· When compliance to rules and regulations is not evident, interventions are put in place.

APPENDIX C

Review of Leadership Studies

In addition to the extensive research base detailed on page 196, two recent reports have supported the validity of the Marzano School Leader Evaluation Model. The 2017 RAND Report, *School Leadership Interventions Under the Every Student Succeeds Act: Evidence Review*, identified the Marzano School Leader Evaluation Model as one of only two leader evaluation models that meet the Every Student Succeeds Act (ESSA) criteria for evidence-based leader evaluation systems.

Additionally, a 2016 Mid-Atlantic REL study, *Measuring Principals' Effectiveness: Results from New Jersey's First Year of Statewide Principal Evaluation*, from the Mathematics Policy Research Institute also reported on the effectiveness of the model based on first-year implementation data of 212 principals in 209 schools. One of the study's conclusions was that principal ratings with the model and median student growth percentiles had moderate to high year-to-year stability.

As noted previously, one of the significant updates to the model is addressed in Domain 6, Resource Management. Research on how a school leader's operational capabilities and resource management practices impact student achievement or school growth is still somewhat scarce. But a 2009 Stanford University study conducted on Miami-Dade Public Schools concluded that:

> time spent on Organization Management activities is associated with positive school outcomes, such as student test score gains and positive teacher and parent assessments of the instructional climate; whereas Day-to-Day Instruction activities are marginally or not at all related to improvements in student performance and often have a negative relationship with teacher and parent assessments. This paper suggests that a single-minded focus on principals as instructional leaders operationalized through direct contact with teachers may be detrimental *if it forsakes the important role of principals as organizational leaders*. (our italics)

Additionally, some researchers have made a distinction between *management* and *leadership* that may be useful here. School leaders must be *leaders*, not managers, even when designing and executing operational systems. Citing 2011 research by Shamas-ur-Reman Toor in the engineering field, Stein (2013), in the *Journal of Leadership Education*, notes three significant themes that emerge in thinking about the difference between leadership and management:

> In his extensive research on the differences between managers and leaders, Toor (2011) concluded that there are three significant themes: "First, leadership pursues change that is coupled with sustainability, while management endeavors to maintain order that is tied with the bottom line. Second, leadership exercises personal power and relational influence to gain authority, whereas management banks on position power and structural hierarchy to execute orders. Third, leadership empowers people, whereas management imposes authority" (p. 318). It is no coincidence, therefore, that America's highest performing schools are the products of good leadership as opposed to effective management.

In this vein, the authors of the 2018 Marzano School Leader Evaluation Model have conceptualized school management of resources and operations as evidence of effective operational leadership.

The Research Base of the Marzano School Leader Evaluation Model

In *School Leadership for Results*, we outlined the research supporting the Marzano School Leader Evaluation Model, which was drawn from four primary documents.

The conceptual framework for the model is based on historical and contemporary research. We also drew on recent public policy initiatives to formulate and refine our theoretical perspective and recommendations. The research draws from four primary documents related to school leadership:

(1) The multiyear Wallace Study conducted and published jointly by the Center for Applied Research and Educational Improvement (CAREI) at the University of Minnesota and the Ontario Institute for Studies in Education at the University of Toronto (Louis, Leithwood, Wahlstrom, & Anderson, 2010)

(2) The 2011 study *What Works in Oklahoma Schools* (Marzano Research Laboratory, 2011) conducted by Marzano Research Laboratory with the Oklahoma State Department of Education over the 2009–2010 and the 2010–2011 school years

(3) The Marzano, Waters, and McNulty meta-analysis of school leadership published in 2005 in *School Leadership That Works*

(4) The Marzano study of school effectiveness published in 2003 in What Works in Schools

The report funded by the Wallace Foundation, Learning from Leadership: Investigating the Links to Improved Student Learning, stands as the seminal examination of the relationship between school leader actions and behaviors and student academic achievement. The report confirmed through quantitative data that effective school leadership is linked to student achievement. It concluded that principals play the central role in leadership, while collective leadership shared between teachers, parents, and other stakeholders plays a contributing part. Researchers found that, for example, "leadership practices targeted directly at teachers' instruction (i.e., instructional leadership) have significant, although indirect, effects on student achievement."

The authors further noted that "leadership effects on student learning occur largely because leadership strengthens professional community; teachers' engagement in professional community, in turn, fosters the use of instructional practices that are associated with student achievement." They added that "the professional community effect may reflect the creation of a supportive school climate that encourages student effort above and beyond that provided in individual classrooms." The report confirmed that school leaders have a profound impact on school culture and that a culture focused on student learning will yield results in improved student performance.

The study *What Works in Oklahoma Schools* conducted by Marzano Research Laboratory (2010) for the Oklahoma State Department of Education also indicated that specific actions on the part of administrators are statistically related to student academic achievement. In addition, Marzano, Waters, and McNulty's Meta-Analysis of School Leadership, published in *School Leadership That Works* (Marzano et al., 2005), which examined the research literature from 1978 to 2001, also found that school leadership has a statistically significant relationship with student achievement. Such leadership can be explained as twenty-one responsibilities of effective school leaders. As the school leader evaluation model developed, these twenty-one responsibilities were redefined as specific actions and subsequently became the original model's elements.

Finally, the Marzano study of effective schools published in *What Works in Schools* (Marzano, 2003) specified eleven factors that schools must attend to if they are to enhance student achievement and the school leadership implications regarding those eleven factors. The Marzano School Leader Evaluation Model was developed based on these key findings, what we believe are best practices within the profession.

APPENDIX D

Further Resources for the Marzano Focused School Leader Evaluation Model

Aligned Evaluation Models

The Marzano Focused Teacher Evaluation Model
  http://www.marzanocenter.com/teacher-evaluation/

The Marzano District Leader Evaluation Model, 2018 Update
  http://www.marzanocenter.com/evaluation-systems/district-leader-evaluation/

The Marzano Focused Non-Classroom Instructional Support Evaluation Model
  http://www.marzanocenter.com/evaluation-systems/non-classroom-evaluation/

Videos and Webinars

Dr. Marzano and Dr. Carbaugh discuss the Focused Teacher Evaluation Model
  https://www.youtube.com/watch?v=4Thc3IZoBJc

Dr. Marzano discusses the Leadership Model
  https://www.youtube.com/watch?v=QYUr7lor3qc

Michael Toth and Robert Marzano discuss Hierarchical Evaluation
  https://www.youtube.com/watch?v=R7GFHVz9Mjo

White Papers

Teaching for Rigor: A Call for a Critical Instructional Shift

Early reports reveal that student scores are dropping on assessments aligned to rigorous state standards. Experts worry that the achievement gap may be widening. And data analyzed by Learning Sciences Marzano Center indicates that teachers are spending less than 6 percent of classroom lessons teaching the cognitively complex skills students need to succeed.
http://www.marzanocenter.com/essentials/

Teaching for Rigor: Three Challenges for School Leaders

The Marzano Center Essentials for Achieving Rigor instructional model provides school leaders with resources, support, and the confidence they need to succeed.
https://www.learningsciences.com/wp/wp-content/uploads/2017/06/School-Leader-Rigor-Paper-2014.pdf

Common Language, Common Goals: How an Aligned Evaluation & Growth System for District Leaders, School Leaders, Teachers, and Support Personnel Drives Student Achievement

An understanding of a common language and of common goals allows for clear communication across the system, both vertically (from district leader to school leader to teacher) and horizontally (between teachers and instructional support members and between teachers across the district).
https://www.learningsciences.com/wp/wp-content/uploads/2017/06/Hierarchical-Evaluation-2013.pdf

Blogs, Books, and Articles

Articles

"The Principal's Role in Hierarchical Evaluation"
http://www.ascd.org/publications/educational-leadership/apr13/vol70/num07/The-Principal%27s-Role-in-Hierarchical-Evaluation.aspx

Blogs

On Hierarchical Evaluation
http://www.marzanocenter.com/blog/article/hierarchical-evaluation-growth-system-common-language-common-goals/

On School Leader Impact
http://www.marzanocenter.com/blog/article/principals-impact-on-student-learning-the-marzano-school-leader-evaluation-/

On School Leaders and Reflective Conversations
http://www.marzanocenter.com/blog/article/school-leaders-and-reflective-conversations-questions-that-promote-meaningf/

On School Leaders Creating a Vision of Instruction
http://www.marzanocenter.com/blog/article/school-leaders-creating-a-vision-of-instructiontelling-is-not-enough/

Books

Marzano Essentials for Achieving Rigor Series
https://www.learningsciences.com/books/marzano-center-essentials-for-achieving-rigor-10-book-series

Teacher Evaluation That Makes a Difference by Robert J. Marzano & Michael D. Toth

Teacher Evaluation That Makes a Difference describes next-generation teacher evaluation instruments and aligned evaluation systems for school leaders, district leaders, and noninstructional support personnel that are grounded in research

and designed to help educators develop expertise with the ultimate goal of improved student achievement.
https://www.learningsciences.com/books/teacher-evaluation-that-makes-a-difference

Video discussion of *Teacher Evaluation That Makes a Difference*
https://www.youtube.com/watch?v=-GhL1Pv2Brg

Leaders of Learning: How District, School, and Classroom Leaders Improve Student Achievement by Richard DuFour & Robert Marzano

For many years, the authors traveled around, helping educators improve their schools. Their first coauthored book focuses on district leadership, principal leadership, and team leadership and addresses how individual teachers can be most effective in leading students—by learning with colleagues how to implement the most promising pedagogy in their classrooms.
https://www.learningsciences.com/books/leaders-of-learning

School Leadership That Works: From Research to Results by Robert J. Marzano, Timothy Waters, & Brian A. McNulty

What can school leaders really do to increase student achievement, and which leadership practices have the biggest impact on school effectiveness? For the first time in the history of leadership research in the United States, here's a book that answers these questions definitively and gives you a list of research-based leadership competencies.
https://www.learningsciences.com/books/school-leadership-that-works

Technology

iObservation Classroom Walk-Through and Professional Development Platform
http://www.iobservation.com/

LSI Growth Tracker for professional development and Standards Tracker for formative assessment
https://www.learningsciences.com/tech/growth-tracker/

APPENDIX E

Crosswalk for PSEL Standards and the Marzano Focused School Leader Evaluation Model

Alignment: Marzano Focused School Leader Evaluation Model and the 2015 Professional Educator Leadership Standards

Professional Standards for Educational Leaders October 2015 2015 National Policy Board for Educational Administration	Marzano D=Domain E=Element
Standard 1. Mission, Vision, and Core Values Effective educational leaders develop, advocate, and enact a shared mission, vision, and core values of high-quality education and academic success and well-being of *each* student.	D1- E1,2,3 D2- E1
Standard 2. Ethics and Professional Norms Effective educational leaders act ethically and according to professional norms to promote *each* student's academic success and well-being.	D5- E1
Standard 3. Equity and Cultural Responsiveness Effective educational leaders strive for equity of educational opportunity and culturally responsive practices to promote *each* student's academic success and well-being.	D1- E3 D4- E3 D5- E2
Standard 4. Curriculum, Instruction, and Assessment Effective educational leaders develop and support intellectually rigorous and coherent systems of curriculum, instruction, and assessment to promote *each* student's academic success and well-being.	D2- E3,4,5

(Continued)

Standard 5. Community of Care and Support for Students Effective educational leaders cultivate an inclusive, caring, and supportive school community that promotes the academic success and well-being of *each* student.	D4- E3,4 D5- E3
Standard 6. Professional Capacity of School Personnel Effective educational leaders develop the professional capacity and practice of school personnel to promote *each* student's academic success and well-being.	D3- E1,2,3
Standard 7. Professional Community for Teachers and Staff Effective educational leaders foster a professional community of teachers and other professional staff to promote *each* student's academic success and well-being.	D4- E1,2
Standard 8. Meaningful Engagement of Families and Community Effective educational leaders engage families and the community in meaningful, reciprocal, and mutually beneficial ways to promote *each* student's academic success and well-being.	D4- E3,4
Standard 9. Operations and Management Effective educational leaders manage school operations and resources to promote *each* student's academic success and well-being.	D6- E1,2,3
Standard 10. School Improvement Effective educational leaders act as agents of continuous improvement to promote *each* student's academic success and well-being.	D1- E1,2 D2- E2

Works Cited

Andrews, R., & Soder, R. (1987). Principal leadership and student achievement. *Educational Leadership, 44*(6), 9–11.

Anthony, D. W. (2016). *An analysis of principal attrition in a large urban school district.* Retrieved from Digital Repository at the University of Maryland, https://drum.lib.umd.edu/handle/1903/18168

Antunez, B. (2000). *When everyone is involved: Parents and communities in school reform. In framing effective practice.* Washington, DC: Clearinghouse for Bilingual Education.

ASCD. (n.d.). School culture and climate. A Lexicon of Learning. Retrieved from http://www.ascd.org/research-a-topic/school-culture-and-climate-resources.aspx

Balinget, M. (2018, April 10). National math and reading scores remain constant, but disparities emerge. *Washington Post.*

Bass, B. (1985). *Leadership and performance beyond expectations.* New York, NY: The Free Press.

Bass, B., & Avolio, B. (1994). *Improving organizational effectiveness through transformational leadership.* Thousand Oaks, CA: Sage.

Beck, L., & Foster, W. (1999). *Administration and community: Considering challenges, exploring possibilities.* In J. Murphy & K. S. Louis (Eds.), *Handbook of research on educational administration* (pp. 337–358). San Francisco, CA: Jossey-Bass.

Black, P. J., & Wiliam, D. (1998). Assessment and classroom learning. *Assessment in Education, 5*(1), 7–74.

Blankenstein, A.M., Nogura, P., & Kelly, L. (2016, February). *Excellence through equity.* Retrieved from ASCD.org, http://www.ascd.org/publications/books/116070/chapters/Introduction@-Achieving-Excellence-Through-Equity-for-Every-Student.aspx

Blase, J., & Blase, J. (2004). *Handbook of instructional leadership: How successful principals promote teaching and learning* (2nd ed.). Thousand Oaks, CA: Corwin.

Block, P. (2003). *The answer to how is yes: Acting on what matters.* San Francisco, CA: Berrett-Koehler Publishers.

Boulanger, C. (2018, March). (B. G. Carbaugh, Interviewer). Plant City, FL.

Brewer, D. J., & Stacz, C. (1996). *Enhancing opportunity to learn measures in NCES data.* Santa Monica, CA: RAND.

Brooks, D. (2018, March 12). Good leaders make good schools. *New York Times.*

Brown, J. S., Collins, A., & Duguid, P. (1989). Situated cognition and the culture of learning. *Educational Researcher, 18*(1) 32–42.

Bryk, A. S., Easton, J. Q., Rollow, S. G., & Sebring, P. A. (1994). The state of Chicago school reform. *Phi Delta Kappan, 76*(1), 74–78.

Bryk, A. S., & Schneider, B. (2002). *Trust in schools: A core resource for school improvement.* New York, NY: Russell Sage Foundation.

Bryk, A. S., Sebring, P. B., Allensworth, E., Luppescu, S., & Easton, J. Q. (2010). *Organizing schools for improvement: Lessons from Chicago.* Chicago, IL: University of Chicago Press.

Bucy, M., Finlayson, A., Kelly, G., & Moye, C. (2016, May). *The "how" of transformation.* Retrieved from McKinsey.com, https://www.mckinsey.com/industries/retail/our-insights/the-how-of-transformation

Burns, J. M. (1978). *Leadership.* New York, NY: Harper & Row.

Cantrell, S., & Kane, J. (2013). *Ensuring fair and reliable measures of effective teaching.* Seattle, WA: Bill and Melinda Gates Foundation. Retrieved from http://www.metproject.org/downloads/MET_Ensuring_Fair_and_Reliable_Measures_Practitioner_Brief.pdf

Carroll, T. (2009). The next generation of learning teams. *Phi Delta Kappan, 91*(2), 8–13.

Cawn, B., Ikemoto, G., & Grossman, J. (2016). *Ambitious leadership: How principals lead schools to college and career readiness.* New York, NY: New Leaders. Retrieved from http://newleaders.org/research-policy/ambitious-leadership/

Chase, G., & Kane, M. (1983). *The principal as instructional leader: How much more time before we act?* Denver, CO: Education Commission of the States.

Chubb, J. E. & Moe, T. M. (1990). *Politics, markets and America's schools.* Washington, DC: The Brookings Institution.

City, E. A., Elmore, R. F., Fiarman, S. E., & Teitel, L. (2009). *Instructional rounds in education: A network approach to improving teaching and learning.* Cambridge, MA: Harvard Education Press.

Clifford, M. (2012, January). *Hiring quality school leaders: Challenges and emerging practices.* Retrieved from AIR.org, https://www.air.org/sites/default/files/downloads/report/Hiring_Quality_School_Leaders_0.pdf

Clifford, M., Behrstock-Sherratt, E., & Fetters, J. (2012). *The ripple effect: A synthesis of research on principal influence to inform performance evaluation design.* Washington, DC: American Institutes for Research.

Collins, J. (2001, October). *Good to great.* Retrieved from https://www.jimcollins.com/article_topics/articles/good-to-great.html

Davis, S., Kearney, K., Sanders, N., Thomas, C., & Leon, R. (2011*). The policies and* *practices of principal evaluation: A review of the literature*. San Francisco, CA: WestEd.

Deering, A., Dilts, R., & Russell, J. (2003). Leadership cults and cultures. *Leader to Leader Institute, 28*, 31–38.

DuFour, R., DuFour, R., Eaker, T., & Many, T. (2010). *Learning by doing: A handbook for professional communities at work*. Bloomington, IN: Solution Tree Press.

DuFour, R., & Marzano, R. J. (2011). *Leaders of learning: How district, school and classroom leaders improve student achievement*. Bloomington, IN: Solution Tree Press.

Duncan, A. (2013, December 3). *The threat of educational stagnation and complacency*. Retrieved from https://www.ed.gov/news/speeches/threat-educational-stagnation-and-complacency

Edglossary.org. (2013, August 29). *Glossary of Education Reform*. Retrieved from https://www.edglossary.org/continuous-improvement/

Elmore, R. F. (2000). *Building a new structure for school leadership*. Washington, DC: Albert Shanker Institute.

Ericsson, K. A., Krampe, R. T., & Tesch-Romer, C. (1993). The role of deliberate practice in the acquisition of expert performance. *Psychological Review, 100*(3), 363–406.

Freeman, L. (2018, March). (B. G. Carbaugh, Interviewer). Plant City, FL.

Fullan, M., (2000). The three stories of education reform. *Phi Delta Kappan, 81*(8), 581–584.

Fullan, M. (2010). *All systems go: The change imperative for whole system reform*. Thousand Oaks, CA: Corwin.

Fullan, M., Rolheiser, C., Mascall, B., & Edge, K. (2001). *Accomplishing large-scale reform: A tri-level proposition*. Toronto, Ontario: University of Toronto. Retrieved from www.michaelfullan.ca/media/13396045990.pdf

Gehrke, N. J., Knapp, M. S., & Sirotnik, K. A. (1992). In search of the school curriculum. *Review of Research in Education, 18*, 51–110.

Goals 2000: Educate America Act. H. R. 1804—103rd Congress.

Goldring, E., Porter, A. C., Murphy, J., Elliott, S. N., & Cravens, X. (2007). *Assessing learning-centered leadership: Connections to research, professional standards, current practices*. Nashville, TN: Vanderbilt University.

Grace, A. (2015). (B. Carbaugh, Interviewer). West Palm Beach, FL.

Hallinger, P., & Heck, R. (1998). Exploring the principal's contribution to school effectiveness: 1980–1995. *School Effectiveness and School Improvement, 9*(2), 157–191.

Hanover Research. (2014). *Best practices for school improvement planning*. Arlington, VA: Author.

Henderson, A. T., & Berla, N. (1994). *A new generation of evidence: The family is critical to student achievement*. Washington, DC: National Committee for Citizens in Education.

Herman, J. L., Klein, D. C., & Abedi, J. (2000). Assessing students' opportunity to learn: Teacher and student perspectives. *Educational Measurement: Issues and Practice, 19*(4), 16–24.

Herman, R. S. H. (2017). *School leadership interventions under the every student succeeds act: Evidence review: Updated and expanded*. Retrieved from https://www.rand.org/pubs/research_reports/RR1550-3.html

Herrmann, M., & Ross, C. (2016). Measuring principals' effectiveness: Results from New Jersey's first year of statewide principal evaluation (REL 2016–156). Washington, DC: U.S. Department of Education, Institute of Education Sciences, National Center for Education Evaluation and Regional Assistance, Regional Educational Laboratory Mid-Atlantic. Retrieved from http://ies.ed.gov/ncee/edlabs

Horng, E. L. (2009). *Principal time use and school effectiveness*. Stanford, CA: Stanford University, Institute for Research on Education Policy and Practice.

Johnson, S. M. (2010). How best to add Value? Strike a balance between the individual and the organization in school reform. *Voices in Urban Education, 27*. Retrieved from http://www.epi.org/publication/bp249/

Kolata, G. (2007, January 3). A surprising secret to a long life: Stay in school. *The New York Times*. Retrieved from http://www.nytimes.com/2007/01/03/health/03aging.html?pagewanted=all&_r=0

Kruse, S., Seashore-Louis, K., & Bryk, A. (1995). *Building professional learning community in schools*. Madison, WI: Center for School Organization and Restructuring.

Leana, C. (2011). The missing link in school reform. *Stanford Social Innovation Review*. Retrieved from http://www.ssireview.org/articles/entry/the_missing_link_in_school_reform

Leithwood, K., Seashore-Louis, K., Anderson, S., & Wahlstrom, K. (2004). *Review of research: How leadership influences student learning*. Retrieved from http://www.sisd.net/cms/lib/TX01001452/Centricity/Domain/33/ReviewofResearch-LearningFromLeadership.pdf

Levine, D., & Lezotte, L. (1995). Effective schools research. In J. A. Banks & C. A. McGee Banks (Eds.), *Handbook of Research on Multicultural Education* (pp. 525–547). New York, NY: Macmillan.

Little, J. T. (2006). *Professional community and professional development in the learning-centered school*. Washington, DC: National Education Association. Retrieved from http://www.nea.org/assets/docs/HE/mf_pdreport.pdf

Lortie, D. C. (1975). *Schoolteacher: A sociological study*. Chicago, IL: University of Chicago Press.

Lunenburg, F. (2010). The principal and the school: What do principals do? *National Forum of Educational Administration and Supervision Journal, 27*(4), 8.

Lynch, M. (2012, February 13). *What is culturally responsive pedagogy?* Retrieved from https://www.huffingtonpost.com/matthew-lynch-edd/culturally-responsive-pedagogy_b_1147364.html

Makiewicz, M. K. (2011). *An investigation of teacher trust in the principal* (Doctoral dissertation). Retrieved from UMI Dissertations. (Order No. 3465350).

Maxwell, J. C. (2007). *The 21 irrefutable laws of leadership.* Nashville, TN: Thomas Nelson Publishing.

Maxwell, J. C. (2012). *Developing the leader within you.* Nashville, TN: Thomas Nelson Publishing.

Marzano, R. J. (2003). *What works in schools: Translating research into action.* Alexandria, VA: ASCD.

Marzano, R. J. (2007). *The art and science of teaching: A comprehensive framework for instruction.* Alexandria, VA: ASCD.

Marzano, R. J. (2011). Art & science of teaching: What teachers gain from deliberate practice. *Educational Leadership, 68*(4), 82–85.

Marzano, R. J. (2013). *Becoming a high reliability school: The next step in school reform.* Centennial, CO: Marzano Research Laboratory.

Marzano, R. J., & Waters, T. (2009). *District leadership that works: Striking the right balance.* Bloomington, IN: Solution Tree Press.

Marzano, R. J., Waters, T., & McNulty, B. A. (2005). *School leadership that works: From research to results.* Alexandria, VA: ASCD.

Mayer, D. P., Mullins, J. F., Moore, M. T., & Ralph, J. (2000*). Monitoring school quality: Staff satisfaction with administration. An indicators report* (pp. 2000–2030). Washington, DC: US Department of Education, Office of Education Research and Improvement, National Center on Education Statistics.

MetLife. (2012). The MetLife survey of the American teacher. Retrieved from https://www.metlife.com/assets/cao/foundation/MetLife-Teacher-Survey-2012.pdf

Michigan State University. (2004, December). *School climate and learning. Best Practice Briefs.* Retrieved from http://outreach.msu.edu/bpbriefs/issues/brief31.pdf

Mishook, J. (2011). *Supporting the collective practice of teachers.* Annenberg Institute for School Reform. Retrieved from http://annenberginstitute.org/commentary/2011/06/supporting-collective-practice-teachers

Moorman, R. H., & Grover, S. (2009). Why does leader integrity matter to followers? An uncertainty management-based explanation. *International Journal of Leadership Studies, 5*(2), 102–114.

Murphy, J. (2014). *2014 ISLLC Standards for school leaders* (Manuscript in preparation).

National Association of Elementary School Principals. (2016, August 30). *The Every Student Achieves Act (ESSA) implementation: Developing effective principals and other school leaders*. Retrieved from https://www.naesp.org/sites/default/files/ESSA%20Implementation%20-%20Developing%20Effective%20Principals%20and%20Other%20School%20Leaders%20-%208-30-16.pdf

National Conference of State Legislatures. (2015, April 22). *Effective school principals: A lever for school improvment*. Retrieved from http://www.ncsl.org/research/education/effective-school-principals-a-lever-for-school-improvement.aspx

National Policy Board for Education Administrators. (2015). *Professional standards for educational leaders 2015*. Reston, VA: Author.

National School Climate Center. (2007). *The school climate challenge: Narrowing the gap between school climate research and school climate policy, practice guidelines and teacher education policy*. Retrieved from http://www.ecs.org/html/projectspartners/nclc/docs/school-climate-challenge-web.pdf

New England Association of Secondary Schools and Colleges. (2016). *Guide to developing and implementing core values, beliefs, and learning expectations*. Burlington, MA. Commission on Public Schools, Committee on Public Secondary Schools, Burlington.

Newmann, F., & Wehlage, G. (1995). *Successful school restructuring: A report to the public and educators by the Center for Restructuring Schools*. Madison, WI: University of Wisconsin.

No Child Left Behind Act. (2001), Public Law 107–110, §7801[37].

Partnership for 21st Century Skills. (2002). *Learning for the 21st century: A report and MILE guide for 21st century skills*. Retrieved from http://www.p21.org/storage/documents/P21_Report.pdf

Patchin, J. W. (2012a). *A positive school climate makes everything possible*. Cyberbullying Research Center. Retrieved from http://cyberbullying.us/a-positive-school-climate-makes-everything-possible/

Patchin, J. W. (2012b). *School climate and cyberbullying: An empirical link*. Cyberbullying Research Center. Retrieved from http://cyberbullying.us/school-climate-and-cyberbullying-an-empirical-link/

Persell, C., & Cookson, P. (1982). The effect of principals in action. In *The Effective Principal: A Research Summary*. Reston, VA: National Association of Secondary School Principals.

Pierce, P. R. (1935). *The origin and development of the public school principalship*. Chicago, IL: University of Chicago Press.

Pittman, K. J. (2010). College and career readiness. *School Administrator, 6*(67), 10–14. Retrieved from http://www.aasa.org/SchoolAdministratorArticle.aspx?id=13536

Preuss, P. (2003). *School leader's guide to root cause analsysis: Using data to dissolve problems.* Larchmont, NY: Eye on Education.

Programme for International Student Assessment [PISA]. (2012). *PISA 2012 results in focus: What 15-year-olds know and what they can do with what they know.* Retrieved from www.oecd.org/pisa/keyfindings/pisa-2012-results-overview.pdf

Programme for International Student Assessment (2017). *PISA 2015 results (Volume V): collaborative problem solving.* Paris: OECD Publishing.

Robitaille, D. (Ed.). (1993). *Curriculum frameworks for mathematics and science.* Vancouver, Canada: Pacific Educational Press.

Sashkin, M. H. (1986). *A synthesis of job analysis research on the job of the school principal.* Washington, DC: Office of Educational Research and Improvement, US Department of Educational Research and Improvment, US Department of Education.

Schlechty, P. (2009). *Leading for learning: How to transform schools into learning organizations.* San Francisco, CA: Jossey-Bass.

Schmoker, M., & Marzano, R. J. (1999). Realizing the promise of standards-based education. *Educational Leadership, 56*(6), 17–21.

Scholastic, & The Gates Foundation. (2012). *Primary Sources: 2012.* Retrieved from http://www.scholastic.com/primarysources/pdfs/Gates2012_full.pdf

School Leaders Network. (2014). *Churn: The high cost of principal turnover.* Washington, DC: American Institutes for Research.

Scott, A. (2014, October 30). *The high cost of principal turnover.* Retrieved from https://www.marketplace.org/2014/10/30/education/high-cost-principal-turnover

Seashore-Louis, K., Leithwood, K., Wahlstrom, K., & Anderson, S. (2010). *Learning from leadership: Investigating the links to improved student learning.* Retrieved from http://www.wallacefoundation.org/knowledge-center/school-leadership/key-research/Pages/Investigating-the-Links-to-Improved-Student-Learning.aspx

Senge, P. (1990). *The fifth discipline: The art and practice of the learning organization.* New York, NY: Doubleday.

Sergiovanni, T. J. (2004). Building a community of hope. *Educational Leadership, 61*(8), 33–37.

Silins, H. C., Mulford, W. R., & Zarins, S. (2002). Organizational learning and school change. *Educational Administration Quarterly, 38*(5), 613–642.

Sparks, D. (2004). Broader purpose calls for higher understanding: An interview with Andy Hargreaves. *Journal of Staff Development, 25*(2), 46–50.

Stallworth, J. T., & Williams, D. L. (1982). *A survey of parents regarding parent involvement in schools.* Austin, TX: Southwest Education Development Laboratory.

Stein, L. (2016). Schools need leaders, not managers—It's time for a paradigm shift. *Journal of Leadership Education, 15*(2), 23.

Stiggins, R. J. (1994). *Student-centered classroom assessment.* New York, NY: Macmillan College Publishing Company.

Stiggins, R. J. (2016). *An introduction to student-involved assessment for learning* (7th ed.). New York, NY: Pearson.

Strauss, V. (2013, October 24). Five key features of effective schools. *Washington Post.*

Tangri, S., & Moles, O. (1987). Parents and the community. In V. Richardson-Koehler (Ed.), *Educators' handbook: A research perspective* (2nd ed., pp. 519–550). New York, NY: Longman.

Teaching Tolerance. (n.d.). *Being culturally responsive.* Retrieved from https://www.tolerance.org/professional-development/being-culturally-responsive

The New Teacher Project. (2010). Teacher evaluation 2.0. Retrieved from http://tntp.org/assets/documents/Teacher-Evaluation-Oct10F.pdf?files/Teacher-Evaluation-Oct10F.pdf

The New Teacher Project [TNTP]. (2013). *Perspectives of irreplaceable teachers: What America's best teachers think about teaching.* Retrieved from http://tntp.org/assets/documents/TNTP_Perspectives_2013.pdf

Thiers, N. (2017, June). *Making progress possible: A conversation with Michael Fullan.* Retrieved from http://www.ascd.org/publications/educational-leadership/jun17/vol74/num09/Making-Progress-Possible@-A-Conversation-with-Michael-Fullan.aspx

Toch, T., & Rothman, R. (2008). *Rush to judgment: Teacher evaluation in public education.* Washington, DC: Education Sector.

Tooley, M. C. (2015, August 4). *Is effective teacher professional development just a mirage?* Retrieved from https://www.newamerica.org/education-policy/edcentral/effective-teacher-pd-a-mirage/

Tyre, P. (2015, September 26). Why do more than half of principals quit after five years? *Hechinger Report.*

Van Driel, J. H., De Jong, O. (2001). *Investigating the development of preservice teachers' pedagogical content knowledge.* Paper presented at the 2001 Annual Meeting of the National Association for Research and Science Teaching. St. Louis, MO. Retrieved from http://course.zjnu.cn/kcjx/uploadfile/200812322335739.pdf

Walker, D. (2002). Constructivist leadership: Standards, equity, and learning—Weaving whole cloth from multiple strands. In L. Lambert, D. Walker, D. Zimmerman, J. E. Cooper, & M. G. Lambert, *The constructivist leader* (pp. 1–33). New York, NY: Teachers College Press.

Wallace Foundation. (2011, February 22). *Research findings to support effective educational policies: A guide for policymakers.* Retrieved from www.wallacefoundation.org/knowledge-center/school-leadership/key-research/Documents/Findings-to-Support-Effective-Educational-Policy-making.pdf

Wallace Foundation. (2016). *Summary of Tiers I–IV evidence on the effects of school leadership activity*. Retrieved from http://www.wallacefoundation.org/knowledge-center/PublishingImages/Summary-Tiers-I-IV-Evidence--Effects-School-Leadership-Improvement-Activities-chart.jpg

Waters, J. T., Marzano, R. J., & McNulty, B. A. (2003). *Balanced leadership: What 30 years of research tells us about the effect of leadership on student achievement.* Aurora, CO: Mid-continent Research for Education and Learning.

Weisberg, D., Sexton, S., Mulhern, J., & Keeling, D. (2009). *The widget effect: Our national failure to acknowledge and act on differences in teacher effectiveness.* Brooklyn, NY: The New Teacher Project. Retrieved from http://widgeteffect.org/downloads/TheWidgetEffect.pdf

Weisman, L., Allen, L., & Foster, E. (2013). *The multiplier effect.* Thousand Oaks, CA: Corwin.

Wellisch, J., MacQueen, A. H., Carriere, R. A., & Duck, G. A. (1978). School management and organization in successful schools. *Sociology of Education*, *51*(3), 211–226.

Wiliam, D. and Leahy, S. (2007). A theoretical foundation for formative assessment. In J. McMillan, H. (Ed.) *Formative Classroom Assessment: Theory into Practice* (pp. 29–42). New York, NY: Teachers College Press.

Yoon, K. D. (2007). *Reviewing the evidence on how teacher professional development affects student achievement.* Washington, DC: US Department of Education, Institute of Education Sciences, National Center for Education Evaluation and Regional Assistance.

Young, J., & Sheets, J. (2005). *Mentoring principals: Frameworks, agendas, tips, and case stories for mentors and mentees.* Thousand Oaks, CA: Corwin.

www.ingramcontent.com/pod-product-compliance
Lightning Source LLC
LaVergne TN
LVHW080312260326
834688LV00038B/1071